THE IMPACT OF THE ELECTORAL PROCESS

SAGE ELECTORAL STUDIES YEARBOOK

Series Editors

Louis Maisel, *Colby College*
Joseph Cooper, *Rice University*

Editorial Advisory Board

Other volumes in this series:

SAGE ELECTORAL STUDIES YEARBOOK

VOLUME III

The Impact of
the Electoral Process

edited by
LOUIS MAISEL
and
JOSEPH COOPER

 SAGE Publications   Beverly Hills / London

For information address:

SAGE PUBLICATIONS, INC.
275 South Beverly Drive
Beverly Hills, California 90212

SAGE PUBLICATIONS LTD
St George's House / 44 Hatton Garden
London EC1N 8ER

Printed in the United States of America

ISBN No. 0-8039-0709-5 (cloth)
ISBN No. 0-8039-0710-9 (paper)

Library of Congress Catalog Card No. 76-47088

FIRST PRINTING

73820

CONTENTS

INTRODUCTION

I

The organizing focus of this volume of the *Sage Electoral Studies Yearbook* is the problem of linkage. In recent years political scientists have begun increasingly to ask questions regarding the relationship between their findings in their chosen areas of interest and the actual functioning of the political system. This represents a very positive development. A concern with linkage questions broadens the perspectives of individual researchers and promotes cumulativeness in research results. Further, it directs attention to the impacts or payoffs of political action, be they behavioral, policy, or institutional, and in so doing helps to orient research so that meaningful questions are raised and attacked.

Nonetheless, dealing with the question of linkage is never easy. The difficulties that are encountered stem from the inherent complexity of the problem, the current state of knowledge regarding relationships among critical variables, and the continuing competition among a variety of theoretical frameworks for preeminence. Many approaches to the problem of linkage can thus be found in the contemporary literature. Some have attempted to define general theories or frameworks of analysis. Norman Luttberg's schema of linkage models and Theodore Lowi's classification of policy arenas provide familiar examples. Others have sought to formulate and work within the context of partial or middle range theories—i.e., theories that are restricted to explaining particular segments of political life or action and are derived from or tied to data. V.O. Key's path-breaking work on public opinion provides a good example. Finally, many scholars have examined quite particular facets of linkage in highly specific areas of inquiry. The work of Warren Miller and Donald Stokes on the impact of constituency on legislative voting provides a classic illustration.

In introducing this volume, we have no grand theoretical objectives. Our aim is simply to provide a serviceable framework for organizing a group of studies that deal with a basic aspect of the problem of linkage. In essence, our intent is to examine the impact of the electoral process on the functioning of the political system. We thus assume an electoral stage characterized by a set of cultural values and norms, a pattern of beliefs and habits, a distribution of socioeconomic interests, and a set of decision-making structures or arrangements. Given these conditions, we propose to explore the impact of the electoral process in terms of three basic themes: first, the impact of events and behavior at the electoral stage on electoral institutions and outcomes; second, the impact of events and behavior at the electoral stage on the operation and effectiveness of formal governmental institutions; third, the impact of events and behavior at the electoral stage on the substantive character of policy outputs.

II

The articles selected for inclusion in this volume relate directly to the themes outlined above. While we could not hope to present a full examination of the problems involved with electoral linkages, we feel that these articles contribute significantly to our understanding of the impact of the electoral process on both politics and policy.

In the lead article, Gerald M. Pomper asserts that much has been written about the impact of parties on the electoral process but much less about the reverse phenomenon. Analyzing five specific aspects of the electoral process—presidential recruitment, strategies for nomination, campaign finance, national conventions, and electoral behavior—Pomper claims that recent changes have had a profound effect, leading to the decline of political parties, particularly at the presidential level. Parties have lost their traditional monopoly over recruitment of candidates and control of campaign resources and—as voters respond less and less to party appeals—their very legitimacy. Pomper concludes that this change in the role of parties—from quasi-public institution to private association—will eventually lead to a loss of popular control over public policies, the very essence of democracy.

Several of Pomper's themes are explored further in other chapters. Louis Maisel and Gerald J. Lieberman examine the ways in which delegates were elected to the 1976 Democratic National Convention in the primary states. Starting from the party's Charter, which mandates that state delegations fairly reflect the presidential preferences of those participating in the process, Maisel and Lieberman demonstrate that the various plans adopted by the 31 primary states lead to significantly different levels of representation. By recomputing the delegations that would have been chosen under differing rules, they argue that, although Jimmy Carter's nomination would have resulted in any case, the specific rules chosen altered the outcome in seemingly unfair ways, and consequently they propose reforms for future years.

In the final chapter in our first section, Denis G. Sullivan, Jeffrey L. Pressman, F. Christopher Arterton, Robert T. Nakamura, and Martha Wagner Weinberg continue their explorations of Democratic convention behavior begun in 1972. Several of the themes explored in earlier works by Sullivan and his associates—the process of platform writing, the various arenas for decision making, the legitimating nature of the convention itself—are reexamined in light of the Democrats' experience in 1976. While the Carter domination of the 1976 convention led to a different flow of events from that which many observers had predicted, the themes of convention decision making and the value of conventions presented in their earlier works are basically reaffirmed.

Two of the articles that examine the impact of the electoral process on the institutions of government deal with the relationship between congressional elections and legislative voting behavior. The two articles attack the question somewhat differently, but their conclusions are remarkably similar.

Joseph Cooper, David William Brady, and Patricia A. Hurley present a detailed and precise critique of earlier literature on the linkage between congressional elections and legislative behavior. Identifying flaws in conceptualization and operationalization in earlier works, they present a revised model demonstrating the link between strength of party at the congressional district level and voting by Congressmen. Their model proves to have extraordinary explanatory powers for analyzing the records of the House of Representatives from 1896 to 1974.

In exploring the same linkage, David H. Nexon narrows the scope to deal with two subject areas—civil rights and welfare—and a shorter time span—those Congresses sitting from 1952 to 1970. Nexon tests the accuracy with which Congressmen reflect the wishes of their constituents in these two important policy areas, measuring citizens' opinions on these matters and comparing them with their representatives' votes. He concludes that the "responsible party" model of opinion representation has more merit than many critics have given it credit for, but that—at least for the historical period he studied—the model requires modification to account for representation of opinions through party structure and through consensus on salient issues and, in most recent years, a trace of representation without parties. If Pomper's argument regarding the decline of political parties is extended to parties at the congressional level, the implications for changes in the institution of the House because of the electoral process are far-reaching.

Herbert B. Asher's article, which concludes the second section of this book, deals with the role of media on presidential selection. Asher argues that the media's role is an intrusive one which affects the selection process and thus the eventual President. He gives particular attention to how the media contributes to the winnowing-out process during the primary season by setting somewhat artificial standards for evaluating candidates' performances and by structuring citizen perceptions of campaign events.

The three articles which discuss the impact of the electoral process on policy outcomes take very different tacts. David R. Morgan, Samuel A. Kirkpatrick, Michael R. Fitzgerald, and William Lyons examine referenda voting in Oklahoma. Referenda are the mechanisms through which elections most directly affect policy, especially in states in which they are widely used. The data from this article make clear that referenda outcomes are affected by a number of predictable factors—administrative and legal apparatuses and the socioeconomic and political composition of the voting population, among others. This article covers a 30-year period in Oklahoma history and emphasizes the developmental processes throughout the state as reflected in the institutionalization of behavior patterns in these policy-oriented elections.

Shelah Gilbert Leader has explored the policy impact of the two somewhat contradictory electoral strategies pursued by activists in the women's movement. Some feel that it is most important to elect any women to office while others feel that priority should be given to those who take progressive stands on women's issues, regardless of sex. Using data from state legislatures' votes on ratification of the Equal Rights Amendment and a wider range of issues facing recent Congresses, Leader compares the voting records of female and male legislators, controlling for party. She concludes that Democratic women are most likely to support women's issues, Republican men least likely, and that Democratic men and Republican women support the issues that she has studied to about the same extent.

Finally, former President Richard Nixon's top domestic advisor, John Ehrlichman, discusses campaigns in the middle of a President's administration in terms of their effect on domestic policy making. Drawing on his experience from the 1972 campaign, Ehrlichman concludes that, while the upcoming election may alter the timing of some decisions, it also has the positive effect of helping an administration to achieve coordination among those explaining the President's positions. Ehrlichman also examines the proposal to replace the current limit of two four-year terms with a limit of one six-year term, theorizing that such a change would permit Presidents to reach decisions based more on their own personal philosophy than on the weight of public opinion. Looking at the impact of electoral politics at the presidential level then, Ehrlichman emphasizes that the institution of an election is sufficient to guarantee that the public is consulted. His view thus differs from Pomper's conclusion that parties are crucial for maintaining that aspect of democracy.

III

The nine articles collected here explore many aspects of the consequences of the electoral process. Some of the themes are explored in more than one article. Some of the conclusions reinforce each other; others seemingly contradict. We feel that this is as it should be when scholars and practicing politicians are examining mostly uncharted territory. The *Sage Electoral Studies Yearbook* series attempts to provide a forum for political scientists, historians, politicians, journalists, and others concerned with the topic of elections broadly defined, so that they might air their views on common themes.

This is the first volume of the Sage series which deals with the politics of only one country. As Pomper points out in the prefatory remarks to his article, many of the themes discussed and the conclusions reached could apply to non-American situations as well. We felt that a certain coherence would be lost if we divided this volume not only among different types of impact of the electoral process but also among different political systems.

The fourth volume of this series will collect articles which deal with changes in ongoing party systems, seeking to reveal patterns of party evolution and/or decay. The projected fifth volume will be concerned with changes in the electorate over a period of time. We intend to return to our original goal of exploring these themes from a cross-national as well as interdisciplinary perspective.

Finally, this volume is dedicated to our wives. Only rarely are academic careers as disruptive of normal family lives as are political careers, for instance. However, the final editing of this book has been undertaken during particularly disruptive periods, while one of us is in the final stages of an always anxiety-producing tenure decision and while the other is commuting between Texas and Washington, D.C., as he begins a period of government service. These have not been normal times. Our wives have endured increasing breaks from our routines, which themselves are somewhat abnormal, and have done so with an equanimity and perspective that has been most healthy for all of us. We dedicate this book to them with respect and gratitude, but mostly with love.

Louis Maisel
Joseph Cooper
October 1976

To Mary Lou and Frani

Chapter 1

THE DECLINE OF PARTISAN POLITICS

GERALD M. POMPER

Political parties, along with mass elections, have been the hallmarks of modern popular democracy. The relationship between elections and democracy is obvious, even tautological. We do not properly speak of American democracy until the achievement of white male suffrage in the Jacksonian period, or of British democracy until the enfranchisement of the working class in 1867. It is also true that the development of competitive political parties has paralleled, and often preceded, growth in popular participation. Thus, the end of one-party Republican rule in 1824 stimulated America's expansion of the suffrage, as the competition of the parliamentary Liberal and Conservative parties promoted the extension of voting rights to English labor.

The historical union of parties and mass politics continues in modern times. National independence movements are typically led by a political party which sponsors and then employs mass suffrage to further freedom from colonial rule. The Congress party of India, the Mapai in Israel, and the Neo-Destour in Tunisia, are among the many examples provided by the 20th century. Moreover, it is precisely these exemplary movements that have combined their own institutionalization with popular expansion and, thereby, have provided the most stable governments (Huntington, 1968, chap. 7).

I. PARTIES, ELECTIONS, AND DEMOCRACY

The joining of parties and democracy is not only historical but also often viewed as logically necessary. The principles of democracy —popular sovereignty, political equality, popular consultation, and majority rule—require partisan institutions for their realization. James (1974:7) succinctly points to their crucial role in democratic practice:

> The problem is how to organize and structure the relationship of the people to their agent, the government. Only if people control the government are they citizens. If the government can manipulate their responses, the people are only subjects. Classical democratic theorists did not pay a great deal of attention to the problems of staffing and operating the governmental institutions they prescribed. In doing so, they virtually ignored politics, the activities and processes by which governmental policies are developed, influenced, decided, and enforced.

Parties are found to fill this deficiency in prescriptive democratic theory. Once they were regarded as unhealthy challengers of national unity or, at best, tolerated as an undesirable but inevitable product of political freedom. Only recently have they become accepted as an accurate index of the existence of democracy itself, as much a part of its definition as mass suffrage (Hofstadter, 1969). Indeed, Duverger (1954:424f.) concludes, "liberty and the party system coincide. . . . The rise of parties and especially of working-class parties has alone made possible any real and active cooperation by the whole people in political affairs."

In the acknowledged close relationship of parties and elections and democracy, the focus has been on the effect of parties on elections. Parties have been analyzed as fulfilling basic functions for a democratic system. Thus, Ranney and Kendall (1956:505) make "organizing elections" the first of four roles performed by the American party system. "A community, we have learned, needs *some* agency or agencies (a) to define the alternatives open to it, (b) to make clear to the voters what actually is involved in the choice among those alternatives, and (c) to encourage them to use their sovereign power to make the choice for themselves. . . . In the United States, as in the other democracies, the *parties* have taken on these tasks."

Like others, these authors also mention other roles and functions of the parties, such as organizing government, promoting democracy, and nurturing consensus. Some writers have stressed a "constituent" role for parties (Lowi, 1967) or urged a greater influence on public policy (American Political Science Association, 1950). In most of the literature on American politics, however, the stress has been on the electoral functions of the parties—the recruitment and nomination of candidates, the writing of platforms, however vague, and the consequent framing of policy directions, the conduct of campaigns, and the staffing of electoral machinery. "In a word, the parties make the electoral process *work*" (Ranney and Kendall, 1956:505), and this has been the major work performed by the parties.

There is abundant evidence of—and commentary upon—the impact of the parties upon the electoral process. More unique is the impact of the electoral process upon the parties. A political feedback loop has become evident recently, in which the nature and outcomes of elections affect the parties, leading to new influences upon succeeding elections, and further consequences for the parties themselves.

The net result of this process is the decline of partisan politics, most evidently in the choice of the President. The process has now reached the point at which the American political party is little more than one of many groups, not greatly disparate in their influence, which participate in elections. The party has been reduced from a quasi-public agency to a private association. Once a source of power, it has become another contestant for power in the pluralistic system.

THE PARTY PAST

This decline can be easily noticed if we briefly review the position parties held in the electoral process through most of American history, even as recently as the end of the Second World War. Parties then typically possessed either legal or practical monopolies of three vital factors: legitimacy, resources, and recruitment.

The legitimacy of parties was evident in the loyalties expressed by the voters. Americans were fiercely loyal to the two major parties, whatever their labels in any particular historical era. Most voters retained the same party attachments throughout life. Although periodically disrupted at times of critical realignment (Key, 1955), even these realignments could be explained more by generational change than individual conversion (Beck, 1974).

The depth of affection could be located in political humor, which abounds in stories such as that of the Irish family in Boston in which all the children developed well, except for the black sheep who became a Republican. It can be found in the accounts of the "militaristic" period of the 19th century, in which partisans were as devoted to the Republican and Democratic standards as their fathers in the Civil War has been loyal to the Union and Confederacy (Jensen, 1971). It can be found in the aggregate election statistics, in which communities returned virtually the same vote for each faction year after year, and ticket-splitting or "drop-off" in the vote at one end of the very long ballot was almost undetectable (Burnham, 1965). It can be found in modern survey data, in which some 90% of the national samples of the 1950s identified consistently and openly with the major parties (Campbell et al., 1960:124).

Parties classically possessed not only legitimacy, but resources. One resource was access to the ballot itself, as the formal rules (written by party-dominated state legislatures) essentially eliminated nonparty candidates, even after adoption of the Australian ballot. Campaigning resources were also controlled by the parties, most evidently when precinct canvassing and turnout were the principal means of winning votes. The financing needed for elections was another party resource, with money raised and spent by party committees or individuals closely associated with these organizations, and independent organizations existing largely as means to evade unrealistic and unenforceable spending ceilings (Heard, 1962). Patronage provided a means of supplying and multiplying these resources. Spoilsmen reinforced the party monopoly of governmental positions, campaigned for the organization, and contributed to its coffers.

The channels of political recruitment were also dominated by the parties. For most governmental offices in the United States, distinct ladders of political advancement could be located, the rungs of the ladder being held together by the party organizations (Schlesinger, 1966). Distinct regional patterns could be found as well, such as the apprenticeship system practiced by the Chicago Democratic organization (Snowiss, 1966). In the Senate, in the 10-year period after the Second World War, only 9% came to the body without previous political office (Matthews, 1960:51). Party domination of recruitment was evident in the highest office, the Presidency, as well. Except for victorious generals, every national candidate advanced through a number of party positions before receiving his nomination. Precise rules of "availability" existed and served to explain "why great men are not elected president" (Bryce, 1914, vol. 1, p. 80).

Party domination of the presidential electoral process was based on these monopolies of legitimacy, resources, and recruitment. It can be illustrated by the nominations of 1932, the last year before the modern period of presidential races. In the incumbent Republican party, President Herbert Hoover was easily renomiated despite his ineffectiveness in coping with the Great Depression. In control of executive patronage, he was able to keep the state parties in line and to ignore the signs of popular discontent evident in the few, and ineffective, state primaries (Bain, 1960:234f.).

In the Democratic party, Franklin D. Roosevelt used the traditional base of the governorship of New York to win friends in party organizations throughout the nation, while largely ignoring primary contests. A contentious convention was capped by an explicit deal for the Vice-Presidency, bringing Roosevelt the nomination on the fourth ballot (Farley, 1938:132-153). The campaign was conducted through the party organizations, with funds raised by them or closely allied committees, and with the issues largely confined to the conduct of the incumbent Hoover administration. Even though the election would ultimately be seen as one stage in a process of critical realignment, voting patterns showed significant continuity with the recent past: the ecological correlation of the vote, using states as units, reached the considerable level of .85, indicating the persistence of past loyalties even in this period of change (Pomper, 1967:566).

II. THE MODERN ELECTORAL PROCESS

The contrast of this historical sketch with the modern election of the President is so great that we are really dealing not simply with a changed system, but an essentially different process. The differences are evident in five aspects: recruitment, strategies of nomination, campaign finance, national conventions, and electoral behavior. In each, considerable change has already occurred, and the effect of these changes is likely to be further deterioration of the parties in the future.

PRESIDENTIAL RECRUITMENT

Presidential recruitment has changed in both its character and its sources. Campaigns for the White House now begin essentially through a process of self-selection and depend for their success on the development of organizations personally bound to the candidate. In what is perhaps the archetype of the modern campaign, that of John Kennedy in 1960, nine persons were critical: three members of the family, four personal friends and staff members, a public opinion analyst, and but one professional politician, John Bailey (White, 1961:59-63). These persons had not been chosen because of their party positions. They were persons personally selected by the candidate to advance his personal career. As White (1961:63) summarized the process:

> John F. Kennedy in his fourteen years in politics has had many servants, many aides, many helpers. As he has outgrown each level of operation, he has gently stripped off his earlier helpers and retained only those who could go on with him effectively to the next level. These men here assembled were those who had survived a decade of Kennedy selection.

Since 1960, the importance of these personal organizations has become even more evident. Their character has evolved even further from coalitions such as John Kennedy's, based on personal loyalties. Increasingly they are based on relatively formal and contractual relationships, in which the candidate receives the services of strategists, media experts, pollsters, and other experts in exchange for a commercial fee or the opportunity of power. There is "a new kind of loyalty very much like 'bastard feudalism.' No longer does a clever and idealistic young man gravitate automatically into the sphere of a local leader. . . . He can join 'the Kennedys,' or he can attach himself to the retinue of some other 'good lord' who can promise high adventure and reward" (Chester et al., 1969:233).

The sources of presidential recruitment have changed as well. The traditional national candidates, such as Roosevelt, were the governors of large states. Their success in obtaining nominations had many sources, including their ability to evade the difficult decisions of national policy. A more important reason, however, may have been their command of the crucial resources of delegate votes at the national conventions. When state parties controlled their own means of delegate selection, the governor of a large state such as New York could be assured from the beginning of at least 15% of the number needed for victory.

The situation has altered dramatically. In the period since Roosevelt's first nomination, the most important base for presidential candidates has become the Vice-Presidency, once deprecated as "not worth a bucket of warm spit." Every Vice-President in this period has become a presidential possibility, and a third of all nominations for the White House have gone to members of the group. In further contrast to the past, Senators are more likely than governors to receive consideration, and they are almost as common as presidential nominees (Keech and Matthews, 1976:18f.).

In the past quarter of a century, only two governors have received their party's nomination, and both are exceptions that underline the loss of the traditional power of state parties. Adlai Stevenson was not selected because of his influence as governor of Illinois, but because he fit the needs of national party factions and interest groups for a unifying candidate. In 1976, the candidacy of Jimmy Carter is even firmer evidence of the decline of traditional bases of power. He surrendered state power long before the national convention. Although he received home state support, this support was due to a primary victory, rather than to party organization. He essentially lacked a local base of power, while he developed a transcending national constituency. Governors may still be nominated for President, but not because they are governors. To the contrary, they must demonstrate that they are national, not state, figures.

NOMINATION STRATEGIES

The Carter example leads to discussion of the second general change in the presidential electoral process, the new strategies of nomination. The basic change has been from strategies in which coalitions were based on geography, i.e., state parties, to those in which the coalitions are constructed from interest groups, demographic elements of the population, and issue publics. Candidates pursuing a purely geographical strategy have been remarkably unsuccessful, as illustrated by the universal failure of "favorite sons" in 1976. These candidates were unable to carry their home states if they were not viewed as serious national candidates as well. Thus Lloyd Bentsen was shut out in his native Texas and George Wallace seriously challenged in his Alabama domain. Conversely, even serious candidates cannot be assured that they will control their home states, as illustrated by the challenges to Wallace and to Californian Edmund G. Brown, Jr.

Even less successful are governors who seek to maintain control of their state delegations simply for bargaining purposes. Many observers had predicted a bargained Democratic convention in 1976 because of the assumed power of Democratic governors. In the event, no governor was able to maintain this control, as would-be kingmakers such as Hugh Carey in New York or Milton Schapp in Pennsylvania found themselves overwhelmed by the national tides flowing over their personal turfs. Only in the case of California could the governor exercise some control, even while losing a quarter of the delegation, but this relative success required a candidate with more than a parochial home-state appeal.

The presidential nominating campaign has been nationalized. No longer is it true that there are no national parties, only 50 state parties, as the old textbook cliché read. At least for the Presidency it would be more accurate to say that there are no state parties, and perhaps no national parties as well. The state parties have largely and deliberately written themselves out of the presidential nomination. Beset by new and complex rules for the selection of delegates, many state organizations have simply left the choice and mandate of convention delegates to state primaries.

The parties' place has been taken by candidate organizations. As campaigners, these candidate organizations are far different from the locally centered groups of the traditional state parties. By the 1976 campaign, canvassing itself was being handled by out-of-staters. Hundreds of Georgians went to New Hampshire to campaign for Jimmy Carter, while large numbers of Michiganders rang Florida doorbells for President Gerald Ford. That this "carpetbagging" drew little attention and no criticism is quietly impressive evidence of the nationalization of the nominating process, and of its separation from local influences.

Other large national forces are affecting the nominations. A principal means of campaigning is through the mass media. The standing of candidates is now certified not by their support among party leaders or their particular office but by a small group of reporters and commentators for newspapers, magazines, and television. "They are acknowledged experts, well connected in political circles throughout the land. Their reports appear in the nation's most prestigious newspapers and respected news broadcasts. . . . Collectively they are what columnist Russell Baker has called 'the Great Mentioniser,' the source of self-fulfilling stories that a person has been 'mentioned' as a possible presidential nominee" (Keech and Matthews, 1976:13).

The national strategies of candidates are directed toward winning the notice of "the Great Mentioniser" and of the press generally, and then of gaining more widespread public attention. Various tactics will be used to win this attention, since public opinion, and its measurement in the national polls, is usually decisive. Vital issues may be emphasized, as McGovern stressed Vietnam in 1972; or primary victories may be employed to demonstrate an attractive personality, as Carter did in 1976. Whatever the tactics employed, however, their common feature is that they depend little for their success on the support of party organizations.

Standing in the public opinion polls has become decisive in winning presidential nominations. With conspicuous exceptions, such as McGovern and Carter, the leader in the national polls before the primaries almost always goes on to win designation. Furthermore, it is virtually certain that the preconvention poll leader, even an insurgent such as McGovern or Carter, will be victorious in his party. To be sure, poll standings are affected by primaries and by direct support of the state parties, "but the strongest relations are the long-run effects in the opposite direction—the effects of national opinion on winning both the state primary elections and the presidential nomination" (Beniger, 1976:37).

Candidates appeal to geographically diffuse constituencies, not to areal coalitions. The constituencies may be McGovern's opponents of the Vietnam War, or Ronald Reagan's ideological conservatives, or Carter's seekers for governmental purity, or Henry Jackson's laborites. Their common feature is their lack of local coloring. The diminishing impact of geography can also be seen in the convention decisions themselves. Until recently, there was a stable voting structure in both parties, in which the states could be consistently ordered along a single dimension (Munger and Blackhurst, 1965). In the Republican party, factions could be arrayed geographically and ideologically, from conservative to liberal, as in Table 1. Conservative candidates such as Robert Taft or Barry Goldwater received their support from the same end of this spectrum (largely Southern and Midwestern) and liberals from the other end (largely Eastern). In the Democratic party, with the direction reversed, liberals received most support from the Midwest and Far West, conservatives from the South.

This structure has not been evident since 1964. There is limited correlation between the 1968 and earlier results (Pomper, 1971). Furthermore, in the 1972 Democratic and 1976 Republican conventions, the break from past patterns persists. Previous correlations of convention votes over time reached .95. However, the repro-

Table 1. CONVENTION CANDIDATES: DISTRIBUTION OF VOTES FOR SELECTED
CANDIDATES, AS PERCENTAGES OF THEIR TOTAL VOTES[a]

Republican Candidates	Conservative				Liberal	
	I	II	III	IV	V	N
Eisenhower for President (1952)	8.3	6.7	8.3	16.8	59.9	590
Goldwater for President (1964)	28.0	17.1	25.0	22.4	7.5	879
Nixon for President (1968)	27.0	17.2	25.3	12.6	17.9	673
Ford for President (1976)	20.3	6.8	13.9	8.4	50.6	1,122

Democratic Candidates	Liberal				Conservative		
	I	II	III	IV	V	VI	N
Kennedy for President (1960)	28.9	24.5	19.3	25.4	0.5	1.4	685
Johnson for President (1964)	3.0	3.2	5.0	2.5	16.3	70.0	402
Humphrey for President (1968)	15.1	14.7	12.3	18.9	12.9	26.1	1,689
McGovern for President (1972)	30.8	12.0	8.0	33.3	8.3	7.6	1,676

a. All votes are calculated before shifts. Alaska, Hawaii, and the territories are excluded.

ductibility of convention results is only .73 for the Democrats in
1972 and but .60 for the Republicans in 1976.[1] Thus, we find
such anomalies as Midwestern opposition to the liberal McGovern
and support for the more moderate Carter, California support of
Reagan, and Southern and Midwestern endorsement of Ford.

POLITICAL MONEY

The decline of established partisan politics is further promoted by
developments in campaign finance, most particularly the post-
Watergate reform acts of 1974 and 1976. The full effects of the laws
will not be known for some time, and they will certainly be different
from both the intentions of Congress and the expectations of
academic observers. The general effect, however, is already apparent.
It is to shift money, the most vital resource of politics, from the
parties to the control of individual candidates and to nonparty
individuals and groups.

The new law, supplemented by the Supreme Court's interpretive
decision of 1976, takes money away from the parties, while it
provides finances for individuals and outside agencies. The parties are
deprived of money by the limitations on individual contributors who
may not give more than $1,000 to any single recipient. The total

amount of spending by a candidate or party is also limited. While the national party may spend $3 million, its presidential candidate is limited to $20 million, plus adjustments and fund-raising expenses. While these restrictions are easily justified as means of preventing corruption, their effect is to limit politicians rather than to restrict electoral spending generally.

In fact, the law and the Supreme Court do not limit the influence of money in elections—but rather only the influence of party money. Four aspects of the legislation are particularly important. Existing provisions provide for federal subsidies for campaigning, but these subsidies are paid to candidates, not to parties. With the candidates provided seven times the capital that is permitted parties, this provision promotes the increasing separation of national candidates · from the parties. Furthermore, subsidies are paid only to presidential candidates, leaving the rest of the party from Congress to local office fiscally unrelated to the head of the ticket. As interpreted by the Supreme Court, moreover, even the limitations on spending may be ignored by a candidate who declines federal subsidies and raises his own funds. Therefore, candidates of personal wealth or with close connections to such wealth—e.g., a Rockefeller or Kennedy—can still spend unlimited sums. Finally, there is no limitation on contributions or expenditures "independent" of the candidates and parties. Therefore individuals or groups are free to raise and spend whatever they wish, so long as they do not become allied to the political parties. It now becomes ever more to the advantage of political interests to ignore established politicians.

This legislation may become the classic illustration of the dominance of latent over manifest functions. We may doubt that Congress intended to subvert the political parties, but this is the cumulative impact of the finance law. It provides a sufficient explanation of the astounding Republican contest of 1976. The conventional wisdom of politics—and political science—cannot explain the near success of Ronald Reagan. An incumbent President, however chosen, should easily win renomination. In the beginning of the election year, President Ford had achieved a measure of personal popularity; the Vietnam war had ended; there were signs of economic expansion; and the President had the support of almost all important party officials. Compared to Herbert Hoover's position in 1932, there was no reason to doubt his convention success. Nevertheless, Reagan persevered, and the availability of money must be considered a major reason for his persistence. Regardless of party pressure or early primary defeats, Reagan could continue to count on personal contributions, which were doubled in value by federal subsidies. He further benefited from independent expenditures by his sympathizers. The national government thus subsidized insurgency against its own chief executive.

In the Democratic party, with no incumbent leader, the law promoted factionalism, providing support for all comers, regardless of their standing in the party or chances of success. George Wallace, who split the party in 1968, gained proportionately the most federal subsidies, while even Ellen McCormack, running in opposition to the platform, became eligible for federal grants. The Supreme Court's suspension of the law during the vital primary period also affected the race, leaving Morris Udall in debt while allowing Carter, a relatively wealthy candidate, to raise funds privately.

The finance laws reinforce the other developments we have noted. They provide support for the personal, candidate-oriented organizations which now dominate presidential politics. They demand a national constituency, since funds must be raised in at least 20 states to be eligible for federal matching. By ignoring and slighting parties, they promote the general tendencies to emphasize other means of campaigning. They stimulate appeals to ideological and interest groups. Together, surely, these changes do not promote anything resembling a "responsible two-party system." Rather, they foster the turn toward "antiparty government."

THE DECLINE OF CONVENTIONS

New finance laws have accelerated another trend, the elimination of the party nominating convention as a significant decision-making body. No convention since 1952 has taken more than a single ballot to nominate its presidential candidate. Throughout this period, moreover, with the exception of the 1976 Republican confrontation, the winner of the nomination has been determined before the convention actually convened. Only large blunders could have prevented the nominations of such front-runners as Kennedy in 1960 or Nixon in 1968, even though there was a spurious excitement to these meetings.

Once described as "a chess game disguised as a circus," the convention now resembles more a newspaper chess column in which amateurs replay the moves of past masters. Among the reasons for this decline of the convention is the loss of political expertise. The participants at these conclaves never acquired the skill to conduct grand negotiations, or have lost this ability through disuse. Like all talents, that of striking political deals requires practice, but contemporary convention delegates and their leaders have no experience to draw upon. Even the few survivors of a previous age, such as Chicago Mayor Richard J. Daley, find their skills atophied through disuse. Surely the Democratic conventions of 1968 and 1972 were ideal occasions for the emergence of a compromise or dark-horse candidate, such as Edward Kennedy. Yet, in both years, the party's leaders fumbled away the opportunity to choose this likely winner.

The incapacity for negotiation was further demonstrated in 1976. Before the succession of Carter primary victories, there were widespread predictions of a negotiated nomination at the convention. A massive number of primaries, a bevy of candidates, and new rules for proportional division of delegates appeared certain to prevent any one candidate from winning the nomination by storm. Despite all of these favorable institutional factors, however, the party could not forestall the personal drive of one of the least known, and least well-connected, candidates. The likely result of a negotiated convention is further testament to the politicians' lack of control. A brokered convention, it appeared, would quickly turn to Hubert Humphrey, one of its oldest campaigners, who already had been defeated for the Presidency. After decades of growth into the dominant party of the nation, with 35 governors and 62 Senators available, the party would be so unresourceful as to turn to a proven loser. This hypothetical outcome is surely testament to the limited abilities of the pretended "bosses."

Largely without design, the Democrats in 1976 did nominate a candidate with personal appeal, supported by a skilled organization, who could unite the party. This result, however, is more a credit to Governor Carter than to the party. The situation among the Republicans provides still fuller evidence of party decline. With an incumbent President avid for nomination, with virtually all of their elected governors and national officials supporting him, the Republicans still could not prevent the insurgency of Ronald Reagan, nor manage a unifying convention. While the Kansas City conclave did evidence real decision-making power, it also demonstrated the absence of party decisiveness.

The critical agencies in presidential nominations have changed. One of the most vital is the mass media, which appraise candidates, their abilities, and their chances of success. Candidates use the media to appeal directly to vital constituencies, rather than bargaining with party representatives. The media's particular interest in news results in the exaggeration of the importance of discrete events, and their interpretation of these events defines reality. Thus, the New Hampshire primary has been transformed from a minor test of popularity in a minor state to the event which gives a candidate "momentum." Television has further contributed to the decline of the convention by making classic negotiations virtually impossible, for "open covenants openly arrived at" are as difficult to achieve domestically as internationally. Parties do not want to present a messy picture of bargaining to their costless television audience. Instead they seek to present an image of unity and concord, and the result is dullness and impotence.

Party power over nominations has also been displaced by the spread of state primaries which mandate delegate votes. As recently as the 1960s, primaries elected fewer than a third of the delegates and were useful largely as confirmations of the candidates' popular standing and electoral appeal. By 1976, nearly three-fourths of the delegates were chosen in these contests, and they had become decisive. A candidate carrying most, not necessarily all, of the primaries, would win the nomination as did McGovern and Carter. The convention could retain some power of decision only if the voters were clearly divided, as in the Reagan-Ford confrontation. The odds surely are against recurrence of this latter pattern. By removing the party organizations from the nominations, state presidential primaries sever the head of the political party's body—a dangerous condition.

VOTERS AND PARTIES

Electoral behavior provides the final evidence of the decline of the parties. The organized parties have less influence because they have less value to candidates. To win a presidential nomination once brought an aspirant not only ballot position, funding, and campaign workers. Most importantly, it assured him of a substantial share of the vote simply on the basis of the Democratic or Republican label he had won. This label is less helpful today, and candidates therefore need pay less to its manufacturers.

The decreased impact of partisanship is abundantly clear. In answers to standard questions on self-identification, from a third to two-fifths of the American electorate now disclaim affective ties to the parties, and the proportion reaches a majority among the youngest voters (Pomper, 1975:23). There is a general disdain for parties, reflected in the large proportions who see them as contributing little to the maintenance of democratic government (Dennis, 1966, 1974).

Beyond identification, there are multiple indicators in actual behavior of disaffection from the parties. Nearly one of seven 1968 voters cast ballots for the third-party candidacy of George Wallace, and polls during that campaign placed his strength as high as one-fifth of the electorate. Electoral instability is evident as well in ticket-splitting, in defection from the party of self-identification, and in vote switching from one election to the next.

The limited appeal of party loyalty is demonstrated in Table 2, which partitions the electorate of 1972 on various dimensions to reach the core, partisan voter. We first separate the new voters in 1972, since they have not yet been able to develop a history of loyalty. We then successively locate the self-identified independents, those self-identified Democrats or Republicans who voted against their party's presidential nominee, those (of the remainder) who switched votes from 1968 to 1972, and finally those who split their tickets in the congressional race. Of all voters, only about a third passed all of these tests.[2]

These aggregate figures may underestimate the electoral effect of partisanship. More complicated procedures, however, lead to the same conclusion, evidencing an increased effect of issue preferences and candidate appeals. One estimate is that party loyalty, even under favorable statistical assumptions, cannot explain more than half of the variance in the vote (Pomper, 1975:163). Another is that the percentage of pure partisan, issueless voters has declined drastically, from 42% in 1960 to 23% in 1972 (Nie et al., 1976:302). Other analysts place more emphasis on the appeals of candidates, rather

Table 2. COMPOSITION OF THE 1972 ELECTORATE

Group	Percent of Total	(N)
New voters of 1972	15.8	(192)
Self-identified independents (excluding new voters)	23.4	(285)
Defectors from party identification (excluding new voters)	16.0	(195)
Switchers from 1968 vote (excluding previous groups)	4.4	(54)
Ticket-splitters in 1972 (excluding previous groups)	5.2	(63)
Consistent partisan voters	35.2	(429)
Total	100.0	(1,218)

SOURCE: 1972 Election Study of the Center for Political Studies, University of Michigan.

than issues (Kirkpatrick, 1975:268). The common area of agreement is that party loyalty alone cannot be relied upon to win votes.

Candidates will be successful in this situation when they are, or can be made to appear, independent of the parties. Surely part of the success of Jimmy Carter must be explained by the opposition of the very party leaders whose favor was once needed to assure nomination. Similarly, the Republican party designation was crucially affected by crossover votes, Democrats who felt no hesitancy in voting in Republican primaries. Thus, although Ford was the consistent choice of his own party's rank-and-file, he was threatened by these invaders who felt neither loyalty to their "own" party nor repugnance at formally entering the opposition. As strategies outside the parties show success and as voters become uncommitted to maintaining their past loyalties, we can expect further waning of party vigor.

III. THE EFFECT ON THE PARTIES

The state of the parties appears rather pitiful, when sketched in the present time. However, the important point is a dynamic one: the contemporary electoral process stimulates further decline of the parties. The lessons learned in one election become part of the influences in the postelectoral period and in the next contest, leading to acceleration of these trends.

One effect will be on candidate strategies. The success of Carter and Reagan's near nomination will encourage future candidates to emphasize their asserted independence of the party leaders. Indeed, this development was already evident in 1976 when California Governor Brown belatedly entered the presidential primaries, emphasizing his novelty and independence. Insurgency is no longer the crusade of political Don Quixotes; it is the likely path to the political kingdom.

LOSS OF PARTY FUNCTIONS

More generally, we can say that the electoral success of insurgents demonstrates that the political parties have lost their monopoly over recruitment. This loss is evident beyond the presidential level. The last areas to nominate state candidates through party processes were Connecticut and Indiana, but these bastions have fallen, and nomination through the direct primary is now universal. Even attempts by the party leaders to endorse candidates in the primary are now limited. Where attempted, such efforts are likely to be self-defeating, as in New York, where the party endorsement brings a candidate not votes but the burden of charges of "bossism." Nor are party careers necessary to advancement. The ambitious can switch parties, as did Donald Riegle and John Lindsay, or be elected as pure independents, as did Governor James Longley of Maine, or seek high office without previous political experience, as did Senators John Glenn and James Buckley.

Additionally, the party has lost its monopoly over vital resources. Presidential funds, as we have noted, are now independently provided through the federal government, and the 1976 Democratic platform promises similar support for congressional candidates. George Wallace was able to secure a place on the ballot in all of the 50 states, despite the opposition of both major parties, and the Supreme Court has facilitated access by other independent candidates, such as Eugene McCarthy in 1976. Campaigning is now accomplished not by party canvassers, but through the mass media or, locally, by unions and public employees organizations protected from party patronage demands by civil service laws. Delegates to national conventions are elected on the basis of their candidate preference, not as rewards for their loyalty and service to the organization.

As the parties become less able to control these vital resources of the electoral process, the voters respond less to their weakening appeals. The parties then lose their most vital strength, their very legitimacy. Slogans such as "vote for the man, not the party" come to be descriptions of behavior, not only advertising rhetoric. The data of Table 3 point to a nonpartisan electoral future. Five political generations are defined, on the basis of the time they first voted: before the New Deal, during the Roosevelt elections, in the postwar period of 1948 to 1956, the 1960s, and 1972. These generations are then traced over the last four presidential elections. The data show that the proportion of independents has risen considerably and that strength of partisanship has declined (Pomper, 1975:23). They also reveal that this increase has occurred in all political generations and that the increase is greatest among the rising generations in the electorate. It is therefore quite likely that independents will soon constitute a plurality of the nation. The parties are disfavored by the voters. In this situation, they are likely to be ignored by ambitious

Table 3. PARTISAN IDENTIFICATION BY POLITICAL GENERATIONS[a]

	Strong Democrat	Weak Democrat	Inde- pendent	Weak Republican	Strong Republican	(N)
Pre-New Deal						
1960	22.9	23.1	16.6	16.8	20.6	(637)
1964	30.7	20.7	14.6	15.4	18.5	(410)
1968	26.5	25.9	16.9	13.1	17.5	(343)
1972	20.5	24.8	19.6	15.8	19.3	(419)
New Deal						
1960	20.3	25.3	26.8	13.9	13.6	(679)
1964	27.8	26.8	22.5	13.1	9.9	(497)
1968	20.2	26.2	26.4	18.0	9.3	(451)
1972	20.5	26.9	25.3	15.3	11.9	(620)
Postwar						
1960	20.9	27.3	26.9	11.2	13.7	(498)
1964	25.1	27.5	25.9	13.6	8.0	(375)
1968	23.3	25.7	31.5	13.0	6.6	(378)
1972	15.7	25.9	35.3	13.1	10.1	(567)
The 1960s						
1960	3.7	40.7	29.6	11.1	14.8	(54)
1964	22.9	25.7	32.9	12.0	6.4	(249)
1968	11.6	24.9	43.2	14.4	5.9	(354)
1972	8.9	24.8	46.0	13.4	6.9	(642)
New voters						
1972	8.7	27.1	50.9	7.0	5.4	(391)

a. Cell entries are percentages adding horizontally by rows to 100%, except for rounding errors.

SOURCE: Pomper, 1975:23.

office-seekers and to be neglected in such public policies as campaign financing.

THE NEW PARTY STRENGTH

At the same time as the parties have been weakened by these many tendencies, there has been another, apparently countervailing trend. This is the development of strong national party organizations, evident particularly among the Democrats. The party has created a coherent set of national institutions and binding rules which sharply contrast with the traditional portrait of the parties as decentralized and incoherent. It is simply no longer true, as Schattschneider (1942:32f.) wrote in his classic description, that incoherence "constitutes the most important single fact concerning the American parties." Coherence is evident in such indexes as congressional voting, where party unity has recently increased. It is even more evident in party organization.

Over the past 20 years, the national Democratic party has placed a number of restrictions on its once-sovereign state units. Beginning in 1956, state delegations to the national conventions were required to pledge loyalty to the national ticket—a relatively modest requirement. After 1964, racial discrimination in the selection of delegates was banned and was enforced by the exclusion of segregated state units. The most complete changes came as a result of the reform efforts of the McGovern-Fraser commission before the 1972 convention and of its successor, the Mikulski commission. The national party mandated increased and relatively proportional participation in party affairs at all levels by designated demographic groups (particularly racial minorities), women, and persons under 30 years of age. By 1980, the party will actively seek equal numbers of women and men. Further, it required changes in the means of selecting delegates, even when in conflict with state law or party practice, and has now established a complete system of proportional representation in every electoral unit. Delegate fees, early meetings, and irregular practices have been abolished, and these bans have been effectively enforced.

The party has also created itself as a national body, rather than as a collection of state units. Membership in the national convention is no longer based principally on electoral votes, a reflection of the states as constituent elements, but now equally weights the contribution of these states to a national Democratic vote. Similarly, the national committee once acknowledged state sovereignty by giving equal representation to all states, but now is weighted by the size of states and includes representatives from all branches of federal, state, and local government.

For the first time in American political history, the Democrats in 1974 adopted a national party charter, which gave permanent existence to the party, and provided for mid-term conferences of the party, giving it a visible existence other than during the four days of a presidential nominating convention. New organs of party government were created, including a national finance council, a national education and training council, and a judicial council to settle disputes and interpret party rules. The rudiments of a full governing structure are now in place, including the traditional legislative, executive, and judicial branches.

The national party is able to exercise these powers in the absence of legal constraints. In the 1972 Democratic convention, important credentials disputes turned on the right of the convention to exclude delegates from Illinois and California duly elected under state law. In both instances, these delegates were barred because the credentials committee ruled that they failed to meet some of the new reform rules. A critical decision of the Supreme Court upheld the right of the party to self-government because of "the large public interest in allowing the political processes to function free from judicial supervision" (*O'Brien* v. *Brown* 409 U.S. 1, 1972).

The independence of political parties was further acknowledged in a later case involving the Republicans. A challenge brought against the national party disputed the allocation of convention delegates, arguing for application of the "one-man, one-vote" principle, in the same fashion as the apportionment of state or congressional representatives. The Circuit Court of Appeals, later upheld by the Supreme Court, declined to intervene, declaring the party free to organize "in the way that will make it the most effective organization . . . without interference from the courts" (*Ripon Society* v. *National Republican Party* 525 F.2d. 567, 1975, cert. denied 96 S.Ct. 1147, 1976).

These decisions are important in themselves, for they seem to conflict partially with the earlier position of the Supreme Court which recognized political parties as virtually a formal part of government. It was for this reason that the "white primary" was abolished, even when no state law was involved (*Smith* v. *Allwright,* 321 U.S. 649, 1944; *Rice* v. *Elmore,* 165 F.2d. 387, 1947). In these recent cases, however, the parties are permitted actions which are contrary to state law or which are different from principles of representation applied to formal governmental institutions. The result is to make the parties, at least on the national level, autonomous and potentially strong institutions. At the same time, the parties, as we have argued, are becoming weak influences in the political process. There is a seeming contradiction in the existence of strong institutions of little effectiveness.

THE PARTY AS PRIVATE ASSOCIATION

The apparent contradiction can be resolved if we recognize that we are witnessing the transformation of American political parties. One element of the transformation is structural, an internal shift of power from state to national parties. While state parties are losing their functions, national parties are developing as coherent organizations. While state parties are not able to control national decisions such as the presidential nomination, national parties are more able to control state decisions such as the selection of convention delegates.

A more basic transformation is occurring as well, altering the place of parties generally in American politics. In the scholarly literature, and even in practice, parties held a special place among the many contestants for power and were recognized as the major intermediate associations between the citizen and the government. While multitudes of interest groups attempted to influence government, the political party was unique as an aggregator of interests, for "no interest group or alliance of such groups has supplanted the party as a device for mobilizing majorities" (Truman, 1951:272).

In contemporary America, it seems more accurate to describe the political party as little more than another private association or interest group. Like other associations, such as the American Medical Association, it attempts to influence elections, but both groups have only marginal effects. Like other associations of a nominally "private" character, it successfully claims independence from governmental regulation. The courts have long been hesitant to interfere with the internal organization of churches or unions. Now the courts have extended similar freedom, based on the same First Amendment principles, to the parties. This reluctance to prescribe party rules suggests that the organization of the Democrats and Republicans is no more politically relevant than the structure of the Episcopal Church or the United Mineworkers.

In elections, the parties are becoming only one of many actors, not the chief contestants. Parties are wooed by ambitious candidates, but so are the mass media. Parties contribute funds to these candidates, but so do private individuals and interest groups. Parties campaign for their nominees, but so do labor unions, and often more widely and more effectively. Parties sponsor candidates, but so do conservationists, business groups, and ideologues of various persuasions.

Even in their most characteristic functions, nominations, the formal party organizations lack an exclusive position. Delegates to the national conventions are successfully sponsored by these organizations in some places, such as Cook County, Illinois. Success is also achieved by interest groups, such as the 1976 Labor Coalition Clearinghouse, which chose over 400 Democratic delegates, by ideological groups such as New York liberals, and, most decisively, by candidate factions acting outside of or in opposition to the established parties. Once won, a party nomination must be supplemented by endorsements of interest groups, the media, and factional leaders. Eventually, with the increase in electoral instability, a party label on a candidate may come to have no more effect than a union label on clothing.

The nonpreferred position of the parties has now been partially incorporated into federal law. When Congress adopted a revised finance law following the Supreme Court's 1976 decision, a vigorous effort was needed to allow parties to receive contributions in the same manner as other political committees. The final statute does give some particular recognition to the parties, since individuals may contribute up to $20,000 to the parties, while they are limited to $5,000 in gifts to other committees. Nevertheless, the law still places the parties in the same juridical position as other private groups, even if it is more well-endowed for purposes of electioneering. However, parties are limited in their spending—giving them a less advantageous position than other committees, which may spend freely.

More generally, the political parties are being incorporated into the overall American system of "interest group liberalism" (Lowi, 1969, chap. 3). The liberal model sees politics as a struggle of competing interests. Government is neither to grant privileges nor to handicap any group in this struggle. Government is to be an arbiter, to maintain the competition itself. Its role "is one of ensuring access particularly to the most effectively organized, and of ratifying the agreements and adjustments worked out among the competing leaders and their claims" (Lowi, 1969:71).

This model explains many actions of American legislatures and bureaucracies and the character of policy outputs. We now see its application to the electoral process itself. Parties are permitted access, but so are other groups. Government encourages this access through financial subsidies, but no distinction is made among those seeking funds on the basis of their adherence to party principle or discipline. The goal becomes participation for its own sake. Individual participation is encouraged through widespread primaries easily subject to crossovers and insurgencies. Candidate participation is encouraged by easy access to campaign subsidies and "equal time" on the mass media. Group participation is encouraged by permitting independent committees to solicit funds and spread propaganda. New social movements are encouraged through easy placement on the ballot and postelection subsidies. Government does not limit access to the political competition, nor regulate the organization of the competitors, but rather seeks only to stimulate more activity.

The defect of interest group liberalism as a general mode of government is its neglect of policy outcomes. Its application to electoral politics evidences the same defect, for it deprives the parties of a continuing, substantive meaning. Party programs then vary with the character of the particular activists and candidates of a specific time, rather than providing a persisting opportunity for voter judgment. To be sure, the national parties are more organizationally coherent and better able to enforce a measure of internal discipline. What the parties increasingly lack is a palpable reason for coherence and discipline. "There is therefore no substance. Neither is there procedure. There is only process" (Lowi, 1969:97).

Many social trends have promoted the decline of partisan politics in the United States. At root, however, the decline can be traced to a theoretical failure, the placement of the parties within the ideology of interest group liberalism. The place of parties has not been fully considered, even by those most concerned with party reform. These advocates have championed the liberal solution of greater popular involvement in party decisions, while also seeking strengthened national organizations (Ranney, 1975). No contradiction between these aims was seen, as even the notable Schattschneider committee called for both centralized and open parties, arguing, "Clearly such a degree of unity within the parties cannot be brought about without party procedures that give a large body of people an opportunity to share in the development of the party program" (American Political Science Association, 1950:18). Today, the contradictions between these two goals are increasingly apparent. Parties can be both hierarchical and participatory only if they are also irrelevant.

The special place of parties must be rethought—and reclaimed. Ultimately, this revival of partisan organizations is properly the concern of advocates of representative government itself. The parties have provided the basic means of aggregating social interests, of simplifying choices for a mass electorate, and of permitting responsibility to be fixed for governmental achievements and failures. They have permitted the voters to make at least a retrospective judgment on public policy and occasionally to provide direction for the future (Key, 1966). In the context of the 1976 elections, it is difficult to see these functions being fulfilled. While a Jimmy Carter may enforce unity on the Democrats, this is a personal triumph, implying no permanent responsibility of the party. Among Republicans, the most basic agreement between Ford and Reagan was that neither had any responsibility for the actions of a twice-elected President of their party. Can elections without parties then be anything but short-term choices of particular candidates and their idiosyncratic policies?

The ultimate cost of the decline of parties is the loss of popular control over public policies and the consequent inability of less privileged elements to affect their social fate. "Political parties, with all their well-known human and structural shortcomings, are the only devices thus far invented by the wit of Western man which with some effectiveness can generate countervailing collective power on behalf of the many individually powerless against the relatively few who are individually—or organizationally—powerful" (Burnham, 1970:133). The policy result of party decline will be a fundamental conservatism, with no alternate agency available to generate the political power of a popular majority.

Elections will surely continue, for they have demonstrated their social utility in investing rulers with legitimacy. Social movements will periodically express the discontents of neglected and disadvantaged groups. Grievances will be heard and responded to from time to time by sensitive · individual leaders and by legislators concerned over their personal or their constituents' futures. The republican form will persist, even while alienation further develops.

Yet, if the decline of partisan politics continues, if parties become only one among many participants in elections, much will be lost. We may identify the losses as choice, as clarity, as diffuse support, or as the effective aggregation of political interests. But, in a single word, the loss will be that of democracy.

NOTES

1. The correlation is calculated as a Democratic comparison of McGovern's support, by states, with that of the combined Kennedy, Humphrey, and Stevenson vote in 1960, and a Republican comparison of Ford's support with that of Eisenhower in 1952. These were judged the most comparable previous convention alignments. The 1976 roll call is found in the *Congressional Quarterly Weekly Report,* 34 (August 21, 1976), p. 2313.

2. The figures in Table 2 were calculated to eliminate overlapping of the various categories, so that the ticket-splitters, for example, are only those voters who otherwise meet all tests of party loyalty. In the total sample, however, many persons do manifest more than one of these behaviors. Overall, independents constituted 30% of the 1972 sample: 27.1% defected from their self-identified party; 27.3% were party switchers from 1968 to 1972; and 29.5% split their presidential-congressional tickets.

REFERENCES

American Political Science Association, Committee on Political Parties (1950). "Toward a more responsible two-party system." American Political Science Review, 44(supplement).

BAIN, R. (1960). Convention decisions and voting records. Washington, D.C.: Brookings Institution.

BECK, P. (1974). "A socialization theory of partisan realignment." Pp. 199-219 in R.G. Niemi (ed.), The politics of future citizens. San Francisco: Jossey-Bass.

BENIGER, J.R. (1976). "Winning the presidential nomination: National polls and state primary elections, 1936-1972." Public Opinion Quarterly, 40(spring):22-38.

BRYCE, J. (1914). The American commonwealth (3rd rev. ed.). New York: Macmillan.

BURNHAM, W.D. (1965). "The changing shape of the American political universe." American Political Science Review, 59(March):7-28.

––– (1970). Critical elections and the mainsprings of American politics. New York: Norton.

CAMPBELL, A., CONVERSE, P., MILLER, W., and STOKES, D. (1960). The American voter. New York: Wiley.

CHESTER, L., HODGSON, G., and PAGE, B. (1969). An American melodrama. New York: Viking.

DENNIS, J. (1966). "Support for the party system by the mass public." American Political Science Review, 60(September):600-615.

––– (1974). "Trends in public support for the American political party system." Paper presented to the annual meeting of the American Political Science Association, Chicago.

DUVERGER, M. (1954). Political parties. New York: Wiley.

FARLEY, J.A. (1938). Behind the ballots. New York: Harcourt, Brace.

HEARD, A. (1962). The costs of democracy. Garden City: Doubleday Anchor.

HOFSTADTER, R. (1969). The idea of a party system. Berkeley: University of California Press.

HUNTINGTON, S. (1968). Political order in changing societies. New Haven, Conn.: Yale University Press.

JAMES, J. (1974). American political parties in transition. New York: Harper and Row.

JENSEN, R. (1971). The winning of the Midwest. Chicago: University of Chicago Press.

KEECH, W., and MATTHEWS, D. (1976). The party's choice. Washington, D.C.: Brookings Institution.

KEY, V.O. (1955). "A theory of critical elections." Journal of Politics, 17(February):3-18.

––– (1966). The responsible electorate. Cambridge, Mass.: Harvard University Press.

KIRKPATRICK, S. (1975). "Candidates, parties and issues in the American electorate." American Politics Quarterly, 3(July):247-283.

LOWI, T. (1967). "Party, policy and Constitution in America." Pp. 238-276 in W.N. Chambers and W.D. Burnham (eds.), The American party systems. New York: Oxford University Press.

––– (1969). The end of liberalism. New York: Norton.

MATTHEWS, O. (1960). U.S. Senators and their world. Chapel Hill: University of North Carolina Press.

MUNGER, F., and BLACKHURST, J. (1965). "Factionalism in the national conventions, 1940-1964." Journal of Politics, 27(May):375-394.

NIE, N.H., VERBA, S., and PETROCIK, J. (1976). The changing American voter. Cambridge, Mass.: Harvard University Press.

POMPER, G. (1967). "Classification of presidential elections." Journal of Politics, 29(August):535-566.

――― (1971). "Factionalism in the 1968 national conventions." Journal of Politics, 33(August):826-830.

――― (1975). Voters' choice. New York: Harper and Row.

RANNEY, A. (1975). Curing the mischiefs of faction. Berkeley: University of California Press.

RANNEY, A., and KENDALL, W. (1956). Democracy and the American party system. New York: Harcourt, Brace.

SCHATTSCHNEIDER, E.E. (1942). Party government. New York: Holt, Rinehart and Winston.

SCHLESINGER, J.A. (1966). Ambition and politics. Chicago: Rand McNally.

SNOWISS, M. (1966). "Congressional recruitment and representation." American Political Science Review, 60(September):627-639.

TRUMAN, D.B. (1951). The governmental process. New York: Knopf.

WHITE, T.H. (1961). The making of the President 1960. New York: Atheneum.

Chapter 2

THE IMPACT OF ELECTORAL RULES ON PRIMARY ELECTIONS: THE DEMOCRATIC PRESIDENTIAL PRIMARIES IN 1976

LOUIS MAISEL
GERALD J. LIEBERMAN

When the platform committee for the 1976 Democratic National Convention met in its preconvention session, the spirit was one of harmony and unity; the result was a moderate platform to which only one minority report, and that on a fairly noncontroversial subject, was attached. When the 1976 rules committee met in its preconvention session, the spirit was the same, but the result was quite different. The draft rules dealt with basic philosophical conflicts over the means of delegate selection for future conventions. Eight minority reports, some of which dealt with topics that had provoked heated debate, were attached to the committee's final report. That contrast should be instructive.

AUTHORS' NOTE: This research was made possible, in part, by a grant from the Social Science Research Committee of Colby College. We would like to take this opportunity to thank Ruth Streeter, who served as our research assistant; Congressman Donald Fraser, Rhodes Cook, Steven Lieberman, and Charles Hauss, who made substantive criticisms of an earlier draft of this paper; and John Sweney and Charles Bassett, who provided invaluable editorial assistance. Obviously, we alone are responsible for any errors which remain in this work; those who reviewed it earlier saved us from many more. Carol Amez and C. Blake typed draft upon draft of this chapter with speed and accuracy which was much appreciated.

By the time the convention's committees met, in mid-June, Governor Jimmy Carter's nomination was assured. Few wanted to raise the kinds of open conflicts which could possibly jeopardize his chances for victory in November. The spirit of harmony and unity prevailed, and the moderate platform was adopted. Rules committee members were acutely aware, however, that their deliberations would affect future conventions as well as the 1976 session. Theirs was the first opportunity to assess the impact of the rules under which Governor Carter had achieved nomination and to determine if these rules should be modified for the calls to future conventions. Delegate selection rules are not neutral: they affect the changes of different types of candidates in differing ways. The rules committee in 1976 was staking out the ground for future presidential nominating contents.

I. INTRODUCTION

In this paper we will attempt to assess, in a systematic way, the impact of the various rules under which states selected their delegates to the 1976 Democratic National Convention. The Charter of the Democratic party mandates that each state delegation fairly reflect the presidential preferences of those participating at all stages in the selection process. However, each state party is free to adopt its own rules for delegate selection if those rules conform to certain broad guidelines. State rules are subject to review by the Compliance Review Commission (CRC) of the Democratic National Committee (DNC). The rules accepted for 1976 resulted in wide and sometimes confusing variations in the process by which state delegations were to achieve fair reflection of presidential preferences. Some states used proportional representation while others used derivatives approved by the CRC. We will examine the degree to which delegations chosen by methods other than proportional representation did or did not fairly reflect the presidential preferences of those selecting the delegates. It is first necessary to clarify the issues raised by the complexity of the nominating process.

Seventeen states held no primaries at all; rather, Democrats elected their delegates to the National Convention at state conventions.[1] Although the exact process varied, most states used some sort of tiered system of caucuses and conventions, starting at the local level, with delegates to each higher level reflecting the presidential preferences of those who had elected them. We will not be dealing with the convention states. Though some of the problems we raise would apply to some of the convention states as well, sufficient data on presidential preferences at the lower levels are not available, and thus analysis of the way the conventions systems worked would of necessity be either impressionistic or theoretical, but not analytical.

Instead, we will concentrate on those states which held primary elections in order to choose delegates to the New York City convention.[2] Variations among these states are still considerable. Primary participants perform two separable tasks in the delegate selection process. First, they determine to which presidential candidates, if any, delegates to the national convention will be pledged. Second, they determine who those delegates will be. Many of the debates at the rules committee meeting were centered around the latter problem. Should the rules be amended to assure that minorities or women be more strongly represented at the national convention? How could the rules be so amended? These questions were extensions of the desire to open the Democratic party to groups which had been traditionally underrepresented, a concern given impetus because both women and minorities were less well represented in 1976 than they had been in 1972 or at the Charter conference in 1974. While questions of demographic representation are important for those examining the functioning of conventions (see, for example, Sullivan et al., 1974:1-16), they are not central to our study. Rather we will concentrate solely on those rules which determine how well the delegate selection process allows the presidential preferences of those participating in the primaries to be reflected by the preferences of those chosen as delegates.

The Charter of the Democratic party, adopted in Kansas City in 1974, states explicitly that delegates to presidential nominating conventions should be chosen in such a way as to "assure that delegations fairly reflect the division of preferences expressed by those who participate in the Presidential nominating process" (Charter of the Democratic Party, 1974, article II, section 4.ii). This mandate is reflected in the "Rules for Delegate Selection" (1975:6) issued by the DNC.

The Call of the 1976 Democratic National Convention shall include provisions that assure that the delegates to the 1976 Democratic National Convention be chosen in a manner which fairly reflects the division of preferences expressed by those who participate in the presidential nominating process in each state, territory, and the District of Columbia. At all stages of the delegate selection process, delegations shall be allocated in a fashion that fairly reflects the expressed presidential preference, uncommitted, or no preference status of the primary voters.

It is clear from the legislative history that these selections were written in order to avoid "winner-take-all" primaries. In 1972, the convention declared flatly that "in 1976 there can be no winner-take-all" when it adopted the rules committee's report. Some "winner-take-all" primaries, most notably California's, were permitted in 1972, with the clear understanding that they would be eliminated by 1976. This mandate was never revoked.

Through a somewhat loose interpretation of this mandate, however, 13 states were permitted to use "loophole" primaries in 1976. Such primaries are de facto "winner-take-all" primaries at the district level. Voters cast ballots directly for delegate candidates, usually voting as many times as there are delegates to be elected, and those delegates with the greatest number of votes win. Past experience has shown that voters tend to cast their votes for delegates supporting the same presidential candidate. Thus, if three presidential candidates were competing for five delegates in a district, each would file a slate of five delegate candidates. It is very likely that the top finishers in this hypothetical primary, in which each voter is permitted to vote for up to five delegate candidates, would all be pledged to the same presidential contender, even though that contender's delegates' percentage of the total votes cast might be only 40%, while the other candidates' delegates polled 35% and 25%. Five delegates pledged to a plurality winner, with none for either of the two losers, is far from proportional representation.

"Loophole" primaries were approved by the Mikulski Commission and declared valid in the Delegate Selection Rules (1975:6). In October, 1975, Robert Strauss, chairman of the DNC, ruled that the credentials committee would not hear any challenges based on nonproportionality of representation.

Lengle and Shafer (1976) have already discussed the effect of "winner-take-all" versus districted versus statewide proportional delegate selection rules on the power of various states within the Democratic party and on the fates of particular candidates. Rhodes Cook, in an early assessment of the 1976 primaries, has declared that the new rules have had little impact (Cook, 1976). In this paper we focus on the differences between strict proportional representation and "loophole" primaries in terms of how well the delegates so chosen reflect the preferences of the voters casting primary ballots and in terms of what types of candidates each system is likely to benefit or hurt.

The 1976 rules vary from strict proportional representation in another way as well. Rule 11, dealing with "Fair Reflection of Presidential Preferences," contains the following proviso: "except that preferences securing less than fifteen percent (15%) of the votes cast for the delegation need not be awarded any delegates" (Delegate Selection Rules, 1975:6). A number of states, both primary and caucus states in this instance, have adopted the 15% minimum eligibility requirement or in some cases a lower one, e.g., 5%. When the number of delegates to be chosen is large, minimum eligibility requirements have the effect of depriving of delegates those who otherwise would qualify for them, straying from strict proportional representation. The 15% minimum eligibility requirement was instituted to diminish the possibility that fringe candidates would obtain some delegates. However, when a large number of serious candidates are competing, as was the case early in the 1976 primary process, minimum eligibility requirements tend to magnify narrow victories for those who win and unduly penalize those who fall just below the limits. We will explore the effects of 15% and 5% eligibility requirements, again in terms of how they influence the representative nature of the process and the chances of certain candidates.

In order to assure that public and party officials and underrepresented minorities were given a chance to attend the national convention, the Delegate Selection Rules (1975:7) and the Charter (article II, section 4.vi) allow for the selection on an at-large basis of up to 25% of the delegates chosen in primary states, provided again that those so chosen reflect the presidential preferences of those participating in the process. In some states (e.g., Massachusetts) the presidential preferences expressed in the popular vote statewide were used to determine the distribution of at-large delegates. In others, however, the presidential preferences of the delegates already selected were used to apportion those chosen at large (e.g., New York). The effect of this procedure is to disenfranchise further those voting for certain minor candidates, particularly those whose strength is just above the minimum eligibility requirement but is spread unevenly throughout the state. In that case, although these candidates would win some delegates at the district level, they would not gain the delegates due them from those chosen at large. This impact of this procedure will be examined as well.

Finally, another factor influencing the delegate selection procedure is the method of apportionment used. An apportionment method must be used to distribute national convention delegates among the various states, territories, and the District of Columbia and among the various districts within each state. Apportionment must also be used to distribute delegates among the various presidential preferences receiving support at the state or district level. We are concerned only with the method of apportionment used to allocate delegates among the presidential preferences.

A number of recognized apportionment methods, each having a different effect, are available. In 1976, the Democratic party used the Hamilton method of apportionment for distributing delegates among the presidential preferences (see Lindsay, 1974). Recently M.L. Balinski and H.P. Young (1974; 1975:701-730) have developed a new apportionment method which mathematicians feel improves upon the Hamilton and all other methods. In Section IV, we will briefly examine the history of apportionment methods and analyze the impact that adoption of the Balinski and Young method might have.

The delegate selection rules used by the Democrats in 1976 thus raised a number of important questions. How would each of the various rules used affect the delegate selection process had it been used exclusively? Which rule is most representative? Which least? Which rule affects what kinds of candidates? How many voters are disenfranchised under the various systems? The purpose of these rules, in theory, is to select a candidate at the Democratic National Convention who would have been the choice of those Democrats who participated at all levels in the presidential nominating process. In our final section we will look at some reforms which have been given new life because of the arduous process which led to the 1976 convention. Serious proposals either for a series of regional primaries or for one national primary are now before the Congress. We will analyze these as well as the systems currently used in suggesting changes for future years.

II. METHODOLOGY

We examined the primary votes and the delegates selected in 30 states—all primary states except New Jersey, from which neither official nor unofficial returns are available. (See Appendix on Data Sources.) However, the choice of which particular vote to look at and what interpretation to give to that vote was far from a simple matter. The variety in the connections between primary vote and delegate selection complicated the process.

In general, our goal was to examine that vote through which the voters could most clearly express their preference for a presidential nominee. Which particular vote we chose varied from state to state.

The simplest choice was in those states in which presidential preference votes were binding as far as the selection of convention delegates was concerned. For example, this was the case in Kentucky, Massachusetts, and Michigan, each of which chose their delegates in proportion to the vote cast in presidential preference primaries, though the procedure for selecting the actual delegates varied and the minimum eligibility requirements were not the same.[3] In these cases, we chose the presidential preference vote.

The situation was somewhat more confusing in states which held presidential preference polls and delegate elections on the same day, but based the apportionment of delegates among the presidential preferences on the votes for delegates, not those for presidential preference. Typically this was the situation in "loophole" states, such as New Hampshire, Illinois, and Maryland. In these states, normally we used the vote on presidential preference.

The determination of which vote more accurately reflects the presidential preference of the voters is problematical. Generally, we felt that votes cast directly for presidential contenders measured this preference more accurately; therefore, that vote was used. Delegate votes could be affected by many factors—particularly popular or unpopular delegate candidates, confusing ballots, and/or rules which excluded some candidates from one ballot or the other. In a few states, however, we felt it preferable to use the votes for delegates. For instance, in Illinois, the differences between the presidential preference ballot and the delegate selection ballot reflected strategic choices by the candidates. There, Sargent Shriver entered the "beauty contest" but filed delegate slates in only a few districts, in deference to the wishes of Chicago Mayor Richard J. Daley to run slates pledged to the state's favorite son, Senator Adlai E. Stevenson

III. We felt that the Stevenson votes accurately reflected the desire of Illinois Democrats to give Mayor Daley more power at the convention. The Illinois and Pennsylvania situations were the most complex ones with which we dealt because the presidential contenders filed slates only in those districts in which they judged they would run well. This picking and choosing made it most difficult to assess the statewide preferences of those participating in the election. We estimated these preferences by totaling votes cast for delegates pledged to each contender throughout the state, but any use of this analysis must be undertaken with great caution.

In four states—Alabama, New York, Louisiana, and Texas—no presidential preference poll accompanied the selection of delegates. Each of these states ran a "loophole" primary, though the Alabama situation was unique in that only one delegate was elected per district, thereby making proportional representation impossible, and in that victors in the delegate elections had to achieve a majority of the votes cast in order to avoid a runoff election. Our analysis of the returns from elections of this type is based upon summing the votes cast for the delegates pledged to the various presidential contenders, a procedure similar to that used in Illinois. Thus, we were examining what percentage of the total votes cast each contender received. Unless we could demonstrate that each voter cast all of his/her votes for a contender's entire slate, an assumption we examine below, we cannot determine exactly what percentage of the voters chose each candidate.

Finally, in some states such as Vermont, the presidential preference primary was not binding on, and was not held at the same time as, delegate selection. While it is possible to determine the composition of the delegations that these primaries would have elected under each of the various sets of rules, we could not determine the relationship between the actual apportionment of delegates among the presidential candidates and the votes cast in these primaries. Often different candidates were involved in the two processes.

Once we had determined which primary vote to use in each state, we analyzed how the delegates to the national convention would have been apportioned among the presidential preferences under strict proportional representation, proportional representation with a 15% minimum eligibility requirement, proportional representation with a 5% minimum eligibility requirement, and the "loophole" system.[4]

Our hypothetical analysis of results under a "loophole" system was based on the assumption that a "loophole" primary was in fact "winner-take-all." That is, we assumed that the candidate receiving a plurality of the votes would receive all of the delegates. This would be the case if each voter case all of his/her votes for delegates on one candidate's slate and did not "cross over" to vote for delegate candidates on any of the other slates. From experience we know that this is often, though not always, the case. In the 1976 presidential primaries, one preference won all of the delegates from 19 of the 23 congressional districts in Ohio, from 30 of the 39 in New York State, and from 15 of the 24 in Illinois. We felt that we were justified in examining these votes as if the leader had won all of the delegates in all of the districts because this is the logical extension of the "loophole" process and because variance from "winner-take-all" at the district level is caused by factors extraneous to presidential preference, notably the popularity or unpopularity of particular delegate candidates.

After arriving at these alternative apportionments of delegates, we compared them with each other and with the apportionment of delegates under the system actually in use in each state. We developed two measures to compare different delegate selection procedures. Several delegate selection rules effectively disenfranchise large groups of voters. All procedures designed to distribute delegates among presidential preferences according to primary results are, of necessity, only approximations of ideal representation, some varying from the ideal more than others. These two factors, amount of disenfranchisement and degree of misrepresentation, appear to be the main evidence of the differing effects of the delegate selection rules. Our two indices were designed to measure these factors.

A voter in a primary can be disenfranchised if his/her vote is ignored. According to our assumption about voting patterns in "loophole" primaries, the presidential preference receiving a plurality of the vote receives all of the delegates. A voter who chooses any other preference is therefore disenfranchised. No matter which minority preference he/she votes for, that vote will not alter the outcome. In addition, he/she has no voice in choosing the actual delegates selected. With a 15% or a 5% minimum eligibility requirement, voters who prefer candidates not reaching these minimums are disenfranchised. If the preference for which a vote is cast does not receive enough votes to exceed the eligibility requirement, then the vote is discarded, even if that preference would have received some delegates were no minimum imposed.

Our measure of voter disenfranchisement simply counts the number of voters in a primary who are disenfranchised in one of these ways in the several districts. This figure is expressed as a percentage of the total vote cast in the primary. Although this is a simple measure, it provides a good indication of how thoroughly the apportionment resulting from a set of delegate selection rules reflects the wishes of the entire electorate.

To measure how closely the distribution of delegates to the various presidential preferences reflects the actual distribution of the votes among those preferences, we devised a Fair Reflection of Presidential Preference Index (FROPP Index).[5] In each primary state and for each set of delegate selection rules, we computed the absolute value of the percentage of the votes for each preference minus the percentage of the delegates for that preference. We then added the numbers so obtained and divided the sum by two to arrive at the FROPP Index for that state for that set of rules. As a formula, the FROPP Index =

$$\frac{1}{2} \sum_{i=1}^{n} \mid \% \text{ votes for preference i} - \% \text{ delegates for preference i} \mid .$$

If a particular preference i is overrepresented, the $\mid \%$ votes for preference i $- \%$ delegates for preference i $\mid$ measures the amount of overrepresentation. Similarly, if preference i is underrepresented, then the absolute value obtained measures the amount of under-representation. Since the total amount of overrepresentation must be exactly equal to the total amount of underrepresentation, the factor of $\frac{1}{2}$ in the FROPP Index allows us to interpret it as either the amount of underrepresentation or the amount of overrepresentation. Alternatively, the FROPP Index measures the percentage of the voters whose votes were incorrectly reflected by the distribution of delegates. Thus, the FROPP Index measures the deviation from the ideal.

Other indices could be proposed to measure fairness. Our first reason for preferring the FROPP Index was that it seemed simple and intuitively reasonable. Our second reason was more technical. The index of fairness chosen determines which means of distributing delegates among the presidential preferences will yield the best results under that measure (Huntington, 1928; Balinski and Young,

1975:707). Essentially, for each of the major apportionment methods, an index can be chosen which shows that delegates distributed under that system are the most fairly distributed. We chose the FROPP Index because the Hamilton method of apportionment, the method actually in use in 1976, is the fairest apportionment method as measured by the FROPP Index.[6]

The FROPP Index measures the percentage of the votes incorrectly reflected by the distribution of delegates. Thus, it ranges from 0 to 100, with 0 the ideal (and normally unobtainable) apportionment. Within a state, delegate selection rules yielding lower FROPP Indexes are fairer. Differences in the FROPP Index from one state to another reflect additional factors, such as the number and relative strengths of the presidential preferences competing in those states and the number and size of the districts in the states. It would be fallacious to compare the fairness of different delegate selection procedures by using the FROPP Indexes from different states. As noted above, for technical reasons, the FROPP Index is also inappropriate to decide which apportionment method is the fairest way to distribute delegates among the various presidential preferences. Congressman Charles W. Gillet (Republican, New York) pointed to this fact in a debate over reapportioning the House after the 1900 census: "It has been abundantly proved that mathematics cannot determine any apportionment [method] which shall be universally fair and equal" (Congressional Record, 1901:742).

III. THE IMPACT OF ELECTORAL RULES

We can quickly deal with the question of allocating at-large delegates. Some states, such as New Hampshire, elect no delegates at large. Others, such as Idaho (3) or Wisconsin (10), elect relatively few. In these states, under most apportionment methods, it is irrelevant whether the at-large delegates are chosen so as to reflect the presidential preferences of those casting votes in the primary or to reflect the preferences of those delegates already selected. The results would be the same.

In states with more at-large delegates, the differences for some candidates can be important. In each case we examined, the distribution of at-large delegates according to popular vote yields a lower FROPP Index than would allocating at-large delegates among the presidential preferences in such a way as to reflect the preference

Table 1. A Comparison of the Fairness of Allocating At-Large Delegates to Reflect Preferences Expressed in the Popular Vote or Preferences of Previously Selected Delegates (Representative States)

	FROPP Indexes							
	Reflecting Popular Vote				Reflecting Delegate Preferences			
States	PR	Loop-hole	PR with 15%	PR with 5%	PR	Loop-hole	PR with 15%	PR with 5%
Kentucky	9.47	36.33	21.11	9.47	9.47	40.67	25.45	9.47
Maryland	5.37	30.75	14.49	10.72	7.25	43.96	14.49	12.61
Massachu-setts	11.66	43.20	37.43	14.54	14.54	44.55	37.43	16.47
North Carolina	8.42	36.76	11.70	11.70	11.70	46.59	11.70	11.70

of delegates already chosen.[7] Table 1 presents some representative results. While these differences are not large, because they are all in one direction, subsequent FROPP Indexes will reflect at-large delegates chosen according to the presidential preferences of the primary votes.

Our analysis of primary voting also demonstrates that "loophole" primaries reflect voters' presidential preferences less well than do any of the other systems. For every state analyzed, the "loophole" produces a FROPP Index as high as or higher than any of the proportional systems.[8] (See Table 2.) Looking at the states analyzed in a summary way, the "loophole" system miscasts nearly five times as many votes as does the system allocating delegates according to proportional representation with no minimum eligibility limits. (See Table 3.)

In New Hampshire, the FROPP Index for the "loophole" is almost 14 times what it is for proportional representation with no minimum eligibility. Any of the systems would have been significantly better than the "loophole" for fairly reflecting the voters' choices. Many feel that the New Hampshire primary is given undue prominence because it is traditionally first in the nation. Table 4 reveals that the seriousness of this situation is magnified because the system in use in New Hampshire distorts the voters' actual preferences.

"Loophole" primaries lead to particularly unfair reflection of presidential preferences in such states as New Hampshire and Nevada in which there are not enough districts to make it possible for a "winner-take-all" result in one district to be offset by a similar victory by another candidate in another district. "Loopholes" are also very distorting when candidates' strengths are spread evenly

Table 2. FROPP INDEXES UNDER VARIOUS ELECTORAL RULES

State	Actual System in Use	Proportional Representation	Loophole	PR with 15% Minimum	PR with 5% Minimum
Alabama*	28.07	22.36	22.36	22.36	22.36
Arkansas	5.59	5.59	37.36	25.82	5.59
California	17.31	7.44	34.55	20.52	11.23
District of Columbia	12.76	5.56	60.25	12.76	5.56
Florida	11.14	11.14	15.77	11.14	11.14
Georgia	18.18	2.69	18.18	12.18	2.69
Idaho	7.20	7.20	19.69	19.69	7.20
Illinois	32.99	7.43	32.40	19.02	7.12
Indiana	24.00	7.77	28.05	18.72	3.83
Kentucky	21.11	9.47	36.33	21.11	9.47
Louisiana	15.87	3.37	15.94	8.25	3.37
Maryland	55.32	5.37	30.75	14.49	10.72
Massachusetts	13.46	11.66	43.20	37.43	14.54
Michigan	8.77	5.77	13.28	13.28	7.27
Montana	14.84	10.31	40.08	15.21	10.31
Nebraska	26.43	8.71	30.78	23.24	16.00
Nevada	8.80	8.80	47.26	23.93	14.92
New Hampshire	58.66	5.09	70.42	30.18	5.09
New York	8.55	4.01	8.18	6.12	4.01
North Carolina	11.70	8.42	36.76	11.70	11.70
Ohio	34.55	13.85	35.87	21.91	10.07
Oregon	17.40	7.39	41.89	15.44	12.10
Pennsylvania	20.58	10.00	33.82	22.58	11.68
Rhode Island	11.84	7.67	34.26	11.84	11.84
South Dakota	17.01	12.01	46.96	17.01	12.01
Tennessee	17.93	8.79	22.00	19.83	10.96
Texas	46.13	6.94	37.67	9.33	6.17
Vermont	–	5.22	54.16	23.63	5.22
West Virginia	10.99	4.16	10.99	10.99	4.16
Wisconsin	7.36	7.36	27.75	24.80	9.38

*Alabama has been excluded from subsequent tables comparing the various rules because her allocation of delegates in single-member districts renders any proportional representation impossible.

throughout a state. In that situation the number of districts becomes irrelevant because a narrow loser would lose every district by the same narrow margin. Our analysis reveals that such would have been the case, for example, had Kentucky or North Carolina selected delegates with "loophole" primaries this year. In each case Governor Carter ran evenly ahead of his principal opponent, Alabama Governor George Wallace, and the others throughout the state. His wide victory margins would have been extended even further by a "loophole" system.

While the pattern is clear, in some states the effect of the

Table 3. RATIOS OF FROPP INDEXES FOR "LOOPHOLE" PRIMARIES
TO FROPP INDEXES FOR OTHER SYSTEMS

State	Loophole/ Proportional Representation	Loophole/ PR with 15% Minimum	Loophole/ PR with 5% Minimum
Arkansas	6.68	1.45	6.68
California	4.64	1.68	3.08
District of Columbia	10.84	4.72	10.84
Florida	1.42	1.42	1.42
Georgia	6.76	1.49	6.76
Idaho	2.74	1.00	2.74
Illinois	4.37	1.70	4.55
Indiana	3.61	1.50	7.32
Kentucky	3.84	1.72	3.84
Louisiana	4.74	1.93	4.74
Maryland	5.73	2.12	2.87
Massachusetts	3.71	1.15	2.97
Michigan	2.30	1.00	1.83
Montana	3.89	2.64	3.89
Nebraska	3.53	1.32	1.92
Nevada	5.37	1.98	3.17
New Hampshire	13.85	2.33	13.85
New York	2.04	1.34	2.04
North Carolina	4.37	3.14	3.14
Ohio	2.59	1.64	3.56
Oregon	5.67	2.71	3.46
Pennsylvania	3.38	1.50	2.90
Rhode Island	4.47	2.89	2.89
South Dakota	3.91	2.76	3.91
Tennessee	2.50	1.11	2.01
Texas	5.43	4.04	6.11
Vermont	10.38	2.29	10.38
West Virginia	2.64	1.00	2.64
Wisconsin	3.77	1.12	2.96
Mean =	4.80	1.95	4.43
Median =	3.91	1.68	3.17

"loophole" primary is much less striking than in others. In Michigan, for example, the FROPP Index for the "loophole" is only slightly more than twice that for proportional representation with no eligibility limits. The FROPP Index for the "loophole" is exactly the same as for a system in which the delegates are allocated proportionally but with a 15% eligibility minimum. The Michigan example points to the fact that a "loophole" primary does not result in terribly unfair reflection of presidential preference statewide in the situation in which the strength of the various candidates is spread unevenly throughout a state with a relatively large number of

Table 4. PRESIDENTIAL PREFERENCES OF NEW HAMPSHIRE DELEGATION
UNDER VARIOUS METHODS OF ALLOCATION

Candidate	Actual System in Use	Delegates Under:			
		Proportional Representation	Loophole	PR with 15% Minimum	PR with 5% Minimum
Carter	15	5	17	7	5
Udall	2	4	0	6	4
Bayh	0	3	0	4	3
Harris	0	2	0	0	2
Shriver	0	2	0	0	2
Humphrey (write-in)	0	1	0	0	1
Others	0	0	0	0	0

districts. Thus, in Michigan, Carter and Congressman Morris Udall ran virtually even in statewide voting. Carter narrowly won some congressional districts and won others by wide margins. He narrowly lost some districts and lost others by wider margins. Had Carter maintained his razor-thin statewide advantage over Udall in every district, the "loophole" would have grossly distorted the voters' preferences. The New York State primary produced results similar to Michigan's. In New York four slates—one each pledged to Carter, Udall, and Senator Henry Jackson, and one uncommitted—campaigned statewide. Each had pockets of strength, winning delegates in those districts, and thus avoiding being shut out by the "loophole" system in use.

Even in those states in which the effects of the "loophole" on fair reflection are minimal, however, our index measuring voter disenfranchisement reveals the ill effects that these systems can have. The percentage of voters disenfranchised by "loophole" primaries averaged over 50% for the states we examined.[9] Only in rare states, such as Georgia, Idaho, and West Virginia, where favorite sons won with extremely high percentages of the vote, was the percentage of voters who would have been disenfranchised less than 40%. In Massachusetts, where a large number of candidates split the votes fairly evenly, over three-quarters of those voting would have been disenfranchised at the district level by "loophole" primaries. (See Table 6.) In every state as many or more voters were disenfranchised by the "loophole" as by any system.

Had all states used proportional representation with a 15% minimum eligibility requirement to allocate their delegates, the delegations would have more fairly reflected the presidential pre-

Table 5. DISTORTION OF FAIR REFLECTION OF PRESIDENTIAL PREFERENCES
BY "LOOPHOLE" SYSTEM

Candidate	Actual System in Use (PR with 15% Minimum)	Delegates Under:	
		Loophole	Proportional Representation
a. Kentucky			
Carter	37	44	30
Wallace	7	2	9
Udall	2	0	4
Others	0	0	3
b. North Carolina			
Carter	36	55	35
Wallace	25	6	24
Others	0	0	2

ferences of the voters than under the "loophole" system (as demonstrated in Table 3), but again not so well as under a 5% minimum requirement or under proportional representation with no minimum necessary for eligibility. Again the situation varies from state to state.

Obviously, the 15% eligibility requirement is most distorting in those states in which a large number of candidates competed fairly evenly. In those states candidates who received just below 15% in a district or just below 15% statewide would be ineligible to receive delegates in that jurisdiction. The delegates which would have gone to those candidates had no minimum eligibility requirement been imposed were distributed among those candidates who received slightly more than the required 15%. As a result, the candidates receiving delegates were overrepresented, and those not receiving delegates were underrepresented.

The 15% eligibility requirement would have been most distorting had it been in effect in the early primaries in 1976. In Massachusetts nine candidates' names appeared on the ballot. Senator Jackson "won" the primary with only 22% of the statewide vote. Congressman Udall and Governor Wallace were second and third with 18% and 17% respectively. Each of these three polled fewer than 15% of the votes in some districts. Governor Carter (14%), Senator Fred Harris (8%), Sargent Shriver (7%), and Senator Birch Bayh (5%) all trailed but polled up to or near 15% in some districts.

The commonwealth's primary was run under a system with no minimum eligibility necessary. All nine of the candidates listed on the ballot received at least one delegate. With a 15% minimum,

Table 6. DISENFRANCHISEMENT OF VOTERS*

State	Loophole	Percentage of Voters Disenfranchised Under:	
		Proportional Representation with 15% Minimum	*Proportional Representation with 5% Minimum*
Arkansas	37.36	24.07	3.21
California	40.98	22.80	10.91
District of Columbia	60.25	12.75	1.59
Florida	60.06	13.63	13.63
Georgia	18.18	14.30	1.57
Idaho	19.70	19.70	7.65
Illinois	52.47	23.46	4.49
Indiana	32.05	20.81	2.15
Kentucky	40.67	23.76	9.41
Louisiana	63.42	7.74	1.40
Maryland**	50.69	14.49	9.71
Massachusetts	76.01	46.46	12.08
Michigan	47.36	13.28	5.09
Montana	40.08	15.22	8.97
Nebraska	58.77	23.24	16.00
Nevada	47.26	23.92	8.80
New Hampshire	69.55	28.12	1.63
New York	54.23	9.95	2.27
North Carolina	46.60	11.70	10.63
Ohio	15.87	20.80	5.06
Oregon	65.45	15.45	12.37
Pennsylvania	63.10	28.70	5.86
Rhode Island	67.88	11.84	11.84
South Dakota	58.73	17.38	4.22
Tennessee	22.00	19.33	9.63
Texas	50.75	14.61	1.43
Vermont	54.16	23.64	0
West Virginia	10.99	10.99	0
Wisconsin	60.04	23.54	8.48

*See note 9.
**These figures do not reflect the actual situation in which 283,956 Democrats who voted for Governor Brown in the nonbinding presidential preference poll were not given the opportunity to vote for a slate of delegates pledged to the California governor.

however, Shriver, Harris, and Bayh, as well as Pennsylvania Governor Milton Shapp and antiabortion candidate Ellen McCormack, would have been shut out, and Governor Carter's delegation would have been cut by more than two-thirds. The FROPP Index would have been 3.21 times higher under a 15% minimum eligibility requirement than it was under proportional representation with no minimum. Just over 25% more votes would have been incorrectly reflected in the chosen delegation; 46.5% of the voting Democrats would have been disenfranchised at the district level.

The 15% minimum requirement had its least distorting effect in those states in which very few candidates polled under the 15% minimum but did not reach it. Thus, in New York all four of the slates which campaigned seriously polled over 15% in most of the districts in which they entered. Slightly less than 10% of the total vote was ignored because of failure to reach the 15% minimum. In Rhode Island, three slates—one pledged to Governor Carter, one to Idaho Senator Frank Church, and one listed as uncommitted but supporting Governor Edmund G. Brown, Jr., of California—split approximately 88% of the vote almost evenly. None of the other six candidates on the Rhode Island ballot polled as much as 5% of the vote. Approximately 12% of the voters were disenfranchised by the minimum requirement in Rhode Island. In states in which the political situation resembled New York's or Rhode Island's, the 15% minimum did not distort fair reflection greatly, nor did it disenfranchise large numbers of voters. On the whole, however, while proportional representation with a 15% minimum reflected presidential preferences better than did the "loophole" system, it still penalized serious candidates in some states. By causing candidates who came close to, but did not reach, the minimum to be underrepresented on state delegations, the 15% minimum led to the situation in which presidential preferences of those participating in the primaries were less accurately reflected than under a 5% minimum or under proportional representation with no minimum eligibility requirement.

Table 7. DISTORTION OF FAIR REFLECTION IN MASSACHUSETTS UNDER A 15% MINIMUM ELIGIBILITY REQUIREMENT

	Delegates Under:	
Candidate	Actual System in Use (Proportional Representation)	Proportional Representation with 15% Minimum
Jackson	29	44
Udall	21	30
Wallace	21	24
Carter	16	6
Shriver	9	0
Harris	6	0
Bayh	1	0
McCormack	1	0
Shapp	1	0
Others	0	0

Table 8. RATIOS OF FROPP INDEXES FOR PROPORTIONAL REPRESENTATION
PRIMARIES WITH 15% MINIMUM ELIGIBILITY REQUIREMENT TO FROPP
INDEXES FOR PRIMARIES WITH 5% OR NO MINIMUM REQUIRED

State	PR with 15% Minimum/ Proportional Representation	PR with 15% Minimum/ PR with 5% Minimum
Arkansas	4.62	4.62
California	2.76	1.83
District of Columbia	2.29	2.29
Florida	1.00	1.00
Georgia	4.53	4.53
Idaho	2.74	2.74
Illinois	2.56	2.67
Indiana	2.41	4.88
Kentucky	2.23	2.23
Louisiana	2.45	2.45
Maryland	2.70	1.35
Massachusetts	3.21	2.57
Michigan	2.30	1.83
Montana	1.47	1.47
Nebraska	2.60	1.45
Nevada	2.72	1.60
New Hampshire	5.94	5.94
New York	1.53	1.53
North Carolina	1.39	1.00
Ohio	1.58	2.18
Oregon	2.09	1.28
Pennsylvania	2.26	1.93
Rhode Island	1.54	1.00
South Dakota	1.42	1.42
Tennessee	2.26	1.81
Texas	1.34	2.20
Vermont	4.53	4.53
West Virginia	2.64	2.64
Wisconsin	3.37	2.65
Mean =	2.57	2.40
Median =	2.41	2.18

Very few states used the 15% minimum eligibility requirement.
Minimum requirements were instituted to eliminate fringe candidates
and to divide delegates among only those who were serious
contenders. Our analysis has shown that serious candidates could
have been penalized by the 15% requirement had it been in effect in
a number of early primary states.

The 5% requirement has the desired effect without distorting fair
reflection so much as the 15% figure does. Tables 3 and 8 have
already demonstrated that the 5% minimum eligibility requirement
results in significantly less distortion than either the "loophole" or

the 15% minimum eligibility requirement. Table 9 shows that the distortion from fair reflection under the 5% minimum eligibility requirement would have been only slightly different from that under proportional representation without a minimum. The ratio of FROPP Index under proportional representation with a 5% minimum eligibility requirement to FROPP Index under proportional representation with no such requirement never exceeded 2.00. The two systems resulted in exactly the same allocation of delegates in half of the states analyzed. Thus, if fair reflection of presidential preference is the primary goal, but one still desires to eliminate fringe candidates

Table 9. RATIOS FOR FROPP INDEXES FOR PROPORTIONAL REPRESENTATION PRIMARIES WITH 5% MINIMUM ELIGIBILITY REQUIREMENT TO FROPP INDEXES FOR PRIMARIES WITH NO SUCH REQUIREMENT

State	PR with 5% Minimum/ Proportional Representation
Arkansas	1
California	1.51
District of Columbia	1
Florida	1
Georgia	1
Idaho	1
Illinois	.96
Indiana	.49
Kentucky	1
Louisiana	1
Maryland	2.00
Massachusetts	1.25
Michigan	1.26
Montana	1
Nebraska	1.84
Nevada	1.69
New Hampshire	1
New York	1
North Carolina	1.39
Ohio	.73
Oregon	1.64
Pennsylvania	1.17
Rhode Island	1.54
South Dakota	1
Tennessee	1.25
Texas	.89
Vermont	1
West Virginia	1
Wisconsin	1.27
Mean =	1.17
Median =	1.00

through the electoral system, then the 5% minimum eligibility, not the more commonly used 15%, should be employed.[10]

The last comparisons made examine the relationships between the FROPP Indexes for the systems actually in use in each of the states analyzed and each of the electoral systems we have been assessing.[11] The high numbers in Table 10 show those states in which many more votes were incorrectly reflected than would have been the case under proportional representation or proportional representation with a 5% minimum eligibility requirement. Proportional representation represents the fairest possible reflection of presidential preferences given the fact that states cannot send unlimited numbers of delegates to the national convention. Thus the high

Table 10. RATIOS OF FROPP INDEXES FOR SYSTEMS ACTUALLY IN USE TO
FROPP INDEXES FOR SYSTEMS UNDER EXAMINATION

State	Actual/ Loophole	Actual/ PR with 15%	Actual/ PR with 5%	Actual/ PR
Arkansas	.15	.22	1	1
California	.50	.84	1.54	2.33
District of Columbia	.21	1	2.29	2.29
Florida	.71	1	1	1
Georgia	1	1.49	6.76	6.76
Idaho	.37	.37	1	1
Illinois	1.02	1.73	4.64	4.44
Indiana	.86	1.28	6.27	3.09
Kentucky	.58	1	2.23	2.23
Louisiana	1	1.92	4.71	4.71
Maryland	1.80	3.82	5.16	10.31
Massachusetts	.31	.36	.93	1.15
Michigan	.66	.66	1.20	1.52
Montana	.37	.98	1.44	1.44
Nebraska	.86	1.14	1.65	3.03
Nevada	.19	.37	.59	1
New Hampshire	.83	1.94	11.53	11.53
New York	1.04	1.40	2.13	2.13
North Carolina	.32	1	1	1.39
Ohio	.96	1.58	3.43	2.49
Oregon	.42	1.13	1.44	2.35
Pennsylvania	.61	.91	1.76	2.06
Rhode Island	.35	1	1	1.54
South Dakota	.36	1	1.42	1.42
Tennessee	.82	.90	1.64	2.04
Texas	1.22	4.94	7.48	6.65
West Virginia	1	1	2.64	2.64
Wisconsin	.27	.30	.78	1
Mean =	.65	1.22	2.71	2.92
Median =	.66	1	1.65	2.29

numbers in Table 10 are those states which stray furthest from this fair reflection. In each case, these numbers are found in "loophole" states. All of the "loophole" states, except New York, where the candidates' strengths were unevenly spread and thus offset each other, produced delegations which strayed far from fair reflection of the preferences of those participating in the primary.

The FROPP Indexes obtained for all variants of the electoral rules considered can be compared over our 29 primary states. Because the variances for the FROPP Indexes over the states were quite different for different electoral rules and because it was felt that there were state-related differences, we decided to use a sign test to compare the electoral rules for fairness. The mean values of the FROPP Indexes over the 29 states were 7.56 for proportional representation, 8.80 for proportional representation with a 5% minimum, 18.00 for proportional representation with a 15% minimum, 19.88 for the actual systems used, and 33.26 for the "loophole" system. This led us to suspect that this ordered the rules in decreasing order of fairness. In Table 11, each pair of electoral rules is compared. In each case the hypothesis being tested is that the rule in the row is fairer than the one in the column—i.e., the median of the FROP Indexes is lower. The numerator of the fraction is the number of positive differences. The denominator is the number of nonzero differences. In every case the hypothesis is confirmed at the 0.005 level, except that proportional representation is only fairer than proportional representation with 5% minimum (4/18) at the 0.025 level and there is no significant difference between proportional representation with 15% minimum and the actual system used. Thus, the conclusion is that in decreasing order of fairness the electoral rules are proportional representation, proportional representation with 5% minimum, proportional representation with 15% minimum, the actual system,

Table 11. SIGN TEST ON FROPP INDEXES

	Proportional Representation	PR with 5% Minimum	PR with 15% Minimum	Actual System	Loophole
Proportional Representation		4/18	0/28	0/23	0/29
PR with 5% Minimum			0/26	3/23	0/29
PR with 15% Minimum				12/21	0/26
Actual System					4/26
Loophole					

and the "loophole" system, with all the differences highly significant except proportional representation with 15% minimum versus the actual system.

IV. METHODS OF APPORTIONMENT

In examining the impact of electoral rules on the primary process, we are concerned not only with rules which deviate from proportional representation but also with the apportionment method by which delegates are distributed among the various presidential preferences under whichever set of rules are adopted.

The question of how to apportion representative bodies has long interested both politicians and mathematicians. George Washington's first veto was of a bill to apportion the House of Representatives (Fitzpatrick, 1939:16-17). For this early apportionment fight the lines were drawn between supporters of Hamilton and those of Jefferson. The two apportionment methods under discussion here can be traced to these two men (Ford, 1904:460-471; Syrett, 1966:228-230). The Hamilton method (perhaps better known as the Vinton method or the method of largest remaining fractions) was long used to apportion the House of Representatives and was the method used by the Democrats in 1976. Jefferson's method (also known as the d'Houdt method or the method of greatest divisors) is clearly an ancestor of the Balinski and Young method mentioned earlier.

Daniel Webster (1903:102-123) also made a lasting contribution to the subject of apportionment. He and a Cornell professor, Walter F. Willcox (1916:3-16, 1952:290-302), argued for a method known as major fractions. It was left to E.V. Huntington of Harvard (1921:123-127, 1928:85-110, 1940) to reorganize the subject of apportionment and to put it on a sound mathematical footing. He devised a whole class of apportionment methods, including the Jefferson method, the Webster method, the method of equal proportions (which the House of Representatives currently uses), and two others. Huntington's objective in devising his methods was to avoid the main flaw in the Hamilton method, the Alabama paradox.

The House of Representatives was apportioned by the Hamilton method for most of the 19th century. On October 25, 1881, C.W. Seaton, Chief Clerk of the Census Office, set to Congress the reapportionment figures based on the 1880 census. Seaton applied the Hamilton method for each possible House size from 275 to 350 members. He noted that in a House with 299 members Alabama was entitled to 8 Congressmen. However, in a House with 300 members, Alabama was entitled to only 7 members. This phenomenon, according to which an increase in the number of Congressmen to be apportioned leads to a decrease in the size of some state's congressional delegation, has since been called the Alabama paradox. An apportionment method under which the Alabama paradox cannot occur is said to be "house monotone."[12] The Hamilton method of apportionment, therefore, is not house monotone.

The Alabama paradox—"The atrocity which [mathematicians] have elected to call a 'paradox'... this freak [which] presents a mathematical impossibility" (Congressional Record, 1901: 724-725)—proved particularly vexing in 1901. Congress opted for a House of 357 members. Colorado would have been entitled to three seats for every size House from 350 to 400, except for 357, which only gave her two. The 1901 reapportionment also reduced Maine's representation from four to three, in a House of 357. This led Maine Congressman Charles E. Littlefield to complain:

> Not only is Maine subjected to the assaults of the chairman of this committee [Census Committee], but it does seem as though mathematics and science has (sic) combined to make a shuttlecock and battle door (sic) of the State of Maine in connection with the scientific basis upon which the bill is presented.... God help the State of Maine when mathematics reach for her. [Congressional Record, 1901:592-593]

Several days later, Census Committee Chairman Hopkins answered:

> It is true that under the majority bill Maine is entitled to only three Representatives, and, if Dame Rumor is to be credited, the seat of the gentleman who addressed the House on Saturday last is the one in danger.... [He] takes a modest way to tell the House and the country how dependent the State of Maine is upon him. ... Maine crippled! Maine, the State of Hannibal Hamlin, of William Pitt Fessenden, of James G. Blaine.... That great state crippled by the loss of LITTLEFIELD! Why, Mr. Speaker, if the gentleman's statement be true, ... I can see much force in the prayer he uttered when he said, "God help the State of Maine" (laughter). [Congressional Record, 1901:729-730]

The five Huntington methods, including the method of equal proportions in use by the House since 1930, are all house monotone.

However, they suffer from another serious flaw, namely, that they do not satisfy quota. A state's quota essentially is the number of Congressmen to which its population entitles it.[13] Typically, a state's quota is a fraction—e.g., Maine's present quota is 2.1453. Thus, Maine is entitled to either two or three Representatives, but not one, four, or any other number. In general, a state is entitled to the number of Congressmen obtained by rounding its quota to either the next bigger integer or to the next smaller integer. An apportionment method that guarantees this outcome is said to satisfy quota.

The Hamilton method satisfies quota, but none of the Huntington methods do. In fact, examples can be constructed whereby the Huntington methods produce apportionments that differ from a state's quota by arbitrarily large amounts. Fortunately, this has not yet occurred in the years that Congress has been employing the method of equal proportions.

The new method developed by Balinski and Young (1974, 1975:701-730), a derivative of the Jefferson method, satisfies quota and is house monotone. Moreover, Balinski and Young prove that theirs is the only apportionment method that is consistent and that satisfies these two criteria. Thus, mathematically, it is the best apportionment method. For our purposes, distributing delegates among presidential preferences according to the votes cast in a primary is tantamount to distributing members of Congress among the states according to their population.

In a state primary, with k presidential preferences running and n delegates to be allocated to them, the Balinski and Young method would apportion delegates one at a time. Initially, each presidential preference is assigned no delegates. The Balinksi and Young method would apportion the first, second, third, . . . nth delegate to the "most deserving" preference at each stage. Thus, the first delegate would go to the preference with the most votes. If h delegates have already been apportioned, the (h + 1)st delegate would be allocated to the most underrepresented preference at that stage in the process. This iterative process continues until all n delegates are apportioned.[14]

The Hamilton method is simpler to describe; however, it is simpler to compute only when small numbers are involved. In the hypothetical situation described above, under the Hamilton method one first computes the quota for each preference by dividing the votes for that preference by the total vote and multiplying by the total number of delegates available. One then rounds each quota down to the next smaller integer to obtain the lower quotas of the various preferences. Each preference is awarded its lower quota. Any leftover delegates are apportioned among the various preferences according to which ones have the largest remaining fractions.[15]

The Hamilton method's failure to be house monotone could have an impact on the delegate selection process. For example, suppose that, under proportional representation, the voters in a congressional district with 10 national convention delegates divided 16% for preference A, 37% for preference B, 47% for preference C. This would produce an apportionment of one delegate for A, four delegates for B, and five delegates for C. However, if the congressional district had only nine national convention delegates, the apportionment, given the same division of the vote, would be two delegates for A, three delegates for B, and four delegates for C. It would be advantageous, therefore, for supporters of presidential preference A to have this congressional district lose a delegate. Many variants of this unpleasant phenomenon could occur.

Under the Hamilton method, a clever politician who knew in which districts his presidential preference was likely to run strongest and who understood the Alabama paradox could scheme to choose a convention size that would benefit his favorite candidate. He could aid that preference by arranging to increase or decrease the size of the national or state convention by just a few delegates in order to increase the size of the delegations in which his preference would run highest. This is the kind of game that Congress abandoned after its troubles in the late 19th century.

The Democratic party should follow the Congress's lead and abandon the Hamilton method as well. The Hamilton method's only strong attribute is ease of calculation when numbers are small. With large numbers, such as those involved in state primaries, use of a computer becomes essential in any event. The newly developed Balinski and Young method is not flawed in ways that the Hamilton and all other methods are. Because Balinksi and Young's is mathematically the best method and, with computers, as easy to use as any other, we feel that the Democratic party would be wise to adopt this procedure in the future.

In order to determine what effect changing from the Hamilton method to the Balinksi and Young method would have, we recomputed the composition of each state's delegation under each set of rules examined. One type of difference in the delegate totals for the various presidential preferences did surface. Since both the Balinski and Young and Hamilton methods satisfy quota, they can differ by at most one delegate in any one district. However, a difference of one delegate per district, added over the many districts in some of the larger states, and added again over all the states, might have a substantial effect on national totals.

The Balinski and Young method favors leading candidates, rather than minor candidates. Alternatively, one could state that the Hamilton method gives an advantage to minor candidates. Table 12 reveals that the candidate who won a state would have received more delegates under the Balinski and Young method than under the

Table 12. NET CHANGES FOR SELECTED CANDIDATES BY USING THE BALINSKI AND YOUNG METHOD INSTEAD OF THE HAMILTON METHOD (Based on Proportional Representation)

State	Candidates					
	Carter	Udall	Wallace	Jackson	Harris	Shriver
Arkansas	+ 1	0	−1	0	0	0
California	+ 7	0	−3	−1	0	0
District of Columbia	+ 1	0	0	0	0	0
Florida	0	0	+2	−2	0	0
Georgia	+ 6	−1	−4	0	0	0
Idaho	0	0	0	0	0	0
Illinois	+ 2	0	+1	0	−3	−1
Indiana	+10	0	−3	−7	0	0
Kentucky	0	+1	0	0	0	0
Louisiana	+ 3	0	−3	0	0	0
Maryland	− 1	−1	−2	0	0	0
Massachusetts	+ 1	+2	+4	+4	−3	−7
Michigan	+ 7	+1	−7	−1	0	0
Montana	0	−1	0	0	0	0
Nebraska	+ 1	0	−1	0	0	0
Nevada	0	0	0	0	0	0
New Hampshire	+ 1	+1	0	0	0	−1
New York	− 2	+2	0	+8	−5	0
North Carolina	+ 4	0	−3	0	0	0
Ohio	+ 9	+2	−1	−3	0	0
Oregon	0	−1	0	0	0	0
Pennsylvania	− 1	−3	+2	−4	−1	0
Rhode Island	0	−1	0	0	0	0
South Dakota	0	+1	0	0	0	0
Tennessee	+ 3	−1	−2	0	0	0
Texas	+11	0	−2	0	0	−3
Vermont	0	0	0	0	0	0
West Virginia	0	0	−4	0	0	0
Wisconsin	+ 4	+4	−1	−6	0	0
Totals	+67	+5	−28	−12	−12	−12

Hamilton method; these additional delegates would have come at the expense of the more minor candidates in that state. This finding does not vary if an eligibility limit is imposed.

If one were to accumulate the differences so incurred over all of the primaries, one would see that the candidates whose campaigns never really caught fire—e.g., Harris and Shriver—would have received fewer delegates. Governor Carter, who ran ahead in most of the states he entered, would have benefited most from the change.

The largest observed changes in apportionment within a single state were seen in California. Under proportional representation with no minimum eligibility limit, Governor Brown would have received 14 additional delegates, principally at the expense of Senator Church, who would have lost 16 of the delegates awarded him under the Hamilton method. The winnowing out of minor candidates under the Balinski and Young method is also graphically illustrated in Massachusetts. There Shriver's strength would have dropped from 13 delegates to six.

A change from the Hamilton method to the Balinski and Young method would create a small change in the delegate totals for the leading candidates. One could argue that this change would even have the desirable effect of diluting the strength of fringe candidates; furthermore, it would do so in a less arbitrary way than by imposing minimum eligibility requirements.

In this brief section we have raised only the most obvious points concerning the technical subject of choice of apportionment methods. Without feeling the necessity to marshall the theoretical argument in mathematical terms, we feel that there are sufficient advantages so that the Democrats should adopt the Balinski and Young method in 1980.

V. CONCLUSIONS

Two subjects remain for discussion. First, because political analysts frequently look back, it is appropriate to ask what would have happened had the 1976 primaries been run under one set of rules. What if the "loopholes" had not been permitted? Would Carter have won so easily had proportional representation been in use, without minimum eligibility requirements, in all of the primary states?

Second, because we feel political scientists should look to the future as well, it is appropriate to prescribe the system that we feel should be adopted. We have already stated that the Balinski and Young method of apportionment should replace the Hamilton method. In our final section we will turn to the less technical electoral rules and deal with the nominating system as a whole. What effect will the rules changes adopted by the 1976 convention have? What about regional or national primaries?

What if? Some liberal Democrats, seemingly unwilling to accept the preferences of the voters, claimed that Governor Carter's nomination was the result of "loophole" primaries. According to this point of view, four primaries, all "loopholes," were crucial to Carter's success.

This argument contends that the Carter campaign received its biggest boost by winning in New Hampshire, a "loophole" state. Carter's narrow plurality in New Hampshire was magnified by his winning 15 of the 17 delegates. However, this New Hampshire victory, which established Carter as a credible candidate, was followed by a series of inconclusive primaries. Carter showed strength as a regional choice, winning Florida and North Carolina, but his appeal to the industrial North remained suspect. He ran a poor fourth in Massachusetts, lost to Senator Stevenson's favorite son delegate slate in Illinois, and, on April 6, narrowly edged Udall in Wisconsin while trailing both Jackson and Udall in New York.

One could argue that the Carter campaign might have been on the ropes had it not regained momentum in the next two primaries, Pennsylvania and Texas. These two large states each ran a "loophole" primary. Despite Carter's narrow victory margins, he gained 157 new delegates and effectively eliminated Senator Jackson as a contender. He began in May 1976 as the obvious front-runner. According to those who credit the Carter nomination to the "loopholes," even these magnified victories were not enough to assure his selection. Carter's strength ebbed again from the high point it reached after Pennsylvania and Texas. He continued to win most of the Southern primaries, but he lost to Senator Church in Nebraska and in three Western states, and to Governor Brown in Maryland, Rhode Island, and Nevada; and he barely beat Congressman Udall in Michigan, where he seemed a prohibitive favorite.

Again, it seemed that Carter could be knocked from his lead position on June 8, the day of the final primaries. The press conceded California to Governor Brown and New Jersey to an uncommitted slate. Thus Ohio, another "loophole" state, took on critical importance. Carter won Ohio with 52% of the vote, but because of the "loophole" rules he won 126 of the 152 delegates. His victory was reported as a landslide, his delegate total rose still higher, and his nomination was assured.

Liberal critics of the "loophole" claim that this course of events, and the press coverage of those events, might well have been different had Carter not achieved narrow victories magnified by the "loophole" rules at critical points. We feel that these critics would do well to follow the advice that Congressmen Udall offered when he reviewed his campaign during the speech to the national convention in which he released his delegates: "I am not one who looks back, who says, 'If only . . . ' " Governor Carter won major victories at critical points in the campaign; these victories happened to be in "loophole" states. "Loophole" primaries do distort electoral results, and they are unfair to voters supporting minority candidates. However, the press looks for the popular winner in a primary, not at who wins how many delegates. Carter's victories in these critical states were just that—victories.

The only place where we have any doubt at all about "loophole" primaries affecting the selection process is in New Hampshire. Had New Hampshire's primary been held under proportional representation rules, Carter's commanding total of 15 (out of 17) delegates would have been reduced to 5. Would the media catapult a winner by a narrow plurality, with only 5 delegates to 4 for Udall, 3 for Bayh, and 2 each for Harris and Shriver, into a front-runner? Had the media viewed the New Hampshire results under proportional representation differently, would Carter's Massachusetts campaign strategy have been altered? Would any of this affect the voters in Florida or North Carolina? These questions are unanswerable. Our feeling is that probably the impact would not have been strong enough to significantly alter the results in the next few primaries.

The electoral statistics speak quite loudly. Governor Carter won 19 of the 31 primaries. Some of those were narrow victories, some were near landslide, some in "loophole" states, and some in proportional representation states; but they were all victories. No other candidate won more than four primaries. Carter polled over 6,200,000 votes nationally, nearly three times those of his closest rival, Governor Brown, who accumulated nearly three-quarters of his votes in his native California. Governor Carter received more than twice as many delegates as his nearest rival in the caucus states and nearly twice as many delegates as his nearest rival from the

Table 13. DELEGATES SELECTED AS OF JUNE 10, 1976

	Carter	Wallace	Udall	Jackson	Brown	Church	Uncom.	Others
Chosen in caucus	106	20	69	42	6.5	16	178.5	79
Elected in Primaries	985	148	244	196	226	53	293	157
Loopholes	(555)	(42)	(123)	(138)	(0)	(15)	(248)	(142)
Proportional	(430)	(106)	(121)	(58)	(226)	(38)	(45)	(15)
Total	1,091	168	313	238	232.5	69	490.5	217

proportional representation primaries (and the factor was even larger than that if one again discounts the Brown victory margin in his home state). His lead over all rivals was overwhelming.

Table 14 refutes the theory that momentum picked up in the early "loopholes" carried Carter on to victory. He would have been the clear leader through the first nine primaries—i.e., through Pennsylvania and Texas—under any elctoral system. While Carter certainly did pick up delegates because of the system in use, he did not gain at the expense of any one of the major contenders. No matter how delegates were being selected, the press would have highlighted Carter's six wins in those nine primaries, including the last two, and his win over Senator Jackson in Pennsylvania, despite Jackson's labor and party support, which proved that Carter was a viable contender in any part of the country.

Finally, Table 15 reveals that Carter would still have had an insurmountable lead after June 8 even if all the primaries had been run under proportional representation. Simply stated, Governor Carter was the choice of a large plurality of those Democrats who participated in the presidential selection process. He far outdistanced his early rivals, Shriver, Harris, Bayh, and Jackson; his later rivals, Church and Brown; and his persistent rivals, Wallace and Udall. He did not engender the kind of hatred or fear which would have been necessary to encourage an Anyone-But-Carter movement or a

Table 14. DELEGATES CHOSEN IN FIRST NINE PRIMARIES (Through Texas)

Candidate	Actual System	Proportional Representation	PR with 5% Minimum	PR with 15% Minimum	Loophole
Carter	409	294	299	304	376
Jackson	185	170	168	185	189
Udall	142	154	159	170	139
Wallace	88	121	123	110	53

Table 15. DELEGATES CHOSEN THROUGH JUNE 10 UNDER DIFFERING SYSTEMS
(Excluding New Jersey)

Candidate	Actual System	Proportional Representation	PR with 5% Minimum	PR with 15% Minimum	Loophole
Carter	960	757	778	844	930
Udall	244	283	285	288	217
Wallace	138	217	209	167	90
Jackson	196	192	183	187	189
Brown	226	215	233	265	315
Church	53	98	96	66	76
Byrd	33	28	28	33	33

Humphrey draft. No one else caught the party's fancy. The loss of delegates due to proportional representation probably would not have weakened Carter enough for him to be stopped at the convention. While Carter was not a majority winner, few nominees except incumbents are. He won the nomination because of a broad appeal, not because of the rules of the game.

FUTURE NOMINATIONS

Anyone who watched the 1976 Democratic National Convention had to realize that it was firmly in the hands of the Carter forces. Only once did the convention reach a decision which the Carter camp opposed. The rules committee, 58½ to 58¼, voted to instruct the Commission on the Role and Future of Presidential Primaries, the Winograd Commission, to construe the Charter of the Democratic party so as "to bar the use of delegate selection systems in primary states which permit a plurality winner at any level to elect all of the delegates from that level" (Committee on Rules, 1976:19). Governor Carter urged his delegates to support a minority report which stated that the commission should "analyze and review the use of the so-called 'loophole' primaries . . . and, if appropriate, recommend changes" (Committee on Rules, 1976:25). The convention, by an overwhelming voice vote, supported the majority's position, effectively eliminating "loophole" primaries for the future. Why the convention took this action is beyond the scope of this paper, but we will conclude by examining the effect of this change and others which have been proposed.

In arguing for the minority position before the entire convention, Maryland Lieutenant Governor Blair Lee noted that eliminating the "loophole" would force 13 states to change their laws. The question is what type of system will these states adopt. A look at the latent consequences of "loopholes" is instructive. Besides distorting popular will, the "loophole" also has the effect of boosting the power of political bosses. Strong party leaders use the system to bring large delegations to the convention which are under their control, not pledged to one of the leading candidates. Thus, Mayor Daley ran the Stevenson slate in Illinois; Erie County Chairman Joseph Crangle favored an uncommitted slate in New York; New Jersey regular Democrats backed an uncommitted slate; West Virginians pledged themselves to Senator Robert Byrd.

It is doubtful that these party leaders will give up that strength easily. In some of the "loophole" states, party leaders might favor a return to a caucus system. Such a system is far easier for them to control; it is more to the benefit of party organization. In others, particularly in the Southern states, laws might be changed so as to require runoffs if no majority is attained. The rules committee report does not eliminate "winner-take-all" at the district level if the winner has a majority. It seems clear from the legislative history of the majority report that the elimination of all "loopholes" was desired. However, the exact wording adopted, drafted in the heat of debate by Minnesota Congressman Don Fraser, may well have left another "loophole" to be interpreted by the Winograd Commission. Although "winner-take-all" at the district level did not occur in any caucus states, systems which could have led to those results are not precluded. Thus, the Winograd Commission has significant work to do in interpreting the rules which currently exist.

The mandate for that commission is much broader in any event. The convention accepted the rules committee's recommendation that the Winograd Commission be charged with looking into the entire broad area of the role and future of presidential primaries. The convention also passed a resolution asking the Congress not to involve itself in matters concerning presidential nominations unless and until asked to do so by the parties. If Congress follows this advice, therefore, it will be the Winograd Commission which next examines the persistent calls for either a national primary or a series of regional primaries.

Many politicians felt that the road which led to Governor Carter's nomination in Madison Square Garden was too long, too arduous, too wearing. Seeking to bring rationality to the system, some had already called for a series of regional primaries. An attempt to initiate a New England regional primary was thwarted by a New

Hampshire state law which declared that that state's primary would be held one week before any other. New Hampshire was unwilling to give up her "first in the nation" status, and a regional primary could not work without her cooperation. Two miniregional primaries were held on May 25, a Western one in Oregon, Nevada, and Idaho and a Southern one in Tennessee, Kentucky, and Arkansas. The main argument in favor of regional primaries is that fewer primary days and a decrease in the travel needed to get from one state to the next reduces the strain on the candidate and saves money.

Senate Majority Leader Mike Mansfield and others have extended this logic and proposed that the parties nominate their candidates through one national primary; most national primary proposals have a runoff built in, if a certain plurality is not obtained. Again the rationale would be to reduce the wear and tear on the candidates and the cost of the process. A change to a national primary would be much more fundamental than a change to regional primaries because it would essentially eliminate all caucus/convention states and would render the national convention superfluous. The Winograd Commission will have to deal with each of these proposals.

Time and again Governor Carter has defended the present system, claiming that he enjoyed running in all of the primaries (and in the caucus states) all over the country. In all likelihood, Carter will have a good deal of influence over the Winograd Commission and his opposition to more radical changes will prevail.

Carter's opposition to a regional or national primary system is easy to understand. The national primary penalizes the relative unknown. Carter campaigned hard for over a year before the New Hampshire primary; yet it was only after his win there that the media took him seriously enough that he began to become better known. With a one-shot national primary, the lesser known candidates would have no opportunity to gain momentum. They could not compete and win in states which were small enough so that personal campaigning could work. They could not build name recognition based on early successes in some of these smaller states. Under such a system, the 1976 Democratic nominee might have been any one of a number of prominent politicians, but it certainly would not have been the once obscure ex-Governor of Georgia who raises peanuts.

The regional primary has more appeal, but again it penalizes those who do not do well in whichever region is first. Table 16 shows clearly that different candidates ran better or worse in different sections of the country. It is difficult to speculate how regional

Table 16. PRIMARY VOTE BY REGION (Based on Presidential Preference Vote)

Candidate	Northeast	Middle Atlantic	Southeast	Midwest	Far West
Carter	19.23%	35.37%	54.91%	48.92%	21.18%
Udall	18.22	11.10	3.79	17.70	4.70
Wallace	12.35	9.35	23.58	14.14	2.85
Jackson	18.31	14.14	10.21	3.61	1.22
Brown	1.89	10.74	–	–	52.67
Church	1.66	2.56	0.45	4.77	12.85
Byrd	–	10.76	0.27	–	–

primaries would have come out had they been held in 1976. However, Carter did not dominate any region except for the South. If one looks only at those primaries in which the major candidates were competing, Carter and Udall ran very close to each other in New England, with Udall slightly ahead; Carter received less than 35% of the votes in the Middle Atlantic states, losing New York, Maryland, and New Jersey; Carter and Udall ran very close in the Midwestern states in which they competed, with Carter slightly ahead, but with Church and Stevenson each winning primaries in which Udall was not competing; and Church and Brown won all of the Western primaries. Moreover, one could argue that campaigning would be different if candidates had to campaign in only one region at a time. National issues could well take a backseat to regional concerns. For all of its surface appeal, the concept of regional primaries seems unlikely to be adopted.

Can the system be improved? Should it be made more humane for the candidates competing? We feel that it is possible to achieve a better system if one accepts certain values as desirable.

First, we favor a system in which the presidential preferences of those participating in the selection process are accurately reflected in the delegations sent to the national convention. Thus, we feel that the Winograd Commission should mandate proportional representation, either with no minimum eligibility requirement (preferably) or with a minimum eligibility requirement no higher than 5%, for all states—primary and caucus.

Second, we favor a system in which candidates have the opportunity to become known as the campaign unfolds. We feel that the entire *process* is important, not just the single event of a primary. Thus, we advocate a series of primaries spread over a significant period of time.

Third, we favor a system in which no region—and certainly no single state—automatically has undue influence. We oppose regional primaries and systems which allow states to hold primaries on dates when no others are held.

Finally, we favor a system which tests the national appeal of the candidates and their ability and stamina to wage a long campaign. Perhaps the current system is too chaotic and too taxing, but we would oppose any system which did not adequately test a candidate's endurance and the breadth of his/her appeal.

We feel that the elimination of the "loophole" primary means that some states may decide to go back to a caucus-convention system. A reversal of the tendency toward more and more primaries seems beneficial. The Winograd Commission should then regulate the remaining primaries in line with the values proposed above. The current delegate selection rules are explicit about procedures for caucuses leading to state conventions. Some leeway is left to the states, but basic principles are established at the national level. A similar procedure should be followed for the primary states.

Presidential primaries should be permitted only on the first Tuesday in February, March, April, May, and June of presidential election years. States desiring to hold a primary could choose any of those dates, but no others. The likely result would be four, five, or six primaries, geographically spread throughout the country, on each of five days, with a month between primaries. No region or single state would have too much influence. Candidates would have time to demonstrate their appeal and to gain momentum for their candidacies by campaigning in small as well as large states. A candidate would have to demonstrate a national appeal, not merely a regional one, in order to be treated seriously by the press.

National delegate selection rules should mandate that each state holding a presidential primary must have an on-ballot presidential preference poll and that the delegates to the national convention from each district within a state (the size of which states could determine so long as not fewer than four delegates were elected from each district) and those chosen at large must be apportioned among the presidential preferences according to the results of that poll. Within broad guidelines, the states should be able to decide how the actual delegates to the convention are chosen.

In this paper we have seen the effects of the rules under which the Democrats nominated Jimmy Carter in 1976. We have seen how these rules differ from the ideal intended when the party adopted its Charter. And we have seen how a closer approximation to the ideal would not have altered the outcome of the 1976 nominating process.

The reforms proposed in this current section do not challenge the principle that presidential nominees should be decided upon by delegates meeting in convention; we have not examined that principle. Rather, we have said that, if that principle is accepted, if the basic system does not change, then ours is a better way for it to function.

APPENDIX ON DATA SOURCES

Every scholar has his/her own particular horror story about collecting data for ongoing research. Questionnaires are not returned; important budgetary figures are classified; key participants refuse to be interviewed. We accept these frustrations, note them, and proceed.

Data collection for research on elections has become almost routine. Official returns are published by each state; they are collected in numerous source books such as Dick Scammon's valuable series. To explore the meaning of these statistics we have become used to dealing with Census Bureau publications, roll call votes, and the like. Data manipulation may be necessary, but gathering the raw data has ceased to be a major problem.

Given this background, we were more than surprised that gathering voting returns proved to be the most difficult data collection task we had undertaken. Statewide returns from the presidential primaries were readily available. The press routinely reported these shortly after each Tuesday night's counting. The News Election Service sent the returns out over the wires, and they appeared in papers across the country. But obtaining data at the district level, as was needed for our analysis, proved far more difficult. These data were not routinely available from NES; they were not reported in even major newspapers in the states holding primaries. Moreover, they were not available from normal sources in many of the states until a considerable period of time had elapsed. They were not available from the Democratic National Committee, nor from the various state committees.

The problem could well have been anticipated. Many states were holding primaries for the first time; others were using districts which had not previously been used for primaries. Consequently, no official in these states had assumed the responsibility of collecting and publishing the figures. The returns were tallied on election night and the winners were noted; however, in at least three states, official canvasses were not concluded, and official results were not issued from the responsible state office until some weeks after the Democratic National Convention had adjourned. To the best of our knowledge, statewide totals at the district level have yet (August, 1976) to be issued from a responsible state official in New York or in New Jersey.

The data on which we relied come from many sources. Where available, we have used official election returns. Most typically these are prepared by secretaries of state, but in some states they emanate from other offices. Where official returns were not available, we used the best data obtainable. Often these were complete but unofficial returns distributed by NES or published in the Congressional Quarterly Weekly Reports. In other cases these data were provided to us by friends who were active in one of the candidate's camps or another during the primaries. It is clear to us that some central office should be responsible for gathering the information on which we relied. As the primary process is so important for the political parties, it would seem natural that the elections division of the Democratic and Republican National Committees should assume this responsibility.

Our research would not have been possible without the efforts of many friends who helped us in obtaining the voting returns. John Nelson of the New Democratic Coalition's Center to Save the Reforms and Rhodes Cook of the Congressional Quarterly Service were particularly helpful. Many of those who served with Sandy Maisel on the 1976 Rules Committee helped by sending in the data from their states—Milly Nichols from Rhode Island, Ben Scotch from Vermont, Lieutenant Governor Dick Celeste from Ohio, Ray Jordon from Massachusetts, Mike Bleecher from Wisconsin, John Willis and Joe Gebhardt from Maryland, Fred Furth from California, Mercer Tate from Pennsylvania. We would also like to thank Garry Orren and Bill Mayer at Harvard for sharing their data with us, Joe Cooper and Dick Murray for the Texas results, and Joyce Solo, who pulled Pennsylvania's tally out of a hat the day before this was to go to the publisher. Without the help of all of these people, as well as the staffs of many state committees and the elections division at the Democratic National Committee, we would not have been able to put together the data on which this study is based. Their friendships —and the humorous accounts of some of their incredible efforts to wrench voting returns from a complex bureaucracy—made our particular data collecting horror show much more tolerable.

NOTES

1. These states were Alaska, Colorado, Hawaii, Iowa, Kansas, Maine, Minnesota, Mississippi, Missouri, New Mexico, North Dakota, Oklahoma, South Carolina, Utah, Virginia, Washington, and Wyoming. In addition, Illinois and Texas elected their at-large delegates and Nebraska its alternates at state conventions. The Canal Zone, Puerto Rico, and the Virgin Islands elected delegates at conventions which reflected previously polled presidential preferences; Guam and Democrats Living Abroad elected delegates without reference to presidential preference.

2. California, the District of Columbia, Florida, Georgia, Illinois, Kentucky, Maryland, Massachusetts, Michigan, Nebraska, New Hampshire, New Jersey, Ohio, Pennsylvania, Rhode Island, Tennessee, West Virginia, and Wisconsin all included presidential preference polls on their ballots and chose their delegates without state conventions. Alabama, Louisiana, New York, and Texas all chose delegates through primaries but without presidential preference polls. Arizona, Arkansas, Connecticut, Delaware, Idaho, Indiana, Montana, Nevada, North Carolina, Oregon, South Dakota, and Vermont all operated under systems which used both the primary and the state convention to select delegates.

3. In some cases the actual delegates were chosen in caucuses of the supporters of the various presidential contenders in each district, in others in elections, and in still others in state conventions. Combinations of these were also possible.

The three states chosen as examples also show the variety possible in the use of minimum eligibility requirements. Massachusetts based its allocation of delegates on all of the votes cast, that is, proportional representation with no minimum eligibility requirement. Kentucky is an example of a state in which a candidate needed to receive 15% of the votes cast in the individual districts and in the state as a whole in order to qualify for delegates. The delegates were apportioned proportionally among the candidates meeting this minimum requirement. In Michigan, the 15% eligibility requirement applied for delegates elected at the congressional district level, but the requirement was lowered to 5% for the at-large delegates, who were allocated among the presidential preferences according to the statewide vote. Furthermore, whereas most states ignored the votes cast for preferences receiving less than the designated minimum (dividing delegates in proportion to the votes received among those receiving more than the minimum), Michigan added the votes of those receiving less than the minimum to those cast for "uncommitted," thereby counting them in a way different from that in which they were cast.

4. We are aware that campaigns in the different states might have been conducted differently had different rules been in force. The experience in some of the "loophole" states confirms this supposition. However, more generally, campaign strategy was determined by feelings in national headquarters about how a candidate would fare in one state as opposed to another. It is highly unlikely that candidate decisions on whether or not to concentrate on one state or another were determined by the rules in force in that state. Because there is little evidence that campaign strategy within a state would change radically if the rules changes, we felt justified in examining the hypothetical results under different rules using the actual voting returns. Certainly the actual returns are the best available approximations of what the results would have been.

5. Because this index is used to measure the unfairness of "loophole" primaries, we could have called it the Index of Unfairness of Delegation (IUD). We chose not to.

6. In Section IV (below) we discuss in a more detailed way the meaning of "best" apportionment method. It should be noted that the appropriate measure to use with the Balinksi and Young method is probably

$$\frac{1}{2} \sum_{i, j = 1}^{n} | \text{ (\% delegates for preference j) (\% vote for preference i)/(\% vote} \\ \text{for preference j)} - \text{(\% delegates for preference i)}|.$$

7. In New York State, if the delegates had been selected under a system of proportional representation with a 15% minimum eligibility requirement, the FROPP Index would have been slightly lower if the at-large delegates were apportioned according to the preferences of previously selected delegates than if they were apportioned according to presidential preferences expressed by the voters in the primary. We felt justified in ignoring this one exception, which occurred in only one state and under only one set of rules, because it was the result of candidates not competing in all of the districts, a factor extraneous to the means chosen for allocating at-large delegates.

8. One could argue that reliance on our assumption that "loophole" primaries are de facto "winner-take-all" at the district level stacks the deck and causes the "loophole" to appear unnecessarily unrepresentative. Table 10 (below) compares the actual systems in use with the other systems examined. The FROPP Indexes in the "loophole" states in that table also demonstrate that this system produces delegations which least fairly reflect the presidential preferences of those participating in the primaries.

9. For those states in which no presidential preference vote was taken, and those for which we used the vote for delegates and not the preference vote, the disenfranchisement figures represent the percentage of *votes,* not of voters, which was not counted. In these states voters cast more than one vote, and, of course, it is not possible to ascertain which voters voted across slates and for whom they crossed over.

10. We would argue, however, that there are more appropriate means to discourage fringe candidates than by denying them delegates through an arbitrary minimum eligibility requirement. The most obvious of these would be the denial of matching federal campaign funds to candidates receiving less than a minimum percentage of votes in a series of primaries. Other means—for instance, some dealing with access to the ballot or choice of apportionment method—are also available.

11. One might assume that the ratios should be unitary for at least one of the systems. This is not so, however, for a number of reasons. First, we have presented hypothetical results under "pure" systems while many states used hybrids—e.g., Michigan's employing one eligibility requirement at the district level and another statewide. Second, there is variation in the states using the "loophole," because we assumed slate voting for the purposes of analysis although we realize that some crossover voting did exist. Third, we employed presidential preference votes, while delegates were often selected in separate balloting. This led to major distortions in states such as Maryland, where a leading presidential preference (Governor Brown) could not file a slate of delegates. Vermont has not been included in this analysis because there is no relationship at all—not even temporal—between the "beauty contest" presidential preference primary and the delegate selection by state convention.

12. An apportionment method is said to be house monotone if (in the language of apportioning Congress) an increase in the size of the House always causes every state to receive at least as many Congressmen under the new apportionment as it received before the increase.

13. A state's *quota* is (population of the state/population of the country) x (size of the House of Representatives). For example, using the 1970 census figures, Maine's quota is $(1,006,320/204,053,325) \times 435 = 2.1453$.

14. More precisely, the Balinski and Young method works as follows. The preference with the most votes receives the first delegate. Suppose that h delegates have already been apportioned, giving preference 1 a total of a_1 delegates, preference 2 a total of a_2 delegates, . . . and preference k a total of a_k delegates. To decide which preference is most deserving of the (h + 1)st delegate, one constructs a list of preferences eligible for another delegate and selects the eligible preference that is most underrepresented. Preference i is said to be eligible for another delegate at the level h + 1 if it is underrepresented. The quota for preference i at the (h + 1)st level is (vote for i/total vote) x (h + 1). If a_i, the number of delegates that preference i already has, is less than its quota, candidate i is underrepresented and is said to be eligible for another delegate. If a_i is greater than or equal to the quota for preference i at level h + 1, then preference i cannot be given another delegate without violating quota. One then must compute the ratio (vote for i)/(a_i +1) for each preference i eligible at the (h + 1)st level. This ratio represents the number of voters for preference i that would be represented by each of preference i's delegates if that preference received the next delegate. The eligible preference with the largest ratio is the most deserving and is awarded the (h + 1)st delegate under Balinski and Young's method. One continues apportioning delegates at each stage to the most deserving eligible preference until all of the available delegates have been allocated.

15. The following example demonstrates the functioning of the Hamilton method. If preference A has eight votes, preference B has five votes, and preference C has three votes, then the respective quotas with five delegates to apportion are: (8/16) x 5 = 2.5; (5/16) x 5 = 1.5625; and (3/16) x 5 = 0.9375. The respective lower quotas are 2, 1, and 0. This allocation of delegates leaves two leftover. The leftover fractions are 0.5, 0.5625, and 0.9375. Preferences C and B have the two largest leftover fractions, thereby earning the leftover delegates. In this example the Hamilton method would give two delegates to preference A, two delegates to preference B, and one delegate to preference C.

REFERENCES

BALINSKI, M.L., and YOUNG, H.P. (1974). "A new method for congressional apportionment." Proceedings of the National Academy of Science of the U.S.A., November, no. 11.

——— (1975). "The quota method of apportionment." American Mathematical Monthly, September.

Charter of the Democratic Party of the United States (1974). Washington, D.C.: Democratic National Committee.

COMMITTEE ON RULES (1976). The report of the 1976 Committee on Rules. Washington, D.C.: Democratic National Committee.

Congressional Record (1901). Proceedings and Debates of the 56th Congress, 2nd sess., vol. 34. Washington, D.C.: U.S. Government Printing Office.

COOK, R. (1976). "New primary rules make little difference." Congressional Quarterly Weekly Report, 34(23, June 5). Washington, D.C.: Congressional Quarterly.

Delegate Selection Rules for the 1976 Democratic National Convention (1975). Washington, D.C.: Democratic National Committee.

FITZPATRICK, J.C. (ed., 1939). The writings of George Washington (vol. 32, March 10, 1792-June 30, 1793). Washington, D.C.: U.S. Government Printing Office.

FORD, L.P. (ed., 1904). The works of Thomas Jefferson (vol. 6). New York: G.P. Putnam's Sons.

HUNTINGTON, E.V. (1921). "The mathematical theory of apportionment of representatives." Proceedings of the National Academy of Science of the U.S.A. (7).

――― (1928). "The apportionment of representatives of Congress." Transactions of the American Mathematical Society (30).

――― (1940). "Methods of apportionment in Congress" (Senate Document no. 304, 76th Congress, 3rd sess.). Washington, D.C.: U.S. Government Printing Office.

LENGLE, J.I., and SHAFER, B. (1976). "Primary rules, political power, and social change." American Political Science Review, 70:25-40.

LINDSAY, B.W. (1974). Proportional representation voting methods. Albuquerque: New Mexico Democratic Council.

SULLIVAN, D.G., PRESSMAN, J.L., PAGE, B.I., and LYONS, J.J. (1974). The politics of representation. New York: St. Martin's.

SYRETT, H.C. (ed., 1966). The papers of Alexander Hamilton (vol. 11, February-June, 1792). New York: Columbia University Press.

WEBSTER, D. (1903). The writings and speeches of Daniel Webster (vol. 6). Boston: Little, Brown.

WILLCOX, W.F. (1916). "The apportionment of representatives." American Economic Review, March supplement.

――― (1952). "Last words on the apportionment problem: Legislative reapportionment." Law and Contemporary Problems.

Chapter 3

CANDIDATES, CAUCUSES, AND ISSUES:
THE DEMOCRATIC CONVENTION, 1976

DENIS G. SULLIVAN
JEFFREY L. PRESSMAN
F. CHRISTOPHER ARTERTON
ROBERT T. NAKAMURA
MARTHA WAGNER WEINBERG

I. INTRODUCTION

In recent years, the Democratic party has experienced severe polarization over substantive issues, both foreign and domestic (Miller et al., 1973). Our previous studies of Democratic conventions have shown deep and continuing cleavages, based both on issue positions and on political style (Sullivan et al., 1974; Sullivan et al., 1976). They have also shown increasing strength and institutionalization on the part of special caucus groups—chiefly the Black

AUTHORS' NOTE: We are grateful to our interviewers, who performed with intelligence, enterprise, and tenacity under difficult conditions. The interviewers were Jacqueline Ackerman, Janet Arterton, Michael Baumrin, John Casey, Thomas Cavanagh, Judith Center, Harold Challenor, Paul Coady, Rob Fein, Patricia Hanratty, Robert Kazdin, Marc Levin, Gail Lopata, Donna Malin, Stephen Mandel, Mike McGeary, Stephen Meili, Jared Parker, Roberta Pearson, Kate Pressman, Robert Price, Robert Sholl, Robert Weinberg, and Andrea Wolfman.

We would also like to thank the following members of the Democratic National Committee staff, who were helpful throughout our study: Mark Siegel, Andrea Rosen, Vincent Clephus, and Sheilah Hixson. Carol Casey of the Library of Congress aided us in acquiring lists of delegates. Gilbert Steiner of the Brookings Institution provided office space and other help for Robert Nakamura. Karen Gourdin typed several drafts of the manuscript as well as the final copy. The project was supported by grants from the Ford Foundation and Dartmouth College.

Caucus and the Women's Caucus—who have been hostile to established party leaders.

Based on this experience, one could have expected that the 1976 convention would be a stormy one indeed. Because of certain institutional factors, the prospects for fragmentation and conflict at this convention were particularly strong. It seemed likely that the large number of primaries would make it difficult for any one candidate to amass a majority of the delegates. In addition, there was speculation that rules mandating proportional representation would encourage candidates to stay in the race, even if they did not win many primaries. Finally, many observers thought that new financial rules would increase the chances for fragmentation by placing ceilings on spending (thus preventing a runaway victory) and by providing public funding (thus encouraging candidates not to drop out).

Given these changes in the structure of the process, it seemed likely that there would be multiple candidacies with few dropouts prior to the convention. Early in the campaign, one might have predicted the following scenario. Candidates, none of whom dominated the public opinion polls at the outset of the campaign, would pursue limited strategies. In order to win pluralities in crowded fields, they might narrow their appeals to mobilize groups who felt intensely about issues. Or they might attempt to conserve their time and other resources by running in a limited number of states. Many observers predicted that the logical outcome of these strategies would be a multiballot convention.

At such a convention, we would have expected to find active group caucuses. Each group (women, blacks, labor, and so forth), realizing that there would be a brokered convention, would have sought to get its representatives selected as delegates to the convention. This would have encouraged blocs of delegates who had an overriding commitment to a single issue. If this had happened, candidacies would have been based on issues, group support, and region. Consequently, we might have expected that cleavages in the party would have become deeper.

Of course, the actual Democratic nomination contest and convention in 1976 bore scant resemblance to this scenario. Jimmy Carter locked up the nomination in the days following the final primaries on June 8; there was no serious battle for the presidential nomination at the convention. There were no fights over the platform, which was approved by a nearly unanimous voice vote.

Group caucus leaders, who had raised their voices in protest at the 1972 convention and the 1974 midterm conference, appeared to be happy with the results of the convention. It was indeed strange and surprising to see the usually pugnacious Democrats so unified.

Even though the convention was far from the one that many had expected, it provided us with a laboratory for assessing the models of legitimation, caucus institutionalization, political style, and issue cleavages that we had developed on the basis of our 1972 and 1974 convention research. This essay will go beyond the apparent signs of unity in 1976 to ask the following questions: How as the Democratic party, so long torn by divisions over issues, able to write a platform that so many factions could support? What was the experience at the convention of the special group caucuses? How did they organize themselves and how did they relate to Jimmy Carter as the prospective nominee? What were the roles of the Carter organization and the Democratic National Committee in managing the convention and in encouraging cooperation among the party's various groups? How did Jimmy Carter himself relate to diverse groups of delegates, and how did the delegates in turn perceive Carter? Finally, were the results of the convention viewed as legitimate and desirable by the delegates? Did losers as well as winners find satisfaction in the outcome?

Exploration of the answers to these questions can tell us much about convention behavior as well as about the current state of the Democratic party. But because party conventions involve large numbers of individuals and groups, dispersed over a wide geographic area and often not aware of each other's behavior, conventions are difficult events to study. In order to avoid an interpretation of the convention which, because it was limited to one kind of analysis, did not do justice to the complexity and diversity of the process, we used three different methods to analyze the convention. We sent out preconvention questionnaires, which 300 delegates filled out. In addition, we conducted interviews at the convention. A research team of 29 faculty members and students talked with 75% (330 of 441) of a randomly drawn sample of convention delegates. Finally, faculty members and students were given responsibility for monitoring specific events and organizations at the convention. We observed group caucuses and candidate organizations and also followed the process of platform making. We supplemented these focused observations with interviews of group and organization leaders and political analysts.

This paper represents a preliminary assessment of the results of all three research methods. Because it was completed so soon after the convention, this study necessarily relies most heavily on the data from the preconvention questionnaires and on interviews of elites and observations of their behavior. Though we were able to draw some conclusions about the preferences and feelings of delegates from the delegate interviews, we have not yet begun to analyze all the information with which these interviews provided us, and therefore we have made no attempt to summarize them in this study.

II. FASHIONING THE PLATFORM:
THE TRIUMPH OF ACCOMMODATION

It might have been expected that the platform-writing process would be a site of convention activity particularly susceptible to the outbreak of conflict. The issue polarization which had characterized the party in recent years could be expected to manifest itself here. Also, competing presidential candidates would have incentives to use platform planks to promote their own candidacies. Finally, a wide range of groups within the party—blacks, women, labor unions, and so forth—might be expected to push hard for incorporation of their favored issue positions in the platform.

Because the various candidates and groups disagreed among themselves about both the importance and substance of particular issues, the potential for debate and divisiveness was very real. Yet the platform which was approved by an overwhelming voice vote at the July 13 meeting of the full convention was characterized by less debate and controversy during its development than any Democratic platform in recent memory. In 1972, 20 minority planks had been proposed on the floor of the convention, and two had been accepted. In 1976, by contrast, only one minority plank urging revisions in the Hatch Act was proposed; it was carried by voice vote. The whole process unfolded with no apparent acrimony, heat, or debate.

Why was the process of building the platform characterized by such apparent unity? To understand this phenomenon, one must recognize at least four important underlying factors. First of all, the fact that Carter had all but locked up the nomination before the full platform committee had even met meant that the platform could not be used to bolster other candidacies. Second, a recent party rules change had made it more difficult than ever before for minority planks to be reported out of the platform committee for debate on the floor. Under the old rules, 10% of that committee could vote out a minority plank; but in October 1975 the Democratic National Committee increased that figure to 25% in order to minimize divisiveness at the 1976 convention.

A third factor facilitating accommodation was the fact that the Vietnam War, over which the party had been bitterly divided in 1968 and 1972, was no longer an issue, and no issue of equal salience had replaced it on the party's agenda. Finally, the Democrats had learned from painful experience in 1968 and 1972 about the costs of internal party division and disunity. Our interviews are filled with delegates' resolutions to learn from past experience and avoid such conflicts in the future.

Even given these underlying forces favoring cooperation and accommodation, the final outcome was by no means assured. To understand that outcome, we must examine the way the platform committee and its staff consciously worked to design and carry out a process that facilitated accommodation and compromise.

THE EARLY STAGES

The planning for the 1976 platform actually began in October of 1975, when Michael Barnes, a young Democratic activist and editor of the *Democratic Review,* was hired by Robert Strauss as staff director for the platform committee. Barnes and Strauss were both anxious to avoid the sort of stormy sessions characteristic of the 1968 and 1972 conventions. They also wanted to make certain that the delegates did not feel that the convention had been brokered and "wired" by Strauss. They agreed that their strategy should be aimed at three objectives. First, they wanted to be certain that they would be able to say in good conscience, when the platform was presented, that everyone who had wished it had had access to the process. Second, they wanted to avoid a conflict over the platform on the floor of the convention by making the hearings and the platform committee the site for any battles which would be fought. Finally, they wanted to produce a document around which a majority of the party could rally and which avoided issues of concern to only a small minority. As Barnes put it, "I decided there would be no urban Indians planks if I could help it. Our real hope was for a consensus document, accepted on the floor in the most boring display of party unity we'd ever seen."

To encourage widespread participation, Barnes and the staff began almost immediately to make plans for a series of regional hearings on the platform at which anyone would be welcome to speak. In addition, in an attempt to avoid the possibility that candidates would try to make the platform hearings a political battlefield, the staff asked each candidate to designate a liaison to the committee who would be authorized to speak for the candidate and who would work with the staff throughout the process. Philip Noel, the popular Governor of Rhode Island, was named as chairman of the platform committee.

Thus, by the middle of November, the party leadership had identified a chairman, made linkages with the candidate organizations, worked out an overall strategy, and planned a series of forums for hearing various elements of the party on the subject of the platform. Noel was to resign in May as chairman after being criticized for an alleged racial slur, but by this time he had done most of the groundwork that he and the staff felt was necessary to cement the process as they had initially envisioned it. In addition to planning and publicizing the hearings, Noel and the staff took one crucial preliminary step. Noel held a series of meetings with leaders of a whole series of groups, such as blacks, women, labor, and the elderly to ask them what their concerns on the platform were and to urge them to attend the regional hearings and to speak out on the issues. As one aide to Noel described these sessions:

> We were attempting to do two things—to send out a message that we wanted to listen and that we recognized their legitimacy. We also made it clear that there would be plenty of time for them to get into the act, that we weren't only going to listen during the four days of the convention, and that there would be room for more than just the George Meany's of the world to speak. They [the group leaders] understood what we were saying and telegraphed ahead the major issues with which they were concerned.

Staff aides identified the party's late 1975 issues conference in Louisville as an important turning point in the effort to defuse controversial issues and encourage a spirit of compromise. At this conference the issue of school busing, which appeared to be one of the most divisive issues in the campaign, was discussed heatedly both by leaders of the party and by antibusing advocates. Despite demonstrations outside the Louisville meeting by those who wanted the party to take a stand against busing to achieve integration and despite a rousing probusing speech by George McGovern, neither group "won" on the issue. In fact, neither group was able to have the question put to a vote. As one aide to the platform committee put it:

> To us Louisville was a bellwether. Partisans on both sides of an important issue saw that they couldn't carry the day, that they'd be overwhelmed if they tried to push the party to either extreme. It wasn't a year for those kinds of issues. We could tell that the tone would be geared to compromising and winning the election. Everybody knew that the last time we'd fought we got Nixon—and nothing could be worse than that.

From November until May the staff continued to focus its efforts on pulling as many people into the process as possible while working with a range of groups to find out on which issues they felt most strongly. Four regional hearings were held in different parts of the country at which more than 500 witnesses appeared. At the same time, the staff continued to deal with the groups whom they had initially contacted and with the candidate representatives, as one staff member put it, "walking them through language and compromises, to see how they'd respond, where they'd balk." In April and May, the staff, relying on what it had learned in five months of listening and negotiating, drew up an outline for a first draft of the platform.

THE DRAFTING

The full platform committee held its first meetings in mid-May. Governor Michael Dukakis of Massachusetts was elected chairman of the drafting subcommittee shortly after Philip Noel resigned as chairman of the full committee and after Governor Wendell Anderson of Minnesota was named to succeed him. After these initial meetings, the staff of the committee went to work on the first draft.

It was not until June 3, only a week before the final meetings of the platform committee were to occur, that Dukakis saw the draft which the staff had prepared. The dialogue which occurred in the first meeting of the staff with Dukakis was in many respects a representative expression of the several and often competing goals which the party had set for itself. Dukakis had a mandate from the platform committee to make the platform concise and tight and to avoid "loading it up like a Christmas tree" with issues which would divide the party. The staff, while sharing this goal, had sat through months of hearings and negotiating sessions with groups in the party. The first discussion which Dukakis held with the staff reflected the tension between the competing goals of paring down the platform and making certain that the requests and concerns that groups had expressed during the process did not go unheeded.

Dukakis had two major concerns with the first draft. The first, with which the staff was in agreement, was the rhetoric, logic, and tightness of the writing. The second was with the substance of some of the platform planks. As one observer described the meeting:

> Michael thought the platform was coming out as too much of a grab bag. He would focus in on a statement like the provision of U.S. policy toward Namibia and ask what the hell Namibia was doing in a document that was not supposed to be a laundry list. The staff would then explain that one of the important demands of the black caucus was that explicit reference to U.S.-Namibia policy be included. They kept saying, "We hear you—but we know where the bottom line is."

During the three days after the Massachusetts meeting, Dukakis worked on the platform, carrying with him to Washington a draft shorter by about one-half than the document that he had discussed with the staff. On the evening before the final platform hearings were to begin, Dukakis, Barnes, and two representatives of the Carter organization, Joseph Duffey and Stuart Eizenstat, worked all night to revise the draft. The document with which they emerged was closer in length and style to the original staff draft than to the Dukakis version. As Barnes explained the change:

> Dukakis had tightened it up. But we knew that to have the unity and the support that we'd hoped for, we had to listen to what groups had been telling us. We wanted to avoid a grab bag—but we had to give groups some of the items they wanted, especially those things which wouldn't cause anybody else any problems.

Despite the fact that there had been some disagreement about the length and specificity of the draft, the compromise between the drafters and the staff that was ultimately reached reflected the desire for a document conducive to healing the wounds of the party and responsive to the specific interests of groups which had participated throughout the process.

THE FINAL PLATFORM HEARINGS

The full platform hearings, though not totally placid, were, like the earlier stages of the process, characterized by a high level of agreement and few open battles. After the draft was presented to the full committee, members divided into six task forces to deal with the six sections of the platform. On Monday, June 14, the full committee met to consider the document. It was in the full sessions that the staff and party leaders expected that disagreement over issues would focus more sharply than at any other time during the process. The fact that the process was so smooth can best be explained by looking more closely at the candidate organizations and the groups most closely associated with particular issues.

The groups which had seemed most likely to disrupt the unity and harmony of the proceedings were the competing candidate organizations. But by the time the final platform hearings were held, it was clear that Carter was to be the party's nominee. The Carter organization was represented in the platform hearings by Joseph Duffey and Stuart Eizenstat. These men made it clear that they wanted the product of the meetings to be a document on which Carter could comfortably base a campaign. When amendments on such issues as gay rights and capital punishment were raised in the full committee, the Carter representatives argued against them, saying that they were "inflammatory and emotional" and would only help the Republican opposition if they were included (Congressional Quarterly, 1976:1553).

It is not difficult to understand why the Carter organization was anxious to avoid controversy. The reasons that the other candidates' representatives would go along with the strategy are more complicated. Perhaps the most important of these was best expressed by one of the candidates' representatives:

> Candidates are politicians after all. They knew that the last time we went left, the last time we went to extremes, we lost big. There were no issues as important as Vietnam worth doing that this time. Nobody was going to raise a "here's-my-chin-please-hit-me" issue for the Republicans. We all knew that we had to keep one toe on the 50-yard line.

This willingness on the part of the candidate organizations to live with Carter's wishes for a united front on the platform was reinforced by two other factors. First, several of the candidate representatives felt that they had achieved a substantial number of their own goals on the platform. The representative of one liberal candidate claimed that "the language of the foreign policy plank was totally acceptable to us because it committed us to a $5-$7 billion cut in defense spending." At the same time an aide to Jackson claimed that the foreign policy plank "was a victory for us in the sense that it emphasized the defense of freedom, perhaps the most important symbolic rhetoric in the platform on American foreign policy." Second, the cooperative orientation of candidates' aides was doubtless furthered by the fact that they had been included from the beginning in the process of framing the platform.

Similar explanations apply to the behavior of many of the groups who were pressing for specific issues. These groups had been given a chance to participate in a number of stages of the process. They understood that Carter would be the nominee and that raising difficult issues might work against the election of a Democrat in the fall. In addition, the fact that groups were able to place favored issues in the platform gave group leaders a reason for satisfaction and an incentive to support the whole document.

The desire for unity was clearly evident in the debate on amnesty for Vietnam War resisters. Sam Brown of Colorado, an alternate on the drafting subcommittee, proposed a full and complete pardon for those in "financial and legal jeopardy because of their opposition to the Vietnam War." Despite the opposition of the Carter representatives, who opposed an outright pardon for deserters, the full committee approved Brown's proposal. Brown and Eizenstat then huddled in conference, after which Brown agreed to amend the language to read that deserters would be dealt with on a case-by-case basis. Brown explained that he was not pleased with the new language but added, "You have to give up a bit in order to take control of the Presidency" (New York Times, 1976a).

It is clear that this spirit of unity among Democratic party activists was strengthened by the absence of an issue that split the party down the middle, by the dominance of a single candidacy as the nomination process concluded, and by a widespread determination not to repeat the divisions and defeats of the recent past. But the accommodative behavior was also the result of a sustained effort by party leaders and staff members to involve relevant groups in the process, to listen to their concerns, and to give them some satisfaction in the final document.

III. GROUP CAUCUSES:
THE BUILDING OF POLITICAL BASES

If the party's treatment of issues had changed from 1972 to 1976, the difference in the experience of group caucuses was equally great. The Black and Women's Caucuses demonstrated that they had grown both in their sophistication in dealing with internal organizational issues and in their effectiveness in dealing with external policy questions. And, as was the case in the making of the platform, previously divisive group issues were resolved in a bargaining, nonpolarizing manner. Indeed, it should be noted that the platform process itself contributed to satisfaction and moderation within the group caucuses. A wide variety of groups pointed proudly to their success in placing preferred planks into the platform. (See, for example, Women's Political Times, 1976.) These "victories" enabled leaders to claim credit with followers and enabled the groups themselves to feel that they had won some of the divisible prizes at the convention.

PREVIOUS EXPERIENCES

At the 1972 Democratic convention, group caucuses were formed with the intention of bargaining with presidential candidates and securing candidates' support for group demands. But the experience of those caucuses in 1972 was not a happy one. Although there were meetings during convention week of Black, Women's, and Youth Caucuses, among others, none of these groups was able to influence major decisions at the convention, and most could not even make a sustained claim on the attention of their potential members. Caucus meetings were devoted to listening to candidates' appeals or to general debate on a variety of issues.

The group caucuses' failure to meet expectations in 1972 can be attributed to a number of recurring organizational problems. One of these was the problem of time; because of the fast pace and heavy workload of the convention itself, delegates could not afford the time to attend special caucus meetings. Another problem was that of self-definition; it proved difficult for these groups to set and maintain their own boundaries. For example, the Black Caucus tried to restrict its membership to delegates and alternates, but found it impossible to enforce this restriction. A final and crucial problem for the special caucuses was that other organizations, notably candidate organizations, felt their own goals might be threatened by the existence of strong, independent group caucuses (see, Sullivan et al., 1974, chap. 3).

At the 1974 Democratic miniconvention, however, the experience of the Black and Women's Caucuses was more satisfying. From the beginning of that conference, those two caucuses concentrated their attention on a section of the proposed party charter which spelled out guidelines for challenging delegations on affirmative action grounds. Ultimately, the caucuses were able to persuade a number of other important actors—first some liberal union leaders, then Democratic governors, then party chairman Robert Strauss, and finally a majority of the delegates—to support them in altering the charter section to make affirmative action challenges easier to sustain.

The increase in the effectiveness of the caucuses from 1972 to 1974 can be explained by changes both in the external environment and within the caucuses themselves. Perhaps the most crucial difference in the environment in 1974 was the absence of active candidate organizations which could compete with the caucuses for delegates' time and loyalty. The Black and Women's Caucuses were also aided in achieving their objectives by the internal institutionalization that they were able to develop. In his study of organizational development in the House of Representatives, Polsby (1968) included the following characteristics among his indices of "institutionalization":

(1) [An institutionalized organization] is relatively well-bounded, that is to say, differentiated from its environment.

(2) The organization is relatively complex, that is, its functions are internally separated on some regular and explicit basis.

One important difference between the group caucus experiences in 1972 and 1974 was that, in the latter years, the caucuses were better able to define their membership, to set boundaries between themselves and the outside environment. In 1972, the Black Caucus had found it impossible to limit its own membership. But in 1974, that caucus carefully excluded all but delegates and alternates from its deliberations.

A second difference between the caucuses of 1972 and 1974 was the increased internal complexity and organization that could be observed at the midterm conference. In 1972, both the Black and the

Women's Caucuses had existed merely as forums to hear presidential candidates and to listen to speeches by their own members. But in 1974, both these caucuses had detailed communications networks, and both selected small steering committees made up of prominent delegates (Sullivan et al., 1976, chap. 4).

EXPECTATIONS AND RESULTS IN 1976

With these past experiences in mind, we expected that at the 1976 Democratic convention the group caucuses—particularly of blacks and women—would become further institutionalized. At the same time, the 1972 experience suggested that, at a presidential nominating convention, the strength of candidate organizations would dominate the proceedings and would prevail over group caucus loyalties.

Not surprisingly, our 1976 study showed considerable evidence of organizational strength on the part of the Carter campaign organization. But group caucuses were active as well, although they differed widely in their degree of internal cohesion and external effectiveness. The Black and Women's Caucuses demonstrated further evidence of institutionalization, while the Latino Caucus was forced to grapple with the same sorts of organizational problems that had plagued caucuses in general at the 1972 convention. An interesting new group at this convention was a coalition of labor unions who had chosen to work independently of traditional AFL-CIO channels in the 1976 nomination process. Finally, state delegation caucuses continued to be an important site for the resolution of logistical matters and—in certain cases—for discussion and planning of local political campaigns.

When the Carter organization had a specific preference—on nominations, platform, or rules—it was almost always able to prevail. Unlike the case in 1972, group caucus leaders did not plan to contest candidate organizations for control of the convention. They limited their demands to issues closely related to their own organizational goals.

With the Carter organization strong and with some of the group caucuses demonstrating organizational sophistication and stability, the preconvention and convention periods were characterized by a substantial degree of focused bargaining between Carter and his staff on the one hand and caucus leaders on the other. After examining the performance of group caucuses in 1976, we will consider some of the implications of this bargaining pattern for the broader political system.[1]

BLACK CAUCUS

As it had done in 1974, the Black Caucus at the 1976 convention was able to define its membership effectively and to limit participation to delegates and alternates only. Outsiders were not even allowed into the room as observers at the first caucus meeting on Monday, July 12. But after many delegates complained about their spouses and friends being denied entrance, the caucus' steering committee decided to admit observers to subsequent meetings. These observers were asked to sit in the back of the room and could not debate or vote.

Another sign of institutionalization—the development of specialized leadership—was also much in evidence in 1976. The Caucus of Black Democrats, composed of black elected officials, members of the Democratic National Committee, labor representatives, religious leaders, and members of the black press, selected a steering committee including national black leaders like Julian Bond, Tom Bradley, Richard Hatcher, and Barbara Jordan. Basil Paterson, Vice Chairman of the Democratic National Committee, was named chairman of the caucus.

The Black Caucus could—and did—point with pride to a number of its accomplishments in party committees in the weeks preceding the convention. The party's platform, for example, included a number of the caucus' favored programs in the areas of employment, urban policy, voter registration, national health care, and criminal justice reform, among others.[2] The Black Caucus ascribed these victories to the effective work of caucus representatives on the platform committee. On the convention's rules committee, Black Caucus members were able to persuade Carter staff people to reverse their position and accept the inclusion of "specific goals and timetables for achieving results" in affirmative action programs at all levels of the party.

On the first day of the convention, Monday, July 12, Jimmy Carter met with the steering committee of the Caucus of Black Democrats. Carter pleased the caucus representatives by announcing that he would support the reappointment of Basil Paterson as Vice Chairman of the Democratic National Committee (a reversal of Carter's stand the week before, when he planned to replace Paterson with Ben Brown of his own campaign). The candidate also said that he would support the blacks against attempts to water down the affirmative action rules. In addition he promised to support a proposal for substantial funding for a voter registration drive in the black community and asked for the names of blacks to fill policy-making jobs in the Carter administration (New York Times, 1976b; New York Post, 1976a).

Meetings of the full Black Caucus were held on each day of the convention, following meetings of the steering committee. Attendance at the Monday, Tuesday, and Wednesday meetings averaged approximately 250; the Thursday meeting attracted fewer than 50 people. Caucus leaders used these meetings as an opportunity to talk about the caucus's triumphs in committees and to instruct the delegates on upcoming votes. Whenever the steering committee took a position on an issue, the full body overwhelmingly supported that position.

At the end of the convention, Basil Paterson and other black leaders expressed pride in the level of organization that their caucus had attained. (And they were doubtless happy to hear that the Asian Americans had requested Black Caucus help in their efforts to organize.)

WOMEN'S CAUCUS

The 1976 experience of the Women's Caucus was similar in many ways to the experience of the Black Caucus. Like the blacks, the women were successful in creating boundaries between delegates and alternates on the one hand and outside "supporters" on the other. Credentials were checked at the door of caucus meetings, and delegates and alternates were seated separately from (nonvoting) supporters.

Like the Black Caucus, the Women's Caucus had developed a specialized and stable group of leaders who planned strategy and represented the caucus in outside negotiations. The leadership of the caucus was composed primarily of the heads of the groups that made up the caucus at the convention: the Democratic Task Force of the National Women's Political Caucus, the Democratic National Committeewoman's Caucus (founded in 1974 in an effort to organize and inform committeewomen about women's issues within the party), and the Democratic Women's Agenda (organized in 1976 to mobilize support for and increase awareness of women's issues at all levels of the party). In addition, the leadership included well-known elected officials like Representatives Bella Abzug and Shirley Chisholm.

Although Women's Caucus leaders were generally pleased with the treatment of their concerns in the party's platform (reflecting again the platform makers' success in drafting a consensus document—see Women's Political Times, 1976), they were less pleased with the outcome of the preconvention deliberations of the rules committee. That committee, following the wishes of Carter campaign representatives, watered down a Women's Caucus resolution that would have required future national convention delegations to be evenly divided between men and women. Instead, the committee approved a resolution requiring that after 1976 the call for conventions "shall promote an equal division" between male and female delegates (Washington Post, 1976a). Women's Caucus representatives and their supporters immediately filed a minority plank which would *require* equal division.

As the convention approached, both the women and the Carter organization began to express willingness to negotiate and compromise on this issue. Over the July 4 weekend Jimmy Carter called Bella Abzug and requested a meeting with women leaders to discuss a compromise that would avoid a floor fight. Plans were made for a meeting on Sunday, July 11; the Women's Caucus was to choose a group of 30 negotiators, composed of Democratic national committeewomen, elected officials, rules committee members, and National Women's Political Caucus staff.

The Sunday meeting between Carter and the women's representatives ended in a stalemate on the rules language, although the women were pleased by Carter's pledges to use his influence on behalf of the Equal Rights Amendment and to appoint women to jobs at all levels of a Carter administration. On Monday, a smaller group of Women's Caucus negotiators met again with Carter and this time reached a compromise on the equal division issue. Although the language of the compromise specified that equality was to be "promoted" and not "required," Carter did agree to have the rule take effect at the party's 1978 midterm conference, rather than at the 1980 convention. The women cited as an improvement a new sentence that said, "The national party shall encourage and assist state parties to adopt provisions to achieve this goal [of equal numbers of women delegates] in their delegate-selection plans" (New York Times, 1976c). While the negotiating team was meeting with Carter, other Women's Caucus members were counting votes and preparing a detailed communications network in the event of a floor fight. Caucus activists later observed that such preparations probably helped them convince Carter and his staff that they were organizationally ready to fight the issue out on the floor.

Another bargaining resource for the Women's Caucus negotiators lay in the widespread recognition that a sizable number of caucus members were adamant about requiring equal division and, as a result, were prepared to force a floor fight on that issue. At the daily meetings of the Women's Caucus, Karen De Crow, President of the National Organization for Women (and not a convention delegate) joined others in speaking forcefully against compromise. By insisting to the representatives of the Carter organization that they could not make any binding agreements without a vote of the full caucus, the women's negotiators could use the militancy of many caucus members to their advantage.[3] In fact, the division of opinion in the full caucus on this issue was a very real one. It took repeated appeals by Abzug, Chisholm, and others to build support for the compromise, which was overwhelmingly endorsed at Tuesday's meeting. All of this excitement helped to swell attendance at caucus meetings, which rose from 500 on Sunday to well over 1,000 on Tuesday, before dropping off later in the week.

LATINO CAUCUS

On each day of the convention, a Latino Caucus was called under the auspices of the Spanish-speaking division of the Democratic National Committee. But the experience of this caucus was a frustrating one. The first caucus on Sunday ended because of the lack of a quorum. On Monday, Mexican-Americans loudly protested because the caucus' proposed national issues report did not include mention of the problems of the farm workers and illegal aliens (New York Post, 1976b). By the final day of the convention, the caucus was unable to agree on a Latino platform.

Like the Black and Women's Caucuses in 1972, the Latino Caucus in 1976 was a loose organization without clear boundaries or a well-developed leadership group. As one caucus member remarked: "We have a very loose leadership structure. We're open to the press—open to everybody."

Part of the problem for the Latinos was the extremely heterogeneous character of its potential membership. A caucus activist explained it this way:

This problem is the traditional split—Puerto Ricans versus Mexicans. Then the Puerto Ricans got into a split, statehood for some and commonwealth for others. Another Puerto Rican split is over the Badillo-Velez [congressional primary] rivalry in New York. Then you have the Southwestern Mexican-Americans who are worried about the farm worker situation and amnesty for aliens. They don't understand Puerto Rican statehood issues.

Carter did address the caucus on Wednesday of convention week. But caucus participants were disappointed with the event because there was not the kind of specific bargaining that characterized Carter's communication with women and blacks. As one Mexican-American from California put it: "There's no negotiating. We're just trying to sensitize Carter on issues." In addition, those who attended were unhappy because the media did not give much coverage to the event.

LABOR COALITION CLEARINGHOUSE

In 1972, organized labor at the convention—led by George Meany and the AFL-CIO hierarchy—had been hostile to the new organizational forms represented by the group caucuses. But in 1974, some liberal labor leaders joined the Black and Women's Caucuses in a successful rules battle. Recognizing the value of the caucus as an organizational device, these leaders worked in 1976 to form a caucus of their own.

This new group caucus appeared at the 1976 convention as the Labor Coalition Clearinghouse, a joint effort of nine liberal trade unions. The unions involved in the coalition were among the most politically active in the labor movement—the United Auto Workers (UAW), the Communications Workers of America (CWA), the American Federation of State, County, and Municipal Employees (AFSCME), the International Association of Machinists (IAM), the National Education Association (NEA), the Graphic Arts International Union (GAIU), the International Union of Electrical, Radio, and Machine Workers (IUE), the United Mine Workers of America (UMWA), and the Oil, Chemical, and Atomic Workers (OCAW). the OCAW eventually dropped out of the coalition, leaving eight unions in the group at the convention (Aronson, 1976:113-116).

The coalition, formed to influence the choice of nominee and the platform, had substantial success in electing delegates. Of the 550 to 600 delegates who were union members, 418 were from the eight unions in the coalition. (The National Education Association, with 172 delegates, was the largest group; the NEA also had 93 alternates.) At the convention, the coalition set up an elaborate communications system. From positions at 12 regional desks at the Statler Hilton Hotel, coalition leaders could activate 190 beepers held by coalition members on the floor. And each of 46 state delegations had one or more coalition floor leaders who in turn communicated with other delegates.

With the issue of the presidential nomination already resolved, the coalition's level of organization would appear to have been extravagant for the tasks at hand. But the coalition was able to turn its attention to smaller issues, such as the inclusion in the platform of a plank urging the liberalization of the Hatch Act and the retention of Basil Paterson as Vice Chairman of the National Democratic Committee.

The coalition's ability to elect delegates and organize them at a convention also had implications for union politics outside the Democratic party. The 1976 convention experience caused some observers to predict that the coalition would be able to use its organizational structure and Democratic party standing as resources in future struggles within the labor movement. An example of the impact of these resources was the AFL-CIO executive council's speed in deciding to support the Carter-Mondale ticket, which some observers saw as a response to the possibility that the coalition might shut them out of access to the campaign (New York Times, 1976d).

STATE DELEGATIONS

As they had in 1972, state delegations drew delegates' time and attention because they were the sites of a number of crucial housekeeping functions such as credentialing delegates and passing out gallery passes. But state delegations served other functions as well. For example, the Virginia and Maryland delegations were forums for considerable debate and lobbying in behalf of rival gubernatorial candidates (Washington Post, 1976b, 1976c). The Idaho, Maine, and Minnesota delegations were the locus of campaigns to gain support for favorite sons (Frank Church, Edmund Muskie, Walter Mondale) for Vice President (New York Post, 1976c). And, as in 1972, state delegations were convenient places for candidates to communicate with delegates. Thus, Jimmy Carter made special trips to the New Jersey and California delegations to address delegates who had opposed him in the primaries and to ask for their support.

IMPLICATIONS FOR PARTIES AND THE POLITICAL SYSTEM

The transformation of the Black and Women's Caucuses from formless debating societies in 1972 to well-bounded and well-organized units in 1976 has implications that go beyond the health and stability of these groups themselves. While in 1972 presidential candidates gave brief speeches to these caucuses, in 1976 Jimmy Carter sought—and was able—to enter into concrete and focused bargaining with them. Because they had defined their membership, established leadership structures, and demonstrated organizational capacity, they were taken seriously as bargainers and as representatives of larger groups. Like state and local public and party officials, the Black and Women's Caucuses had become relevant party actors with whom a nominee would have to deal. Because they are based in demographic groups rather than geographic areas, they constitute a new mode of representation within the party.

Having established bases within the party, these caucuses can also be expected to serve as institutional constituencies for future Democratic Presidents. When they consider relevant policy issues and when they fill government positions, Democratic Presidents will have an incentive to work with strong caucus groups through their leaders. Thus, the caucuses' institutional development from 1972 to 1976 may well have implications for presidential bargaining patterns and public policy choices.

IV. MANAGING THE CONVENTION: THE CARTER ORGANIZATION AND THE DEMOCRATIC NATIONAL COMMITTEE

In discussing both the platform and group caucuses, we have seen numerous examples of delegates' desire to build party unity and avoid conflict. This orientation toward unity was so pervasive that it began to seem boring to some people; a number of media accounts described the convention as dull and uneventful.

There is no question that convention sessions lacked the drama of other years. But all this did not mean that the convention simply ran itself, that all convention events had been predetermined. There were possibilities of floor fights over various rules proposals, and hard bargaining was done outside the formal convention sessions. Even in the absence of conflict, the complexity of a convention environment poses problems for those who would manage that environment.

In 1976, two organizations—the Carter campaign and the Democratic National Committee (DNC) staff—sought to undertake this management task. The leaders of both organizations recognized the importance of conducting convention business in an orderly fashion and satisfying the convention participants. In the language of our earlier work (Sullivan et al., 1976, chap. 5), decision makers in the Carter organization and the national party apparatus were concerned with working for a "legitimating" convention.

THE DNC STAFF

The national party staff served as convention host. This involved arranging accommodations, transportation, and delegate credentials. DNC Chairman Robert Strauss or his designees chaired the actual convention sessions and directed the public communication systems in the convention hall. We can see, however, that the role played by the party structure was greatly reduced because the nomination had been resolved prior to the convention. For example, Carter aides became involved in such matters as determining the color scheme used on the podium, producing films to be shown to delegates and the television audience, arranging of convention speakers, and timing convention events. In years like 1972, when the presidential nomination is not resolved before the convention, handling these kinds of details is the job of the DNC staff. In these situations, the influence and power which comes from being in a position to negotiate among candidate organizations over even the most trivial details may be considerable. But in 1976, few real or symbolic battles were fought out in this forum, and the responsibility for making even the most mundane decisions was shared by the DNC and the Carter organization.

The role of the DNC staff in organizing the detailed logistics diminished in the month before the convention. But the DNC still remained a potent force on certain substantive matters. For example, in the middle of June, the Women's Caucus began developing support in the rules committee for equal sex division among delegates at the 1980 convention. Mark Siegel, Executive Director of the DNC, became alarmed and asked Strauss to call Carter personally in order to enlist the help of the Carter organization in combating the women's plank. At the rules committee meeting, the combined effort of the DNC and the Carter whips was instrumental in producing a majority report that did not mention the so-called "50-50" requirement.

Since 1972, Robert Strauss had defined his primary job as promoter of party unity. Many of the factors explaining the growth in party cohesiveness from 1972 to 1976 lay beyond the control of Strauss. But DNC staff members were conscious of the need for unity and handled the tasks that fell to them with this in mind. For example, many of the troublesome issues before the rules committee were deferred until after the election by assigning them to a study commission headed by Morley Winograd, Chairman of the Michigan party. The commission was carefully balanced to insure its acceptance by the party's liberal and labor wings, both of which had been heavily involved in recent party rules issues (Sullivan et al., 1976:34-42). (Mark Siegel had been instrumental in selecting commission members.)

Analysis of delegate perceptions of convention management reinforces our sense that both the Carter campaign and the DNC were important. We asked delegates who they thought was actually running the convention. In many cases, there were parallels between delegates' perceptions and their own candidate commitments. Carter delegates tended to respond that Carter was in control; non-Carter delegates gave a heavier weight to the DNC. A considerable number of delegates saw the complexity of the political relationship between the two organizations. Their comments are quite illustrative:

> "Strauss is running this convention, but he keeps looking over his shoulder because he knows that Carter has all the delegates."

> "The DNC is running it. Yet the DNC is like a little boy taking a big dog for a walk; he asks the dog where he wants to go."

> "Strauss and Carter are in bed with each other, but it's hard to know who's on top."

THE CARTER CAMPAIGN

In the month of June, the Carter organization assumed responsibility both for resolving political disputes that involved convention business and for staging the convention sessions themselves. This shift could be illustrated on many levels, and it was marked even by subtle shifts in nomenclature. For example, Rick Hutcheson, whose formal title is Deputy Campaign Manager, was referred to during the primaries as Carter's "delegate hunter" and "liaison to the DNC." Immediately before the convention he began to be identified as Carter's "convention manager." Also in this period the primary responsibility of Carter strategists such as Hutcheson or Campaign Manager Hamilton Jordan changed from winning the nomination to making that nomination acceptable and legitimate to all parts of the party. Accordingly, they took the lead in persuading such representatives of various wings of the party as Humphrey, Wallace, McGovern, and Church to address the convention.

In addition, members of Carter's staff began to enter into disputes over rules, which had been the cause of severe splits in the party since 1968. In our earlier work on cleavages within the Democratic Party, we found that this conflict came from two distinct problems: a fundamental disagreement over reform of party structure and organization, and polarization on a proparty/antiparty continuum (Sullivan et al., 1976:42-64). There were issues on the agenda of the 1976 convention which could have intensified either of these,[4] but the Carter organization invested its own influence in resolving or at least minimizing these disputes. Carter staff members prevented the combatants from engaging each other in direct conflict. Instead, Carter campaign representatives led the discussion of these potentially divisive questions themselves, making negotiation possible where intragroup conflict might have arisen.

STRUCTURES FOR CONTROLLING THE CONVENTION FLOOR

The most crucial organizational test for the convention managers lay in retaining control of the actual convention sessions. Delegates can be contacted and organized more easily when gathered together in a single hall than when spread out in different hotels across the city. The potential for an unexpected parliamentary maneuver or an inflammatory speech from the podium is always present. Furthermore, these events are likely to occur while gavel-to-gavel coverage conveys the conflict to a national television audience. Accordingly, those who would manage the convention must direct considerable attention to influencing delegate behavior during the convention sessions.

While the staffs of both the Carter campaign and the DNC developed communications networks to coordinate floor action, the system of the Carter organization was much more extensive. It included approximately 400 "whips," each of whom "communicated" with about eight delegates. Whips were organized by delegation and were directed in each delegation by the chairperson of the Carter caucus. The chairpersons reported to fourteen "staff floor leaders." These floor leaders were connected through a special telephone system to high-level Carter strategists in a "boiler room" operation located in trailers off the convention floor. The Carter organization also assigned eight of its top campaign officials[5] to roam the floor at large to resolve any political problems that might arise. Finally, believing in overkill, or at least overlap, the campaign managers designated 14 people—most of whom were delegates—as "public floor leaders," whose job it was to coordinate with the 14 staff leaders, to handle difficulties with troubled delegates, and to relate to the media on the floor.

There are several plausible answers to the question of why the development of such an elaborate structure seemed necessary at a convention in which the major issue, selection of a nominee, had already been resolved. First of all, the Carter organization understood that although Carter had effectively won the nomination a month prior to the convention, large segments of the party were still lukewarm to his candidacy and might demonstrate their disaffection at the convention. The very existence of a strong floor structure could discourage potential challenges. Second, the floor structure could serve as an intelligence operation, giving an early indication of trouble before it arose. Before each vote went to a roll call, the Carter organization had polled the floor so that it knew approximately how the vote would come out.

A third reason for the elaborate organization was that, on most of the issues of party rules to be decided at the convention, the Carter campaign did hold definite preferences and wanted to have those preferences honored.[6] Finally, the Carter campaign staff had to confront the problem of assigning satisfying convention roles to those campaign personnel who had worked hard at running campaigns in many states. The Carter organization solved this problem by giving these people jobs to do, even though this involved overlapping functions and responsibilities. As one Carter aide put it: "I was one of the lucky ones. I had something to do."

The DNC floor structure, on the other hand, extended down only to the level of staff floor leaders, who communicated to the delegation chairpersons or to other specific individuals as the need arose. For the conduct of normal convention business, the delegation chairpersons all had telephones which connected them to the podium. The DNC was able to exercise a large measure of direction over convention business simply by controlling the public address system. The microphones located on the floor beside each delegation's chairperson were turned on only when business on the agenda had to be accomplished.

STRATEGIC BARGAINING

While the Carter campaign organization used its floor operation for the precautionary functions of discouraging challenges and gaining information, the candidate and his aides also engaged themselves in a series of negotiations which were designed to broaden their organization's support. As we have seen, both before and during the convention Carter and his staff met with a range of group caucus leaders—blacks, women, Latinos—and visited certain important state delegations.

In carrying out negotiation and bargaining at the convention, the Carter campaign was advantaged by its ability to bargain with each group separately and sequentially. Representatives from each of the groups came to the Carter suite at the Americana Hotel. The demands of the separate groups were not linked to each other, and separate responses could be made to each. Although the Black and Women's Caucuses cooperated in a number of ways during the convention, the fact remained that Carter had already met the black leaders' rules requests—but not those of the women—before the convention. Thus, unlike the case at the 1974 midterm conference, the blacks and women were not fighting intensely for the same goals. Rather, leaders of each caucus met with Carter separately and discussed separate issues. Each group did win some important concessions from the candidate, but the Carter staff's ability to separate issues in negotiations was an additional resource for its management of the convention.

V. THE PRESENTATION OF CARTER

In our earlier works we have argued that the post-1968 Democratic convention system is a candidate-centered one. Candidate organizations are the central actors within the convention while group caucuses and state delegations play important peripheral roles. The Carter organization, which dominated this convention in the eyes of the delegates, performed all the functions traditionally associated with the party apparatus. Carter aides integrated delegates across state units; they reconciled demands among their followers;

they bargained with outsiders for additional support; and they mobilized a convention majority when needed. (For more on the functions of parties, see Burnham, 1975:277ff.)

In performing these and other functions, the most important resource that a candidate organization has is the candidate himself. Unlike the party apparatus, which it replaces, a candidate organization cannot depend upon the habitual loyalties of followers or a permanent machinery of people with party and official jobs. Instead, a candidate organization is created for the duration of a campaign and held together by individual commitments to a single person. So the way in which a candidate is presented to a convention and the ways he is perceived by the delegates form the most important product of his organization. It is that product which we will now examine in some detail.

This section is divided into three parts. First, we will discuss the delgates' impressions of Carter in the context of his organization's need to maintain its convention majority. Then we will focus on the ways in which Carter presented himself at the convention, using his multifaceted character as a resource. Finally, we will examine some of the discrepancies between what delegates believed about Carter and what the organization would have had them believe.

MAINTAINING THE MAJORITY

Carter delegates were a varied group: early supporters drawn to him as a person, practical politicians who came to him as a front-runner, and finally the supporters of collapsed candidates who wanted both a place on the bandwagon and party unity. Thus, different people had to remain convinced of different things: that Carter was the same person to whom they had originally pledged loyalty, that he was an effective and efficient leader who could win, and that he would be open and responsive to the needs of late supporters.

Much of this analysis is based on the answers to a question in our oral interview schedule. Delegates were given a series of words used by the press to describe Carter and were asked to rate them from +3 for very accurate to −3 for very inaccurate. Interviewers probed for comments, and these were noted on each interview. The words used in the questionnaire were efficient, committed, spiritual, cool, calculating, open, honest, responsive.

Many early Carter supporters apparently felt little need to

reexamine their impressions of Carter. After all, they and their candidate had accomplished what they had set out to do in spite of difficulties. Several delegates whom we interviewed commented on this:

> "He's hung in there in all those primaries against all odds." (a Texan for Carter)

> "Plus 3 on cool. He has weathered the campaign well; remember ethnic purity?" (an Illinois man for Carter)

They attributed his campaign success to Carter's personal abilities:

> "Calculating? Oh yes, he's a calculating man as anybody who gets there is. You've got to be." (a Georgia woman for Carter)

> "He set out four years ago to win the nomination. That's calculating." (a Carter supporter from Michigan)

There were, however, only a few mentions of shared issue commitments between Carter and his supporters. The Carter enthusiasts were more committed to their candidate as a person than as a vehicle for their preferred issues positions.

Many Carter delegates were aware of things about the Carter campaign that they did not like. But often they explained these supposed shortcomings away as campaign necessities rather than as true measures of Carter himself. When they were asked to rank Carter from +3 for very open to −3 for not very open, many of the delegates felt that they should comment on the reasons for their rankings:

> "Plus 1 on open. He had to get elected first of all; he could not articulate all positions in total candidness. I expect that to change now, but he is not an open person by nature."

> "Plus 2 on open. He knows who his enemies are, so he can't be as open as he could be."

> "Plus 1—who's Jimmy Carter [laughs]? But in fairness he's as open as, say, Mo Udall."

Other attributed things they did not like to the campaign organization, distinguishing between the candidate and his advisors:

> "The campaign is a minus 2 [on efficient], but he himself is plus 2."

"Minus 2 on calculating. His organization is calculating, but he is too honest personally."

These are, of course, classic techniques for adjusting to cognitive dissonance. So the impression of Carter, held by many of his supporters, was one of a competent, efficient leader who had—by his exertions and their help—achieved a political miracle. They wanted to be able to minimize the criticism of their candidate, for their own benefit as well as for the benefit of outsiders. By displacing this criticism from Carter to other parts of the process they were able to do this.

Now we will turn to the second element of the Carter majority, the practical politicians who came to him as he achieved front-runner status and those others who came to him at the convention. This group, which includes many party regulars, might be expected to be most concerned with Carter's capacity to win the election. Many of these people expressed admiration for Carter, one politician to another:

"Calculating? Anybody who came from where he was to where he is had to be." (a former Humphrey supporter)

"Efficient? Look at the delegate count." (a former uncommitted from Missouri)

While many were impressed by Carter as a politician, by far the most frequent cynical and joking comments made by these people centered on Carter's commitment:

"Committed? Plus 3 to being President."

"He's committed to himself, plus 3, but not to anything else."

Nearly all of these people, despite their misgivings, were willing to support Carter as the nominee. In fact, one could speculate that a candidate with firm commitments is not attractive to many professional politicians (see Wilson, 1966; Wildavsky, 1971, chaps. 12-14). After all, many of these people came to Carter late in the campaign, so they wanted a flexible candidate who would accommodate them.

While the impression of Carter as an effective professional politician, ready to bring new supporters into the fold, was sufficient for some party regulars, additional enticements were needed for issue activists. A few were simply unwilling to modify their impressions of Carter. Some Wallace supporters were particularly pointed in their criticism of Carter, whom they saw as the antithesis of their candidate:

> "Minus 2 on open. He speaks to one group and they think he is with them and another opposite one and they think he is with them."
>
> "Plus 3 efficient at getting votes *only*!"

Some Edmund G. Brown activists, on the other hand, started making adjustments for Carter as the week progressed. For example, one told us that he thought Carter's Southern background would be a great asset for leadership in civil rights. Another, after hearing Carter address Jerry Brown's California delegation, said she detected "Jerry-like" elements in Carter's speech, particularly in reference to our finite environment.

So far, we have been dealing with the impressions delegates formed of Carter. Impressions about Carter, as a person, were fused with impressions about his convention organization and campaign. This is not surprising; Carter is a newcomer in national politics and as such does not stand apart from the campaign which brought him to the nomination. Most delegates' contacts with presidential candidates tend to be fleeting—a quick visit, a speech, a handshake—while their dealings with the candidate organization is more constant. Furthermore, assessing a candidate by what his organization does seems—to many—more revealing than relying on what he says. Nevertheless, the ways in which a candidate presents himself do have great effect.

CARTER'S OWN PRESENTATION

Carter skillfully used his presentation of himself and his personal attributes to convince others that they ought to support him.[7] He is a complex individual, capable of showing different facets of himself to different groups, leaving each with the impression that he shares at least some of their concerns.[8] At the convention Carter revealed only the appropriate portion of himself in each interaction. It was his capacity to keep these interactions separated from one another, as well as his ability to limit the agenda of discussions to agreeable items, which made his presentation of himself so formidable.

We have already discussed Carter's separate dealings with the group caucuses over issues like future appointments. These negotiations show that Carter had a marked preference for the kinds of concessions which Theodore Lowi (1970) has termed distributive. Distributive goods are those which can be easily disaggregated and given to some individuals without appearing to deprive others. In both cases he stayed away from vast programs, which take things from one group and give them to another (redistributive programs like guaranteed annual income), and from quotas, which also redistribute benefits. Carter's capacity to keep questions of redistribution from arising contributed to the success of his presentation. As the apparent nominee, Carter could set the general agenda for these discussions. After all, his time was extremely valuable, and he was responding to many demands. He could pick and choose among the concerns of groups, selecting those to which he could respond positively.

Carter's capacity to particularize, to show only a glimpse of himself to those with whom he dealt, can be seen in other instances. For example, he was the first presidential nominee to address the Latino Caucus, and he addressed them in Spanish. Several things must have impressed his listeners. First, he knew the language, the common bond of that caucus. Second, he thought them important enough to address, although the caucus had been plagued by poor attendance on the part of its own membership. Third, Democratic party members would see that the party's most important person believed that the Latino Caucus should be taken seriously. In this instance, Carter's concern was conveyed by how and where he spoke. By taking valuable time to attend the caucus, he implied to his listeners that he was willing to spend this scarce resource—and perhaps others—in their behalf. Yet while Carter's time was scarce, no other delegates would deduce that they were deprived because Carter's time was devoted to Latinos rather than themselves. It was a move, then, which would neither deprive nor anger anyone, but would nevertheless yield dividends in support.

Carter's calculated complex appeal extends beyond the organized arenas traditionally associated with Democratic politics. For example, to those who have deep religious convictions, Carter is the first candidate in many years to express similar religious sentiments in public. White and black Southerners, who in so many other ways are at odds, do agree on the importance of their religion. So it is not surprising that they have attached themselves to this facet of Carter and consider him one of their own. Some delegates in our sample were even recruited directly out of their churches to work for Carter.

The candidate's presentation of his own life outside politics also had its attractions for specific delegates. At least two delegates who attended the U.S. Naval Academy said that Carter appealed to them because of that common bond. In addition, several non-Academy delegates cited Carter's career as a naval officer as a sign of his efficiency. Similarly, his background as a farmer, businessman, and nuclear scientist contributed for many to the general image of competence, hard work, and efficiency. One delegate told us that Carter's background as a farmer showed he was honest and a hard worker because "a farmer works for what he gets." Another became a Carter supporter after a long conversation in which Carter demonstrated that the two were distantly related. To each of these people, Carter had shown an aspect that they recognized in themselves.

Thus, each of the groups and individuals with whom Carter dealt came to see him in a slightly different way. Each group felt, with some justification, that it had a special empathy with Carter, that it understood a facet of the nominee in a way that no others in the convention could. Each was, to a certain degree, correct. Where they erred was in believing that the facet of Carter that they understood revealed the structure of the remainder.

EXPRESSIONS AND IMPRESSIONS

Our examination of delegates' impressions of Carter, and the ways in which Carter expressed himself, reveals a number of gaps between campaign presentations and delegate perceptions. The Carter campaign sought to portray its candidate as efficient, committed, honest, and open. Delegates did believe Carter was efficient, but most did not cite his qualities as a governor and businessman, which his organization had stressed. Instead, these delegates referred to his successful campaign organization. While the Carter campaign presented him as an individual with firm and specific commitments—for example, they made available over 90 different position papers through their hospitality suites—delegates again interpreted him differently.[9] Most felt that, if he was committed, it was to himself or to his ambitions rather than to specific causes. While most conceded that he was honest, many felt that he was not particularly open or responsive. Though Carter's appeal was widespread, there were divergences between campaign expressions and delegate impressions.

VI. THE PROBLEM OF LEGITIMATION

One of the more celebrated functions of party nominating conventions is their legitimation of the presidential nominee as a candidate whom all segments of the party can support. Legitimation may be said to occur if the various components of the party believe that the procedures and decisions of the convention were fair and proper and that, as a consequence, the final result should be supported. Political scientists have often commented on the unifying and legitimating functions of conventions. For example, V.O. Key (1964:431) wrote some years ago:

> The convention provides a means for the contending candidates, factions, and interests within a party to consult and agree upon the terms on which they will work together in the presidential campaign. The resulting concert of interests exerts a formidable power throughout the nation.

In our earlier work on the 1972 and 1974 party conventions we identified seven factors which, if present, would produce a legitimating convention. In this section we shall assess, in turn, each of the seven factors for its contribution to our understanding of the willingness of losing factions to come to terms with and accept Carter as the party's presidential nominee. The factors are: (1) the revocability of candidate commitments, (2) the divisibility of prizes at the convention, (3) a professional political style, (4) the expectation of victory in the general election, (5) a low level of issue polarization, (6) multiple group identifications, and (7) a moderately high level of party loyalty.

(1) THE REVOCABILITY OF CANDIDATE COMMITMENTS

In our earlier theoretical work we argued that the growth of national candidate organizations competing for delegate support early in the preconvention period produces intensely committed delegates. The resulting psychological investment, we argued, would make it difficult for supporters of losing candidates to accept the convention outcome.

What we described in our earlier research did not come to pass because the assumption on which it was predicated was not fulfilled. That is, we had assumed a situation in which no one candidate would emerge a clear front-runner. The success of Carter falsified the assumption but did not obviate the need for adjustment on the part of the losers. We still must account for the behavior of the intense Morris Udall supporters (the advocates of liberal activism), the diehard George Wallace delegates, and perennial supporters of Hubert Humphrey and Henry Jackson.

A number of factors combined in 1976 to reduce the intensity of commitment to losing candidates before the convention began. First, there was the early collapse of some candidate organizations and the subsequent withdrawal of their leaders—Lloyd Bentsen, Milton Shapp, Birch Bayh, Sargent Shriver, Fred Harris, Jackson, and Wallace. Second, there was the unexpectedly clear minority status of the remaining candidates—Udall, Brown, and Frank Church. The strong majority enjoyed by Carter prior to the convention put into disarray any plans that the liberal candidates had for profiting from a brokered convention.

The speed with which the tactical situation changed for each of the losing candidate organizations seemed to have had a profound effect on their delegate supporters. In our conversations with delegates we asked about their expectations when they first became delegates concerning a brokered convention and their role in it. Most liberal activist delegates realized early that their candidates could not win a majority in the preconvention period. But they also believed that no other candidate would have a preconvention majority and that they would be soldiers in the service of their candidate at a brokered convention. For example, many Udall delegates originally saw (1) a chance for their man to be the party's presidential nominee, or (2) failing that, a place on the ticket for him as the vice-presidential nominee, or (3) failing that, a role for themselves at the convention supporting Udall in his effort to force Carter into a more liberal issue stance.

For many liberal delegates, the three goals were the substance of a scenario in which they had identifiable roles. As long as the scenario was valid, they were willing to maintain reasonably strong candidate commitments. But as each element of the scenario was disconfirmed and Carter continued to accumulate delegates, the rational incentive for a strong candidate commitment disappeared even before the convention began. The rapid dissolution of their scenarios left many delegates confused and disoriented at the convention.

There were no suitable replacements for the carefully constructed scenarios which had been disconfirmed. Some delegates turned halfheartedly to the platform but discovered either a platform already to their liking or institutional factors preventing a consideration of their "issues" on the floor. Many liberal delegates concentrated on the selection of the Vice President while others attempted to achieve whatever goals they could through the group caucuses. All of these activities did contribute, in the end, to their willingness to accept the outcome. The prizes for which they worked were not major, but they were prizes nonetheless.

(2) THE DIVISIBILITY OF PRIZES AT THE CONVENTION

Unlike the 1974 Charter convention, it is hard to think of a presidential nominating convention as having many prizes or much time in which to work for them. The Presidency is the big prize, and it is easy to upset those denied a chance to obtain it. In a nominating convention, winners and losers are clearly identified, making it difficult for the losers to imagine themselves winners. Yet the platform and Vice Presidency are prizes of sorts. Because we shall deal with the reactions of the delegates to the platform in later sections, we shall restrict our attention here to the vice-presidential nomination.

For a good part of the convention, Carter kept seven names —Walter Mondale, John Glenn, Edmund Muskie, Adlai E. Stevenson III, Peter Rodino, Church, and Jackson—in the air. It was not until 10:00 in the morning of the final day that he announced the selection of Mondale. From the first day of the convention Carter let it be known that *he* would do the selecting and the convention would do the ratifying.

But Carter surely was aware that the vice-presidential nomination is one of the few prizes that the nominee can use to promote party unity. The selection of Mondale did not lessen the intensity of Carter support, and liberals responded favorably to the choice. We were able to assess this effect in a number of ways, but the simplest and most powerful was to examine the changes in attitude toward Carter as the nominee of the party as the convention progressed. We asked delegates to rate Carter (+3 = favorable to −3 = unfavorable) as the party's nominee. Figure 1 shows the changes in attitude toward Carter before and after the selection of Mondale, among Carter and supporters of liberal candidates (Udall, Brown, Church, Harris). Whereas Carter delegates are almost as supportive as the scale allows from the first day to the last day, support for Carter rises sharply among liberal delegates as a consequence of the nomination of Mondale.

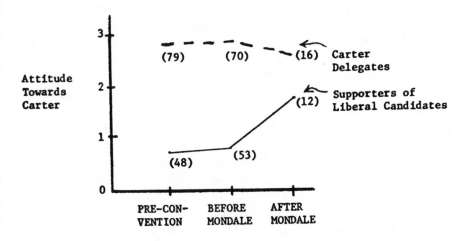

*Attitude toward Carter measured on a +3 to −3 scale with +3 = favorable and −3 = unfavorable. Supporters of liberal candidates are those who preferred Udall, Harris, Brown, Church. (Numbers in parentheses are the numbers of delegates in the sample.)

Figure 1: ATTITUDE TOWARD CARTER AS THE PRESIDENTIAL NOMINEE BEFORE AND AFTER HIS SELECTION OF MONDALE, AMONG CARTER DELEGATES AND SUPPORTERS OF LIBERAL CANDIDATES*

In some ways, then, Carter's selection of Mondale may have allowed liberals to feel powerful. It would be hard to argue, though, that liberals had organized themselves at the convention or had participated in any real way to influence Carter's choice of Mondale. In our recent work in *Explorations in Convention Decision Making* we described the role attributions of power played in the legitimation process. No such mechanism could be observed. Carter acknowledged no power greater than his good judgment. But our data do show that the vice-presidential nomination is a prize capable of contributing to party unity.

(3) A PROFESSIONAL POLITICAL STYLE

In both our 1972 and 1974 studies, we examined the effects of political style on acceptance of the convention outcome. The emergence of the conflict between issue-oriented (ideologically pure) and party-oriented activists had been noted by a number of scholars on political parties (Wildavsky, 1965:386-413; Wilson, 1966, chap. 12). Purists, by definition, pledge themselves to a candidate on the basis of his stand on the issues; professionals justify their commitment in terms of the candidate's capacity to unify the party and win elections. In determining his view of the writing of a platform—the second major function of nominating conventions—the purist arrives at a platform that is correct according to some conception of the public interest or good; for the professional a platform is correct if it placates the losers without alienating the winners and, at the same time, increases the chance of winning the general election.

Our research on the 1972 convention showed that the simple conception of purism-professionalism needs refining. First, purists in one arena are not necessarily purists in another. When members of the McGovern coalition dealt with one another, accommodation and compromise were the order of the day. When the arena shifted from the nomination of McGovern to the issue of party unity, many McGovernites became purists. That is, they saw little need to promote party unity. Second, the regulars were far more supportive of party unity and accommodation as long as the nominee was one of theirs. As soon as it became apparent that McGovern was going to win in 1972, many regulars shed their professional attitudes and donned purist ones (Sullivan et al., 1974, chap. 5).

We continued our investigations of purism-professionalism in our study of the 1974 Democratic midterm convention. The compromise worked out at the Charter convention allowed both purists and professionals to fashion an interpretation of the outcome in which they were victors. The data we gathered at the convention allowed us to refine further the relationship between purism-professionalism and the disposition to support the convention outcome. From our current theoretical perspective, the professional's high concern for party unity is an incentive leading him to search for ways of interpreting political outcomes as advantageous to groups with which he is identified.

Both our 1976 and 1974 measures of purism-professionalism forced the delegate to choose between two values—party unity and issue articulation. The 1974 issues involved Charter issues, while the 1976 convention choice dealt with platform issues. The delegate was asked, "If you *had* to choose, which would be more important? Platform (Charter) issues? Party unity?" Delegates willing to subordinate a correct and forthright platform (the choice in 1976) to party unity were called professionals and those who did the reverse were called purists. Table 1 shows the growth in professionalism from 1972 to 1974 and its stabilization in 1976. And when we

Table 1. GROWTH IN PROFESSIONALISM AMONG DELEGATES TO THE 1972
PRESIDENTIAL, 1974 CHARTER, AND 1976 PRESIDENTIAL
CONVENTIONS OF THE DEMOCRATIC PARTY*

	1972	1974	1976
Professionalism	36%	51%	49%
	(234)	(251)	(249)

*The 1972 measure was different. Delegates were classified as purists or professionals on the basis of their response to an open-ended question. For details see D.G. Sullivan, et al., *The Politics of Representation,* Chapter 5.

examine the distribution of political style by candidate preference in 1976, the results show a striking similarity to 1972 (Table 2).

In 1972 the liberal coalition under George McGovern dominated the convention, and the question of accommodation was faced by the regulars supporting Humphrey-Jackson-Muskie. As we showed in *The Politics of Representation,* neither the regulars nor the McGovernites did much in the way of accommodation and the convention failed to legitimate the outcome. In 1976 the liberal supporters of Udall-Harris-Brown-Church were predominantly purists and, as a consequence, might not have been expected to adjust to the prospect of Carter as the party's nominee.

Our theory predicts that those with the highest level of professionalism (the 1976 supporters of Humphrey and Jackson) should be far more willing to shift to supporting Carter than the more purist liberal delegates. We asked the delegates two questions, one of which measures an intention and the other of which measures an attitude. The first concerns the willingness of the delegate to support a motion ot make Carter's nomination unanimous, while the second measures the delegate's pleasure at the prospect of a Carter first-ballot victory. Figures 2-A and 2-B show changes over the course of the convention in both measures.

Table 2. DISTRIBUTION OF PROFESSIONAL POLITICAL STYLE BY
CANDIDATE PREFERENCE, 1972 AND 1976*

	Wallace	Liberals	Carter	Humphrey, Jackson	Total
1972	35% (17)	11% (109)		45% (109)	175
1976	13% (7)	22% (69)	58% (109)	62% (38)	244

*1972 candidate preference is preference at time of interview; 1976 candidate preference is among candidates perceived to be available at time delegate filled out mail questionnaire. Liberal supporters are delegates preferring Udall, Brown, Church, Harris, or Kennedy in 1976. In 1972 Muskie delegates are added to the total for Humphrey and Jackson.

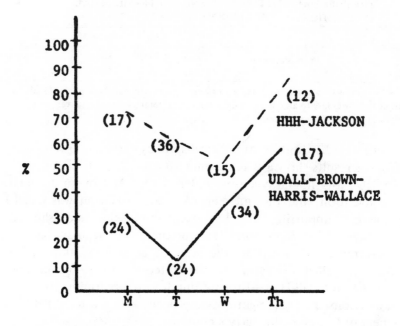

*Candidate preference is candidate most preferred at time delegate was elected or appointed. Delegates were asked, "Are you now pleased that Carter will (has) win (won) on the first ballot?" (Numbers in parentheses are the number of delegates in the sample.)

Figure 2-A: PLEASURE AT PROSPECT OF A CARTER FIRST BALLOT VICTORY AMONG SUPPORTERS OF UDALL-BROWN-HARRIS-WALLACE AND SUPPORTERS OF HUMPHREY-JACKSON*

Both figures show the more professional supporters of Humphrey-Jackson as initially more supportive of Carter than the more purist supporters of Udall-Brown-Church-Harris. The differences are most pronounced on Monday and Tuesday and narrow slightly as the convention draws to a close and delegates begin to report what they did and felt rather than what they intended to do or feel. The increase in expressed pleasure in Figure 2-A among liberal supporters from Tuesday to Thursday (almost 50%) is a most remarkable sign of the convention's ability to contribute to party unity. The convention clearly performed a function for liberals that it did not need to do for the more moderate supporters of Humphrey-Jackson. Members of the latter group came to the convention with a powerful disposition to support the party's nominee (70% expressed pleasure on Monday, and nearly 80% intended to support a motion to make

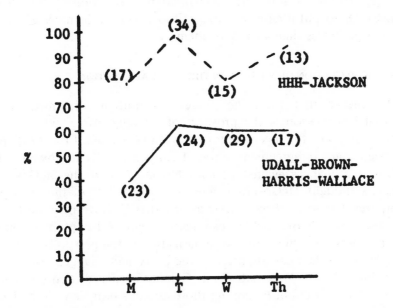

*Candidate preference is measured in same way as described in Table 2-A. Question, "Will (did) you vote to make Carter's nomination unanimous?" (Numbers in parentheses are the number of delegates in the sample.)

Figure 2-B: WILLINGNESS TO SUPPORT A MOTION TO MAKE NOMINATION OF CARTER UNANIMOUS*

Carter's nomination unanimous). The results support both the notion that differences in political style are related to legitimation and the notion that a four-day convention can contribute to legitimation.

Although changes in both our measures support our basic propositions on political style, they also show some interesting differences. Note that, in Figure 2-A, expressed pleasure seems to fall initially for both Humphrey and Udall supporters and begins to rise on Tuesday and Wednesday. But willingness to support a motion making the nomination of Carter unanimous (Figure 2-B) behaves in an opposite manner. Its greatest rise, for both groups, occurs from Monday to Tuesday and seems to stabilize after Tuesday at around 80% for Humphrey supporters and 60% for Udall-Church-Brown-Harris delegates. The cognitive adjustment to the power of Carter (the belief that there is no reason to show behavioral opposition) occurs on Monday, whereas the psychological adjustment (change in attitude toward Carter) occurs later (on Wednesday and Thursday).

Again, as we observed in *Explorations in Convention Decision Making*, attitudinal adjustments seem to be a function of cognitive changes. Or to put it another way, attitudes seem to be more a result of other processes than a cause of them.

(4) THE EXPECTATION OF VICTORY IN THE GENERAL ELECTION

The energy that fuels the process of mutual adjustment and eventual legitimation is the prospect of winning office. When that prospect is poor, the incentive for party unity is weak. In 1972 there had been sharp disagreement among Democratic activists concerning McGovern's chances against Richard Nixon; 72% of the McGovern delegates thought McGovern would win, while 72% of the Muskie-Humphrey-Jackson delegates were as sure that McGovern would lose. The disagreement over which candidate might best exploit Nixon's weakness was a further source of polarization in the party.

In 1976 the tactical situation of the party had changed considerably since 1972; Watergate and Gerald Ford's difficulties had produced a mild euphoria among those assembled in New York. The expectation that the party might reoccupy the White House, coupled with the tactical success of Carter, acted to heighten the value of party unity.

At the New York convention in 1976, unlike the situation at Miami in 1972, supporters of Carter and supporters of Udall-Church-Brown-Harris agreed that Carter could defeat either Ronald Reagan or Ford in November. Of course, supporters of the losing candidates also told us in interviews that "their man" could win too. But for most delegates the central issue—whether the likely nominee of the party could win the general election—had been resolved even before the delegates had gathered in New York.

(5) A LOW LEVEL OF ISSUE POLARIZATION

Supporters of some of the losing candidates—Wallace, Udall, Harris, Church, and Brown—claimed that profound differences existed between their candidates and Carter. During the latter stages of the primaries, Udall spoke of the necessity to represent the "liberal" position at the convention. But in 1976 the "liberal" position was a bit more complicated than it was in 1968 and 1972, when Vietnam was a dominant issue. As we have described in an earlier section, the platform was constructed to represent the

Democratic party's centrist tendencies in which extreme positions on busing, amnesty, and so forth did not appear. One might expect, then, that delegates representing Wallace or the liberal candidates would push at the convention for the incorporation of their own issue positions into the platform. We have earlier explained some of the institutional factors responsible for the absence of such actions. Still, the delegates might have been expected to have talked to us about their deepest wishes for a "correct" platform. After all, a majority of Wallace and liberal candidate supporters had said that a correct and forthright platform was more important than party unity.

Our interviews offer some additional insights into the causes of the failure of liberals to be more vocal about issues at the convention. First, many of the purist supporters of liberal candidates liked the platform. A female Udall supporter from Kentucky said:

> Issues are important. I am issue oriented. . . . We should force the party to address itself to [the] needs of the people.

But when she was asked about the 1976 platform, she went on to say:

> I'm pleased with this one in general. . . . Many things fought for in McGovern [years] are partially in there. It's more liberal than I expected.

Also, some liberal delegates did not believe the platform to be of great importance. Another Udall delegate from Michigan told us:

> Pragmatically, it [the platform struggle] is to iron out differences between factions of the party. It is something we as a party must be able to live with internally. But externally, it means just about nothing—outside the party.

It should be pointed out, however, that only a minority of liberals (around 30%) felt that the platform was not important.

There was a small minority of liberal delegates who were disturbed because specific measures like gay rights were not included. But, overall, the level of satisfaction was strikingly high, given the expressed concerns of liberal delegates that their own issue positions were not being represented to the convention.

The Wallace supporters had a more precise idea of what ought to be in and out of the platform. Although their perceptions were not always accurate, they expressed their views with economy and precision. One Massachusetts Wallace supporter said:

> Take out busing, abortion, and the Panama Canal plans. I think they are wrong.

The delegate went on to express a desire for a comprehensive platform. When asked what should be excluded, he said:

> Only very minor things. It [the platform] should be a thick document.

More than other delegates, Wallacites were strongly issue-oriented and saw the platform as a device for expressing their issue concerns.

The solution to our puzzle concerning the failure of the liberal issue activists to pursue issues at the convention lies in a combination of factors: (1) the makers of the platform created a centrist document satisfying even to many of the liberal delegates; (2) some liberal delegates thought the platform of small importance and thus were not too upset that it failed to represent their issue positions precisely; (3) none of the losing candidates present at the convention chose to focus on any one issue in the platform, and thus delegates dissatisfied with the platform—like the Wallacites—had no spokesman; (4) the institutional rules made it difficult to bring a minority report to the floor where the issue might occupy center stage at the convention; and (5) there was no simple issue like the Vietnam War in 1968 and 1972 which could galvanize the delegates. Either the issues were unifying ones, like full employment and a national health-care system, or too complex, like the environment and energy policy. The potentially divisive issues—amnesty, abortion, busing—stayed in the background.

And underlying all the above were the pervasive memory of the divisive effect of the 1972 convention and the prospect of a unified party winning the White House. As one liberal delegate told us:

> People have burned themselves out ... sick of the GOP administration. They've been willing to curb their normal fractiousness. ... It's too self-destructive.

(6) MULTIPLE GROUP IDENTIFICATIONS

The legitimating role played by multiple group identifications is far more subtle and complex than any of the previous factors we have discussed. And to grasp the role of groups in the legtimation process, one has to understand first how delegates see themselves as politicians. It is valuable to remember that politicians seek power for themselves *and* for groups they represent (or identify with). Of course, they want other things, but, as they all learn, the acquisition of power is the key to getting the other things. If groups that a politician represents continually suffer losses, the politician's reputation for power—and thus his power itself—suffer as well. A politician must improve the power position of groups he represents if he is to maintain his own. Winning an election means little to the delegate-politician if the groups that he represents have little claim on the newly elected President. Therefore, he is driven to evaluate convention outcomes in terms of gains and losses for the groups he represents. To maintain their self-esteem as effective politicians, delegates must find groups that they represent (or identify with) who are advantaged by the outcome.

The larger the number of groups that the delegate represents, the more probable it is that he can discover a constituent group advantaged by a particular outcome. The drive for party unity acts as an incentive; the multiple groups of the delegate are alternative pathways toward an integrative solution, one consistent with the delegate's desire for party unity and the success of his constituent groups. The appearance, if not the reality, of power is necessary if the politician-delegate is to support the convention outcome.

The question posed in this section can be reduced, then, to the following: How did the group identifications of the supporters of the losing liberal candidates—Udall, Church, Brown, Harris—promote their acceptance of the outcome? In our 1972 and 1974 research we identified two basic kinds of groups—regular and reform. The delegate's configuration of group identifications tends to be either a reform or a regular one.

Thus in a legitimating convention both regular and reform groups would appear powerful to their followers. For example, in 1974 women identifying with the Women's Caucus supported the convention outcome because they thought that caucus efforts had produced it. Noncaucus women identified with groups on the regular dimensions—DNC, labor, etc. And they were able to attribute power, and thus success, to the efforts of the regular groups at the convention. As a consequence, both caucus and noncaucus women were equall satisfied with the outcome.

In 1976 liberal candidate supporters—unable to attribute power to their own candidate organizations—had to look elsewhere. As we have already discussed, the platform was one place they did look and found some satisfaction. They could not look to groups located on the regular dimension because most liberal candidate supporters did not strongly identify with any of the regular groups. But, as was the case in 1972, there were links between candidate supporters and the group caucuses—Women's, Black, Labor Coalition, and Latino. The group caucuses are located on the reform dimension and tend to attract those delegates least strongly identified with party and most issue conscious.

In our interviews with delegates we asked them to describe their activities (intended or past) at the convention in terms of working with the Carter organization for a unified convention, raising issues as caucus participants, or staying within their state delegations. Table 3 shows the distribution of activity by arena for supporters of losing candidates—Humphrey-Jackson, Wallace, Udall-Brown-Church-Harris.

The 1976 results parallel those for 1972 and 1974. Liberal candidate supporters tend to be more reform-caucus-oriented than the more professional supporters of Humphrey-Jackson. Without effective leadership from their candidate organizations in 1976, the liberal delegates focused their attention on the group caucuses (38%) or the Carter organization (27%). Humphrey-Jackson delegates, on the other hand, devoted little attention to the caucuses (7%) and divided their time between supporting Carter (46%) and working in state delegations (34%).

Table 3. PRINCIPAL ARENAS OF ACTIVITY BY SUPPORTERS OF
LOSING CANDIDATES*

	Liberal Candidate Supporters	Humphrey-Jackson	Wallace
Follow group caucus (Black, Women, Latino)	38% (21)	07% (02)	18% (02)
Follow Carter to promote party unity	27% (15)	46% (12)	08% (01)
Work in state delegation to promote unity	21% (12)	34% (09)	27% (03)
None of the above	14% (08)	12% (03)	45% (05)
	100% (56)	100% (26)	100% (11)

*Candidate preference was candidate preference when delegate elected or appointed. Arenas were: (1) follow Carter organization helping them insure a unified convention; (2) raise issues through group caucuses with which Carter must deal; (3) work through my state delegation to maintain local party unity.

Both caucus leaders and followers experienced some measure of success. And the followers were able to attribute power, and thus task achievement, to groups with which they were identified. Identification with the Black and Women's Caucuses was up slightly over 1974, from 33% to 44% for women and from 60% to 70% for blacks.

Both blacks and women came to the convention expecting their caucus groups to be powerful. The Carter organization reinforced their sense of power by scheduling appointments early in the week with Black and Women's Caucus leaders. And as the week progressed, there was a general perception of goal achievement. We were able to measure the attribution of power for women (there were not enough blacks in our sample for analysis) by asking delegates which groups they thought would generally be most powerful at the convention. Not surprisingly, 90% of all delegates chose the Carter organization as most powerful. But the delegates' choice of the second and third most powerful groups did reveal a secondary power structure organized around the caucus groups, party regulars, COPE, the Labor Coalition, and some state delegations. Table 4 shows how caucus and noncaucus women perceived their own and each other's power.

Table 4 shows that caucus women saw their own group as powerful and the party regulars only a little less so (52% to 48%). Noncaucus women, on the other hand, attributed little power to the Women's Caucus (21%) and a great deal to party regulars (79%). As in 1974, each faction saw its group as powerful and its opposite as less so.

Table 4. ATTRIBUTION OF POWER BY CAUCUS AND NONCAUCUS WOMEN TO REGULARS AND WOMEN'S CAUCUS*

Attribution of Power to:	Caucus Women	Noncaucus Women
Women's Caucus	52%	21%
	(13)	(10)
Party regulars	48%	79%
	(12)	(38)
	100%	100%
	(25)	(48)

*A caucus woman was defined as one who chose the Women's Caucus as one of the three most important groups with which she identified at the convention. Attribution of power was measured by presenting each delegate with a list of 14 groups expected to be powerful at the convention and asking each delegate to rank order the three most powerful. Where both party regulars and Women's Caucus were mentioned, the delegate was classified by the group with the highest rank.

The relative success of the caucus groups at the convention allowed the self-identified liberal supporters of Udall-Brown-Church-Harris to feel some measure of power and, in turn, contributed to their expressed satisfaction with the outcome. And again, as was the case in 1974, the nonzero sum nature of the conflict allowed those identified with party regulars to feel powerful and successful as well.

(7) A MODERATELY HIGH LEVEL OF PARTY LOYALTY

The final variable in our theory of legitimation deals with the effect of party loyalty or identification on the disposition to support the convention outcome. We have argued in prior sections of the paper that the delegate's desire for party unity is a function of both his expectation of victory in the general election and his party loyalty. We have kept track of fluctuations in party loyalty at each convention since 1972. Table 5 displays the changes.

As Table 5 shows, the level of party identification is far higher in 1976 than it was in 1972 (an increase of 14% in the percentage of strong identifiers). Party identification performs an especially important function for those who did not feel at home with the caucus efforts and who failed to align themselves with the eventual winner. Thus, the Humphrey-Jackson delegates valued party unity in 1976 because they were strong Democrats who saw a good chance for the party to occupy the White House for the first time in eight years.

Table 5. PERCENT EXPRESSING A STRONG IDENTIFICATION WITH THE DEMOCRATIC PARTY*

	1972	1974	1976
	63%	88%	82%
	(234)	(284)	(287)

*The measure is an adaptation of the standard University of Michigan question, "Generally speaking, do you think of yourself as a strong or not strong Democrat, Independent, or what?"

VII. CONCLUSIONS

SUMMARY

Although the Democratic party has been torn by deep cleavages in recent years, the party's 1976 convention exhibited impressive signs of unity, with no open conflicts over nominations, platform, or rules. This unity was facilitated by the dominance of the Carter candidacy, the bright prospects of victory in November, the bitter memory of past divisions, and the disappearance of the Vietnam War as a divisive issue. But party unity was also the result of a series of negotiations and accommodations involving a wide range of party actors.

In framing the platform, for example, party officials and platform committee staff worked together with leaders of diverse party groups to fashion a document which provided a measure of satisfaction to each of those groups. The ability to lodge favored positions in the platform enabled group leaders to claim organizational successes and increased their disposition to support the final document. At the convention itself, the Black and Women's Caucuses showed new sophistication in controlling the caucuses internally and in bargaining effectively with other groups. In 1972, those groups had existed as large debating societies; in 1976 group leaders were able to engage in concrete negotiations with the nominee.

The stress on unity and accommodation did not mean, however, that the convention merely ran itself. There were a number of threats of conflict, and there were also diverse logistical activities which had to be carried out. The Carter campaign organization worked with Democratic National Committee staff to avoid conflict and manage convention business. Carter's staff members recognized the advantage which negotiating separately with various groups gave them. The candidate's own ability to make a wide range of specific appeals to specific clusters of delegates made this strategy even more effective. Our interviews showed that delegates, viewing Carter in a variety of different ways, supported him for a variety of different reasons.

All of this resulted in a convention that, unlike the cases of 1968 and 1972, could be considered a legitimating convention. In 1976 a large number of delegates were already disposed to accept the outcome of the convention, but, for others, the convention experience itself increased their willingness to support the result. Consistent with the theoretical model developed in our previous work, we found that the following factors contributed to legitimation: (1) the willingness of delegates to detach themselves from commitment to candidates, (2) the existence of multiple prizes at the convention, (3) a professional political style, (4) the expectation of victory in the general election, (5) a low level of issue polarization, (6) multiple group identifications, and (7) a moderately high level of party loyalty.

IMPLICATIONS

At recent Democratic party conventions, candidate organizations have been dominant. In 1976, as we have seen, the Carter campaign organization exercised substantial control over convention business and was viewed by a large majority of the delegates as the most important group at the convention. This model, with a dominant candidate organization, presents a sharp contrast to the classic model of convention decision making, in which the decisive bargaining takes place between hierarchical state delegations, dominated by party leaders.

In 1976, Jimmy Carter emerged from the primaries with a substantial lead and had virtually secured the nomination a month before the convention began. It is worth considering the implications of this kind of situation both for the nomination process and for the role of party conventions in that process.

If a single candidate emerges from the primaries in a dominant position, then the strategic environment is dramatically changed for a number of actors. The candidate is able to command media attention and becomes the center of communication for the various groups within the party. Just as a President's special vantage points give him power in the bargaining process, so a candidate's status as prospective nominee leads a variety of actors to seek his approval (Neustadt, 1960). Party regulars develop a stake in his success and begin to coordinate their activities with his. Platform and rules committee negotiations center on the prospective nominee's preferences. Interest groups seek his favor as a way of satisfying their policy demands.

Like a President, the leading candidate can engage in a range of intersecting negotiations, and he can often turn these negotiations to his own advantage (Schelling, 1960). He can make himself a sought-after source of information about others' intentions, and he can argue that concessions in one area would upset a carefully arranged balance in another. Finally, he can argue that undue conflict in the party can only help the other party in the general election.

In the case of early single-candidate dominance, the process of intraparty bargaining and legitimation can be moved forward in time. In 1976, some of the most important functions of conventions —selecting the nominee, framing the platform, agreeing on party rules, stimulating dialogue among groups, and building legitimation— were in fact carried out in the weeks preceding the convention.

If convention functions can be fulfilled in the preconvention period, do we really need a convention at all? The emergence of Carter in 1976 gives the question a special relevance. For many, the 1976 convention seemed to be an example of much ado about nothing. But before we dismiss out of hand the utility of conventions when the choice of nominee is a foregone conclusion, we should recognize that holding the convention may still be important in facilitating legitimation. Delegates may draw some satisfaction from divisible prizes such as platform planks which express their policy preferences, opportunities to hear their leaders, a vice-presidential nominee who is one of their own, and rules changes which they hope will work to their advantage in the future. Even though these prizes may seem pale in comparison to the prize of the presidential nomination, they may still contribute to the losing delegates' willingness to support the final outcome. Delegates are also given an opportunity to change their candidate commitments while remaining honorable. Thus conventions can help satisfy what we have identified as the preconditions for legitimation. Our data show that the convention experience itself increased the willingness of many delegates to accept the party's nominee.

More broadly, conventions can assist in performing certain important party functions—agenda setting, integrating groups within the party, and constraining the policy choices available to the nominee. In 1976, a wide range of groups within the party did come together to write a platform that was surprisingly satisfactory to all of them. If the party had not had to produce a platform at the convention—and to present that platform on national television—the pressures for intergroup cooperation would have been greatly reduced.

Not only does the convention provide an arena in which groups bargain with each other; it is also the site of negotiations between party groups and the nominee. These negotiations serve two functions. They place constraints on the nominee, who must make himself acceptable to groups. And they serve to reassure groups by allowing them to become familiar with the candidate.

Still, it might be argued, such constraints could have been applied in the absence of a convention. Meetings could and would occur between the nominee and group leaders. But the existence of the convention serves to increase the groups' strength as negotiators. For one thing, the convention provides a site for group members to gather in numbers and organize themselves. A further advantage for the groups stems from the fact that the convention is nationally televised and reported upon by a total press corps of 10,000. Thus, both group leaders and the candidate know that dissatisfied participants can easily voice their discontent to the nation simply by calling a press conference. In these ways, the existence of a convention contributes to the ability of party groups to bargain with, and to constrain, the nominee.

If conventions can perform these functions even when they are dominated by a single candidate, they are even more important when support is fragmented among numerous candidates. In such situations, conventions can serve as arenas for bargaining among diverse party elements.

But the forging of agreement among all these groups is not an easy task. And our previous research has shown that legitimation at party conventions is very difficult to achieve. It remains to be seen how durable the unity displayed by the Democrats in 1976 will be.

METHODOLOGICAL APPENDIX

We arranged our interviews, as much as was possible given the inherent difficulties in the task, so that each day's interviews constituted a random selection of the entire 441-person sample. Thus, for example, delegates interviewed on Monday would be a representative sample of convention delegates. Delegate names were grouped and randomly ordered by hotel. Interviewers assigned to a particular hotel were instructed to work their way down the list. However, as we had anticipated, the pressures of time forced us to deviate from what we considered an optimal research design. We were able to gain access to the convention floor and ask delegates in our sample to move to the convention periphery where they could be interviewed. Obviously, we tried to get as many delegates as we could from any one state with which we were in contact on the floor. This meant that for particular hours or half-days certain states were heavily overrepresented in our sample. Thus we have had to take precautions in removing the effects of this interviewing procedure on our measures of change over time. We have done so by ensuring that no state is overrepresented in any one time period for measures dealing with change over the course of the convention.

NOTES

1. We are grateful to the following members of our research team for their insightful caucus observations: Patricia Hanratty (Women's Caucus), Robert Weinberg (Labor Coalition), and Andrea Wolfman (Black Caucus).

2. The caucus sent members a leaflet, "Analysis of Caucus of Black Democrats Issues in the Democratic Party Platform," which detailed the platform's incorporation of caucus issue positions.

3. Thomas C. Schelling (1960) showed how such "constraints" can often work to a negotiator's advantage, by making it appear harder for the negotiator to compromise.

4. Examples of such issues were proportional representation in primaries, the equal sex division requirement, and the composition of the 1978 midterm conference.

5. Hamilton Jordan, Jody Powell, Ben Brown, Pat Caddell, Gene Pokorny, Joe Duffy, Frank Mankiewicz, and Ted Sorensen. The last four of these were assigned to specific sectors of the convention floor, leaving the first four to rove freely around the floor.

6. One question was decided against the preferences of the Carter campaign: the Winograd Commission was directed to mandate only proportional representation primaries for 1980. However, Rich Hutcheson claimed that the Carter organization had not pushed too hard for its position. "It's not a make-or-break issue," he remarked.

7. We are using the terms and method of analysis developed by Erving Goffman (1959).

8. For a discussion of Lyndon Johnson's use of his personality, see James David Barber (1972). A similar discussion can be found in the discussion of Woodrow Wilson as a "power-seeker" by Alexander and Juliette George (1956).

9. The list of specific position papers ranged from highly controversial items like abortion and amnesty to items like Radio Free Europe and railroad reorganization. Individual items could be ordered from the campaign itself. Carter was personally concerned with the ways in which his commitments were portrayed; he did not want to be seen as a rigid individual but rather one whose commitments were real but flexible (explicitly referring to James David Barber's categories of presidents). (See Broder, 1976.)

REFERENCES

ARONSON, B. (1976). "A new coalition is born as labor looks for a candidate." Democratic Review, July-August.

BARBER, J.D. (1972). The presidential character. Englewood Cliffs, N.J.: Prentice-Hall.

BRODER, D.S. (1976). "Carter would like to be an 'active-positive.' " Washington Post, July 16.

BURNHAM, W.D. (1975). "Party systems and the political process." In W.N. Chambers and W.D. Burnham (eds.), The American party systems (2nd ed.). New York: Oxford University Press.

Congressional Quarterly (1976). "Peace prevails as Democrats write platform." June 19, p. 1553.

GEORGE, A., and GEORGE, J. (1956). Woodrow Wilson and Colonel House. New York: Dover.

GOFFMAN, E. (1959). The presentation of self in everyday life. New York: Doubleday Anchor.

KEY, V.O. (1964). Politics, parties, and pressure groups (5th ed.). New York: Thomas Y. Crowell.

LOWI, T. (1970). "Distribution, regulation, redistribution: The functions of government." In R. Wolfinger (ed.), Readings in American political behavior. Englewood Cliffs, N.J.: Prentice-Hall.

MILLER, A.H., MILLER, W.E., RAINE, A.S., and BROWN, T.A. (1973). "A majority party in disarray: Political polarization in the 1972 election." Paper delivered at the annual meeting of the American Political Science Association, New Orleans.

NEUSTADT, R.E. (1960). Presidential power. New York: John Wiley.

New York Post (1976a). "Carter 'sincerity' convinces blacks." July 13.

——— (1976b). "Hispanics: Fractured, frustrated." July 14.

——— (1976c). "Their no. 1 concern is the no. 2 job." July 14.

New York Times (1976a). "Democrats shape a platform aimed at uniting party." June 16.

——— (1976b). "Carter makes peace with black leaders and reviews pledge of high-level jobs." July 13.

——— (1976c). "Compromise reached on women's role." July 13.

——— (1976d). "AFL-CIO pledge support to Carter." July 20.

POLSBY, N.W. (1968). "The institutionalization of the U.S. House of Representatives." American Political Science Review, (March):144-168.

SCHELLING, T.C. (1960). The strategy of conflict. New York: Oxford University Press.

SULLIVAN, D.G., PRESSMAN, J.L., and ARTERTON, F.C. (1976). Explorations in convention decision making: The Democratic party in the 1970s. San Francisco: W.H. Freeman.

SULLIVAN, D.G., PRESSMAN, J.L., PAGE, B.I., and LYONS, J.J. (1974). The politics of representation: The Democratic convention 1972. New York: St. Martin's.

Washington Post (1976a). "Democratic unit defers to Carter." June 21.

——— (1976b). "Carter's campaign in Va. fuels feud of Miller, Howell." July 15.

——— (1976c). "Marylanders hold 'convention' of their own at Garden." July 15.

WILDAVSKY, A. (1965). "The Goldwater phenomenon: Purists, politicians, and the two-party system." Review of Politics, July.

——— (1971). The revolt against the masses. New York: Free Press.

WILSON, J.Q. (1966). The amateur Democrat. Chicago: University of Chicago Press.

Women's Political Times (1976). "Women's concerns recognized in Democratic platform." July.

Chapter 4

THE ELECTORAL BASIS OF PARTY VOTING:
PATTERNS AND TRENDS IN THE
U.S. HOUSE OF REPRESENTATIVES, 1887-1969

JOSEPH COOPER
DAVID WILLIAM BRADY
PATRICIA A. HURLEY

Party voting in the Congress has long been a topic of great concern to political scientists. From the time of Woodrow Wilson and Abbott Lawrence Lowell numerous authors have devoted their energies and attention to elucidating its character and determinants. Yet, despite the attention this question has received, current understanding of its facets and causes still suffers from a number of serious defects.

Large gaps in our knowledge of the basic historical record continue to exist. From work that has been published it is clear that there has been considerable variation in congressional party voting over time (Turner and Schneier, 1970; Shannon, 1968). Nonetheless, the published data are fragmentary and incomplete, with the result that vital information bearing on the character and patterns of change is not readily available or accessible.

In addition, insufficient attention has been paid to the fact that assessing the impact of party on congressional voting is a complex, multifaceted problem rather than a simple, unidimensional one. To say this is not to imply that the difficulties that exist are not known. In his pioneering work many decades ago Stuart Rice (1928) developed an index of likeness to complement his index of cohesion because he recognized that the index of cohesion simply measured agreement within a party and was therefore insensitive to interparty conflict. Nor is it to disregard the valuable work of men such as Duncan MacRae (1970) and John Grumm (1964). Nonetheless, the point remains that commonly used measures are too often applied without adequate recognition of their limitations as sources of evidence upon which to base general assessments of party strength. Equally, if not more important, little has been done empirically since Rice's time in terms of either simple or sophisticated measures to explore the various facets of party voting and determine their interrelationships.

Last, but certainly not least, after decades of research the causes or determinants of variation in congressional party voting are still subject to considerable controversy. The thrust of the modern literature on legislative voting both in Congress and the state legislatures has been to cast doubt on the traditional view that electoral interests and opinions and legislative voting are closely linked (Jewell and Patterson, 1973; Miller and Stokes, 1963). In the more specific case of party voting the concomitant trend has been to undermine belief in the primacy of electoral interests or alignments and to suggest that other determinants may be as important or even more important. Thus, for example, the recent literature emphasizes such determinants as personal attitudes and orientations, cues from fellow members, executive pressure, structural features, majority size, leadership strategies and skills, etc. (Kingdom, 1973; Brady, 1973; Ripley, 1969; Mayhew, 1966; Wahlke et al., 1962; McCally, 1966; Moore, 1969). In general, such research has established that party voting is a product of more than constituency influence. Nonetheless, the overall result has been to produce a highly contradictory and inconclusive set of findings (Fiorina, 1974; Shannon, 1968). At this point in time, neither the role of electoral factors as determinants of party voting nor their relative importance vis-à-vis nonelectoral determinants can be assessed in a clear and coherent manner.

The aim of this paper is to assist in remedying each of the problems or defects that we have identified. To facilitate the attainment of such an objective, we shall, however, focus our attention on the U.S. House of Representatives and restrict our causal analysis to the problem of variation in the overall level of party voting.[1]

The remainder of this paper is accordingly organized into four parts. The first section discusses the character and pertinence of various measures of party voting and presents and interprets the historical record of the late 19th and 20th centuries in terms of these measures. The next two sections deal with the linkage between electoral factors and party voting. In these sections our object is both to demonstrate that current approaches to this linkage have biased results and to present a model which reconfirms the impact of external determinants on the basis of improved conceptualization and operationalization of the problem. The final section seeks to develop the implications of our findings both for the role of party in the Congress and for the further study of legislative party voting generally.

I. PARTY VOTING IN CONGRESS

The four most commonly used measures of party voting in Congress are the index of cohesion, the party vote score, the party unity score, and the index of likeness. As indicated above, the index of cohesion is simply an overall measure of partisan unity or cohesion on roll call votes.[2] The party vote score is a measure of the degree to which the parties differ from one another on roll call votes. As initially formulated by Lowell (1902), it measures the percentage of the time that 90% of one party oppose 90% of the other on roll call votes. In recent decades, however, party votes have generally been measured as the percentage of the time that 50% of one party opposes 50% of the other on roll call votes (Turner and Schneier, 1970). The party unity score measures unity or cohesion on party votes. As currently used, it measures the degree to which fellow partisans vote together on roll calls in which 50% of one party oppose 50% of the other.[3] The index of likeness is similar to the party vote score in its object. It focuses on division or conflict and measures the degree to which the parties differ from one another on roll call votes.[4]

PATTERNS AND DIMENSIONS

As is clear from our brief descriptions of these measures, they tap different facets or dimensions of the impact of party on voting. With the exception of the party unity score, they focus either on unity or conflict. The party unity score taps both dimensions, but in a circumscribed fashion. Certainly, both these facets or dimensions are important. High overall unity in a context of low divisiveness does

DIVISIVENESS

	High	Low
High	Comprehensive Impact (A)	Segmented Impact (B)
Low	Impaired Impact (C)	Negligible Impact (D)

U N I T Y (left axis label)

Figure 1: MODAL PATTERNS OF PARTY VOTING

not testify to the strength of party as a determinant of voting. Similarly, high degrees of divisiveness combined with restricted degrees of internal unity would indicate severe elements of weakness in the strength of party as a determinant of voting. Moreover, not only are both facets or dimensions important, they also appear to be highly interrelated. Thus, as has been suggested earlier, the patterns that these relationships assume pose a critical problem for students of party voting to explore and resolve. Abstractly, four broad modal or archetypal patterns can be conceptualized, if overall unity as identified by the index of cohesion is treated as one primary dimension and divisiveness or conflict as identified by the party vote score or the index of likeness is treated as a second primary dimension. These four patterns are presented in Figure 1.

Cell A, in which both unity and divisiveness are high, represents a pattern in which party has a strong and comprehensive impact on voting. Cell B, in which unity is high but divisiveness is restricted, represents a pattern in which party has a strong impact on voting in some areas but not in all areas. Cell C, in which divisiveness is high but unity restricted, represents a pattern in which party serves as an important basis of division on issues generally but exhibits substantial weaknesses in internal cohesion and discipline. Cell D, in which both unity and divisiveness are restricted, represents a pattern in which party has only marginal importance as a determinant of voting. Parties rather tend to disintegrate into factions and voting tends to be characterized by highly fluid and transitory factional combinations.

HISTORICAL ANALYSIS

If we turn now to the actual historical record, data on all four measures have been gathered for the 50th through the 90th Congresses (1887-1969) by running an Accum I program on all roll call votes in each of these 41 Houses. The results are shown in Tables 1 and 2. The strongest trend evident in the data confirms the impression conveyed by more scattered evidence that already exists in published form.[5] Over the course of this century there has been a clear and substantial decline in the strength of party as a determinant of voting. This is more evident in the measures that focus on divisiveness or conflict than on the unity measures, but it is apparent in both. We should note, however, that we might expect the unity measures to lag behind the divisiveness measures since the index of cohesion gives credit for intraparty agreement that derives from bipartisan agreement and the party unity score cannot by definition fall below 50. Aside from the overall trend, Tables 1 and 2 indicate that the years from 1910 to 1940, the years from the overthrow of House Speaker Joe Cannon to the accession of Speaker Sam Rayburn, stand as a period of transition from the high scores of the era of party government to the far lower scores of the contemporary, decentralized House. In addition, the data indicate that the decline in party strength, though continuing, has not occurred at a steady rate, but rather has proceeded at different rates in different decades. For example, it was checked somewhat by the Warren Harding landslide in 1920 and the emergence of the New Deal coalition in the 1930s.

Yet, despite the importance of these data for understanding the historical record, it is significant for other reasons as well. Tables 1 and 2 also cast light on the scope and relevance of particular measures and on the relationships that exist between unity and divisiveness as facets or dimensions of party voting.

In the former regard, we have already pointed out that the divisiveness measures present a more severe picture of the character of the decline than the unity measures. It is equally true that even measures that tap the same facet of dimension of party voting differ significantly in their results. This is not surprising given the nature of

Table 1. MEASURES OF PARTY UNITY IN THE HOUSE, 1887-1969

	Average Index of Cohesion		*Average Party Unity*	
Congress	*Republican*	*Democratic*	*Republican*	*Democratic*
50 (1887-1889)	77.8	58.9	88.5	77.2
51 (1889-1891)	86.2	70.5	93.5	86.9
52 (1891-1893)	73.8	55.9	79.6	76.2
53 (1893-1895)	73.3	73.0	86.1	85.1
54 (1895-1897)	58.0	67.3	82.2	86.9
55 (1897-1899)	84.3	74.6	93.2	89.3
56 (1899-1901)	83.8	73.8	94.2	89.5
57 (1901-1903)	87.6	75.1	93.4	87.2
58 (1903-1905)	83.9	83.2	92.8	93.2
59 (1905-1907)	79.1	80.9	88.7	92.5
60 (1907-1909)	89.3	78.6	93.0	88.4
61 (1909-1911)	67.4	78.5	85.3	89.8
62 (1911-1913)	73.5	69.8	89.2	88.1
63 (1913-1915)	72.0	63.2	87.8	83.6
64 (1915-1917)	72.1	67.0	87.0	85.1
65 (1917-1919)	67.3	72.9	79.9	85.0
66 (1919-1921)	75.4	67.2	86.3	82.0
67 (1921-1923)	76.1	70.8	88.1	85.9
68 (1923-1925)	73.9	59.4	83.5	81.9
69 (1925-1927)	72.5	55.3	86.0	74.7
70 (1927-1929)	65.1	64.6	81.8	80.5
71 (1929-1931)	68.1	67.5	86.1	85.1
72 (1931-1933)	57.0	60.0	78.6	81.0
73 (1933-1935)	70.2	68.3	88.5	85.5
74 (1935-1937)	68.0	64.4	85.8	83.5
75 (1937-1939)	68.7	56.6	87.0	80.4
76 (1939-1941)	74.2	65.4	87.6	83.1
77 (1941-1943)	72.3	62.9	85.4	81.5
78 (1943-1945)	73.0	59.9	85.9	79.6
79 (1945-1947)	69.4	64.4	84.7	79.5
80 (1947-1949)	76.5	65.1	89.6	82.6
81 (1949-1951)	67.6	63.0	81.2	80.1
82 (1951-1953)	65.2	61.8	79.0	75.4
83 (1953-1955)	73.8	60.9	83.7	76.7
84 (1955-1957)	61.4	68.8	77.7	80.1
85 (1957-1959)	56.9	59.9	74.5	77.8
86 (1959-1961)	62.3	62.5	80.8	80.1
87 (1961-1963)	64.3	73.2	80.8	83.0
88 (1963-1965)	67.4	73.5	81.9	83.1
89 (1965-1967)	70.4	70.6	80.7	80.3
90 (1967-1969)	68.3	67.9	78.7	75.3

Table 2. MEASURES OF PARTY CONFLICT IN THE HOUSE, 1887-1969

Congress	Average Index of Likeness	Percent Party Vote 90% vs. 90%	Percent Party Vote 50% vs. 50%
50 (1887-1889)	58.7	8.7	51.1
51 (1889-1891)	32.7	42.5	78.9
52 (1891-1893)	61.0	4.2	45.4
53 (1893-1895)	59.6	6.1	44.8
54 (1895-1897)	46.1	24.8	68.5
55 (1897-1899)	30.8	50.2	79.8
56 (1899-1901)	31.0	49.8	77.2
57 (1901-1903)	42.6	38.9	67.0
58 (1903-1905)	21.7	64.4	89.7
59 (1905-1907)	35.9	34.6	73.5
60 (1907-1909)	50.1	26.3	57.1
61 (1909-1911)	37.1	29.4	79.2
62 (1911-1913)	46.9	23.0	59.5
63 (1913-1915)	49.6	19.9	61.4
64 (1915-1917)	51.5	21.7	58.6
65 (1917-1919)	65.9	9.4	42.7
66 (1919-1921)	63.8	14.9	44.9
67 (1921-1923)	50.3	35.2	59.9
68 (1923-1925)	51.9	13.4	58.7
69 (1925-1927)	63.7	5.3	43.7
70 (1927-1929)	61.8	5.6	48.6
71 (1929-1931)	50.9	13.6	58.2
72 (1931-1933)	61.1	13.8	57.7
73 (1933-1935)	42.3	18.9	70.6
74 (1935-1937)	51.8	14.2	59.9
75 (1937-1939)	49.3	11.8	63.9
76 (1939-1941)	44.9	17.6	71.4
77 (1941-1943)	62.8	10.5	41.5
78 (1943-1945)	59.5	9.6	49.4
79 (1945-1947)	61.3	12.1	48.1
80 (1947-1949)	58.0	12.7	44.8
81 (1949-1951)	62.1	6.5	50.9
82 (1951-1953)	59.4	4.9	64.1
83 (1953-1955)	65.7	5.4	44.9
84 (1955-1957)	68.9	6.7	42.3
85 (1957-1959)	67.5	5.2	49.2
86 (1959-1961)	61.2	5.0	52.8
87 (1961-1963)	63.0	5.8	48.8
88 (1963-1965)	60.7	8.6	51.7
89 (1965-1967)	66.8	1.8	47.1
90 (1967-1969)	74.2	2.9	35.8

these measures. But it highlights the limited utility of measures we commonly rely upon without much forethought of the constraints that exist.

In the latter regard, Tables 1 and 2 testify to the dependencies that exist between the facets or dimensions of party voting and to the nature of the patterns that actually occur. Congresses such as the 55th (1897-1899) and the 56th (1899-1901) exemplify the modal pattern represented in Cell A of Figure 1. We may note that the Republicans, who controlled and organized these Congresses, had cohesion scores substantially above 50 and that the likeness scores in these Congresses were substantially below 50. In contrast, Congresses such as the 89th (1965-1967) and 90th (1967-1969) exemplify the modal pattern represented in Cell B of Figure 1. In these Congresses the Democrats, who controlled and organized the House, registered cohesion scores substantially above 50. However, the likeness scores in these years were also well above 50.

No Congresses in Tables 1 and 2 come close to satisfying the requirements of Cells C and D in Figure 1. In the case of Cell D this result can be attributed to the time period of our data. Our expectation is that Congresses in periods of party disintegration, such as the years between 1817 and 1825, would provide examples of the modal pattern represented in Cell D. The fact that no Congresses in our data approach the requirements of Cell C is more significant. Though even abstractly there were grounds for doubt that this pattern could be realized, it remained theoretically possible that party could serve as a basis of division on a large number of issues while still lacking the ability to mobilize high levels of support in any consistent or comprehensive manner. This possibility may now be discounted; high levels of divisiveness do not seem to combine with restricted levels of unity. In sum, then, it would appear not only that unity and divisiveness are highly interrelated but also that unity exists as a necessary, though insufficient, precondition of divisiveness.

The relative importance of unity as opposed to divisiveness can be put to another and perhaps more severe test if we narrow our conception of unity and measure it by the party unity score instead of the index of cohesion. If we so interpret our data, a number of conclusions can be drawn. On abstract or logical grounds it might have been conjectured that a reduction in the proportion of issues that divide the parties would enhance or at least not impair unity on the smaller proportion that continued to do so. But this clearly is not the case. The decline of party as a determinant of voting in this century has involved both a reduction in the proportion of partisan issues and a decline in the ability of majority party leaders to mobilize their forces on such issues. Nonetheless, even when one takes the limited range of the party unity score into account, unity appears more resistent to decline than divisiveness. Moreover, though standards for high levels of agreement must be more demanding in the case of the party unity score, here too the same dependencies between unity and divisiveness seem to obtain. Majority party unity scores of 75 or more are associated with both high and low divisiveness scores. However, high divisiveness scores are not associated with low party unity scores. We may conclude once again that unity and divisiveness are highly interrelated and that unity seems to be the more influential or determining facet or dimension.

II. PARTY AND CONSTITUENCY REVISITED

In seeking to fulfill the remaining objectives of this article, attention must first be given to the literature that deals with the linkage between electoral factors and party voting. This literature is extensive and focuses quite understandably on constituency impact. As a body of research, it is, to be sure, not without its drawbacks. Actual results have been disappointing (Fiorina, 1974; Shannon, 1968). Moreover, the primary goal has been to explain variation in party voting among individual members, and much of the research concerns the state legislatures rather than Congress (Keefe and Ogul, 1973; Jewell and Patterson, 1973). Nonetheless, this literature constitutes the necessary starting point in any attempt to improve understanding of the determinants of overall levels of party voting in Congress.

In part, this is true because the underlying problems of conceptualizing party and constituency are similar and are the basic findings of relevance to all legislatures in the system. In large part, however, the need to assess the existing literature on the linkage between constituency and party voting derives from its limitations. Though research on constituency impact has yielded highly inconclusive and inconsistent results and though research on nonelectoral determinants has yielded some important insights and findings, students of party voting should not conclude that henceforth they can discount the influence of electoral factors. Even a cursory inspection of the existing literature suggests that the results that have been obtained may be more an artifact of the manner in which the key variables have been conceptualized and operationalized than a valid reflection of reality. In sum, then, for both positive and negative reasons, it is necessary to preface any attempt to design and test a model that will explain variation in overall levels of party voting in Congress with an examination of current approaches to and findings regarding constituency impact.[6]

CATALOG OF APPROACHES

Perhaps the oldest and most familiar approach to the linkage between constituency factors and party voting at both the national and state levels is to presume a strong and direct relationship between them (Flinn, 1964). What is hypothesized is that members vote together or in conflict largely or primarily on the basis of the character of their constituencies. Such an hypothesis, in turn, involves an implicit assumption regarding party: that it has little or no independent effect as a determinant. Though in recent decades this view has usually been advanced simply for heuristic purposes, conceptualization and operationalization of the key variables generally do not vary in any critical regards among proponents and opponents of the thesis (Froman, 1963; Derge, 1958; Truman, 1959; Dye, 1961; Markus, 1974). Constituency is conceptualized in global or generalized terms and operationalized through reliance on objective measures of overall socioeconomic constituency characteristics. In contrast, since party is regarded as a resultant or effect, differences between the concepts of party and party voting become blurred. Party thus tends to be conceptualized as a voting stance and is operationalized through measures of party loyalty or measures of policy positions or orientations.

Skepticism that party voting could be explained in terms of what V.O. Key (1961) has called "the simple constituency pressure model" has led to three other approaches. One of these approaches assumes that party has impact or influence as a determinant, but treats party and constituency as distinct and largely opposing determinants. This approach, in short, treats party not only as an effect but also as a determinant that is both separate from and in conflict with constituency.

This approach may be termed the dual pressure theory. Two broad or general variants exist in the literature. The more traditional variant is represented by Julius Turner both in his original work (1951) and the more recent update of it by Edward Schneier (Turner and Schneier, 1970). In Turner's treatment, party as an independent variable is conceptualized as some aggregate of shared policy positions or orientations, organizational loyalties, and leadership pressures. As a dependent variable it is conceptualized as a distinctive form of voting behavior. In both cases, however, the measures are the same—that is, various measures of intraparty unity and interparty conflict. Constituency is conceptualized in global or generalized terms and operationalized in terms of objective socioeconomic measures of overall constituency characteristics. On the basis of such conceptualization and operationalization Turner proceeds to examine levels of party voting over time as indicators of the strength of party pressure and then turns to the impact of constituency, which he treats as a separate and highly conflicting source of pressure.

Turner's work has had a great impact on research and shaped the conceptual frameworks of many subsequent students of party voting (Patterson, 1962; Rieselbach, 1964; LeBlanc, 1969; Wiggins, 1967; Erikson, 1971a; Markus, 1974; Deckard and Stanley, 1974). Nonetheless, in the past decade a more sophisticated variant of dual pressure theory has emerged (Clausen, 1973; Stone, 1965; Clausen and Cheney, 1970). In this variant the key variables are conceptualized in much the same manner as in Turner. However, researchers in this category view party more exclusively in policy terms and see it essentially as a set of shared policy positions or orientations. In addition, they typically regard broad ideological predispositions as an underlying element of such policy content and treat ideology as a basic and important factor despite its limitations in the American setting. Finally, representatives of this variant are far more sensitive to the need for clear and distinct measures of the key variables, and they try to operationalize party and constituency in a manner that avoids confusion and ambiguity. The technique that they commonly employ is to seek to hold constituency constant by focusing on cases of partisan turnover and examining the degree of change in voting on policy issues that results. The guiding assumption is that stability in voting under such circumstances can be attributed to constituency impact and change that are congruent with partisan voting patterns to party impact. This technique has thus been used to assess the relative impact of party and constituency and to argue that party as an aggregate set of shared policy orientations exists as a distinct and significant determinant of party voting.

The remaining two approaches differ from the first approach by assuming that party exists as a determinant of party voting and from the second approach by treating party and constituency as factors that overlap without being identical or reducible to one another. In short, adherents of these approaches regard party as an electoral entity that is rooted in constituency, as an entity that is based on and unites constituency interests. Moreover, they assume that the impact of constituency on party voting is mediated through party as an electoral force.

One such approach seeks to find the linkage in the competitive or partisan aspects of party as an electoral force. Most of the research in this category focuses on the individual level and treats the size of electoral margins as the independent variable and the measures of party loyalty and/or partisan policy positions or orientations as the dependent variable (Keefe and Ogul, 1973; Shannon, 1968). To a lesser degree, however, the relationship between the competitiveness of state party systems and overall levels of party voting has also been explored (Jewell and Patterson, 1973).

A second approach of this type seeks to find the linkage between constitutency factors and party voting in the substantive or aggregative aspects of party as an electoral force, in party as a substantive political coalition. Here research with few exceptions has focused on explaining variation in party voting among individual members, and the guiding presumption has been that the more "typical" a constituency is of a particular party the higher the degree to which its elected representative will vote with his fellow partisans. Or, to put it another way, what is assumed is that the degree of fit between party as a factor within a particular constituency and party as an aggregate electoral force can be used to predict party loyalty or voting choices in accord with partisan policy positions or orientations (MacRae, 1952; Sorauf, 1963; Dye, 1961).

This last approach may be called the degree of fit theory, and, as in the case of dual pressure theory, several variants exist. In its most prevalent form, reliance is placed on objective socioeconomic measures of overall constituency characteristics both to establish the distinctive pattern of interests that characterize party as an aggregate electoral force and to establish the distinguishing characteristics of particular constituencies (Shannon, 1968). A second, but far less common, variant attacks the problem of operationalization in political rather than socioeconomic terms. In this variant, measures, such as the percentage of the party vote for President or the direction and degree of the margin between the congressional and presidential vote, are typically relied upon as indicators of the degree of fit (LeBlanc, 1969; Waldman, 1967; Weinbaum and Judd, 1970; Flinn and Wolman, 1966; Markus, 1974).

PROBLEMS IN SIMPLE CONSTITUENCY THEORY

All these approaches, however, contain serious deficiencies in conceptualization and operationalization. These deficiencies help to explain the muddled state of research findings regarding the relationship between constituency factors and party voting. Moreover, they preclude drawing any quick or facile negative conclusions regarding this linkage.

Results of tests of the first theory are highly mixed, if not negative (Key, 1961; Flinn, 1964; Broach, 1972). Fellow partisans from different types of districts often vote together; conversely, opposing partisans from the same type of constituency often vote in conflict. Nor is it surprising that the simple constituency pressure theory cannot adequately explain party voting. To do so, a theory must at a minimum accord adequate recognition both to electoral choice and to party as an electoral force. The simple constituency pressure theory can do neither.

It is true, of course, that, in part, elections impact subsequent legislative voting on the basis of aspects or features of particular constituencies that exist as absolute or consistent constraints. Some constituency interests are indeed so pervasive and important or so isolated and important that any and all successful candidates will espouse and later defend them. But it is also true that elections serve as a medium of linkage between voters and legislators because they involve choice between or among candidates with opposing policy orientations. In each of these cases the mediating role of elections derives both from the discipline of the electoral process and from the tendency of members to internalize values and interests that are widely shared throughout their constituencies or within the core groups that provide them with most of their electoral support (Miller, 1970; Sullivan and O'Connor, 1971; Segal and Smith, 1972; Erikson, 1971b). But the point remains that the impact of elections on legislative voting through electoral choice is at least as substantial as the impact through absolute or consistent constituency representation and far more critical to the successful functioning of a modern democratic order (Clausen, 1973; Stone, 1965; Markus, 1974). Yet it is precisely this type of impact that a global and objective approach to constituency necessarily discounts. Such an approach treats members as if they responded simply to an overall and objectively defined constituency, whereas in fact they respond as much, if not more, to a segmented and political constituency that they themselves participate in defining (Dexter, 1957; Fenno, 1975). Indeed, the more heterogeneous the constituency the more this is true.

Nor is it only the fact that the simple constituency pressure theory does not take adequate account of electoral choice that undermines its explanatory power. This source of error combines with another to compound the difficulty of securing positive results. If constituency factors are to be tied to party, it is not sufficient merely to take the segmented and subjective dimensions of constituency into account. The political coalition that elects and sustains a particular partisan in office varies in character from the political coalitions in other districts that sustain fellow partisans in office and from the aggregate of such coalitions. Moreover, the compatibility or incompatibility of the component elements of the aggregate varies over time. Thus, whether approached as a problem of explaining variation in overall levels of party voting or differences in the degree of party voting among particular partisans, what is essential is that party itself be treated as an electoral variable in order that an accurate estimate of the degree to which constituency factors contribute to or inhibit party voting can be secured and a sound or valid basis for confirming the relationship or linkage can be provided. Once again, however, this is something that is beyond the reach of the simple constituency pressure theory. It cannot relate the strength of party at the legislative stage to the strength of party at the electoral stage. Ironically enough, because it correctly perceives party to be a resultant of electoral forces, it is led to treat party incorrectly as merely a product or sum of particular constituencies, conceptualized and measured in overall and objective terms. The inevitable consequence is to combine and confuse both those aspects of constituency that contribute to party voting and those that do not.

PROBLEMS IN DUAL PRESSURE THEORY

The second approach accords party as well as constituency recognition as a pressure or determinant, but treats them as distinct and rival causal factors. As a consequence, it too produces inconclusive results and discriminates against positive findings.

The more traditional variant, as represented by Julius Turner's work (1951) and the recent update of it (Turner and Schneier, 1970), relies on the same indicators to measure party pressure and party voting. To do so, however, is to fail to confirm party's status as a separate and distinct determinant. Indeed, this gap becomes all the more serious given the full range of Turner's findings. For though he treats constituency pressure as a conflicting source of pressure and explains party disunity in terms of it, he also finds that constituency pressure can "combine with" party pressure to reinforce party voting. In contrast, the greater care in operationalization displayed in the more contemporary variant serves only to intensify the bifurcation of party and constituency (Clausen, 1973; Stone, 1965; Clausen and Cheney, 1970). However, it is by no means clear that the impact of party is wholly separate or distinct from that of constituency, even if it is measured as if this were the case. As just noted, even Turner's work suggests the existence of overlap as well as conflict.

Such problems or limitations reflect more basic conceptual deficiencies in what we have called dual pressure theory. Adherents of this approach conceptualize party as some aggregate of policy positions, loyalties, and leadership pressures that exists apart from any base in constituency interests and viewpoints. The instincts that motivate such an approach are sound. What lies at the heart of this approach is the view or feeling that the bases of party strength in the electorate are broader than particular constituency interests and viewpoints and, in fact, largely in conflict with them. In short, the primary assumption, though implicit, is that party as an aggregate of electoral interests and viewpoints is qualitatively different from and not reducible to any sum of the interests and viewpoints of particular constituencies. Thus, party is identified and treated directly in policy or substantive terms not because it is not seen as a derivative of electoral interests and viewpoints but to avoid the distortions that are felt to be connected with rooting it in constituency. In addition, this approach seeks to recognize that party has both ideological and organizational dimensions: that it is not an aggregate of interests or policy positions in a physical or mechanical sense, but rather a structured social entity which rests on shared ways of looking at and assessing issues and has independent organizational impacts of its own at the electoral and legislative levels.

Nonetheless, dual pressure theory presses such insights beyond their range of application and in so doing converts them into sources of error. It is true that party has both ideological and organizational reality. It is also true that party aggregates interests and viewpoints that are broader than the confines of particular constituencies. Geographical locations do not vote. Rather, the residents within them do and these residents vote in terms of regionally and nationally defined interests and viewpoints rather than merely in terms of local or parochial concerns.[7] Be that as it may, it is still a mistake to treat party and constituency as distinct and rival sources of pressure. If those who approach party as a sum of particular constituencies, conceptualized in overall objective terms, are in error, then to conceptualize party as separate from and in conflict with constituency does not correct the error. So treated, constituency continues to be approached as a location, though now more narrowly and consistently interpreted in highly particularistic, negative terms. Party, in contrast, is reified. By being removed from any roots in individual constituencies, it is left hanging in indeterminate space.

Yet, in reality, discrete constituencies serve as the electoral units for legislative parties, and party members in the legislature respond to and are sustained by such constituencies. Moreover, since values, beliefs, and interests are not uniformly distributed geographically, the status of discrete constituencies as electoral units affects the mix and strength of the interests and viewpoints represented at the aggregate as well as the constituency level. This is not to deny what we have already asserted. The dominant political coalitions within individual constituencies are based upon and reflect broader concerns than those of a particular location. Still, if constituency boundaries are not controlling, they are a source of influence. If the residents of constituencies vote on the basis of concerns that extend beyond constituency boundaries, the fact that the legislative party as an aggregate is a set of constituency coalitions and not a set of interests and viewpoints aggregated on a national basis remains of critical importance. It means that the legislative party cannot validly be separated from its constituency roots.

Dual pressure theory's assumption that party should be separated from constituency is thus an inevitable source of bias. In the first variant it leads Turner to assume what he ought to prove. Measures of party voting are read as measures of party's independent strength as a determinant. The fact that constituency contributes to, as well as conflicts with, party voting is discounted, and, insofar as constituency is seen to have positive effects, these effects are treated as secondary or subsidiary to party pressure. Nor is this surprising, despite the absence of any direct test of party's impact on voting apart from constituency. Since Turner assumes such impact from the start as a fundamental axiom, he feels no need to test it and simply proceeds to interpret the empirical evidence in terms of his preconceptions.

The second variant operationalizes party at the electoral as well as the legislative level and thereby permits a test of the hypothesis regarding the policy results of partisan turnover. However, the fact that this hypothesis can be tested does not mean that the relative impacts of party and constituency have been properly conceptualized or measured. On the contrary, by attributing stability in policy voting in cases of partisan turnover to constituency, this variant reduces constituency to its most particularistic and parochial features as a location and restricts its impacts to those that serve as absolute and consistent constraints on voting. Similarly, by attributing change in policy voting in cases of partisan turnover to party, it attributes to party, as opposed to constituency, impacts that depend upon and involve significant change in the character of dominant political coalitions within particular districts. In sum, then, this variant cannot avoid understating the impact of constituency because it attributes all the impacts of electoral choice to party, conceived and measured as a factor apart from and in conflict with constituency. In so doing, it too assumes what it ought to prove.[8]

PROBLEMS IN POLITICAL APPROACHES

The final two approaches have also yielded unsatisfactory results. Those who have investigated the relationship between electoral margins and party loyalty and/or partisan policy orientations have produced a confusing and highly conflicting set of findings (Fiorina, 1974). Similarly, exploration of the relationship between overall levels of party voting and the competitiveness of state party systems has produced mixed results (Jewell, 1955; Jewell and Patterson, 1973). Authors who have emphasized the substantive or aggregative aspects of party as an electoral force, rather than its competitive or partisan aspects, have had their problems as well. Those who have relied on objective measures to apply the degree of fit approach to explain variation in party voting among individual members have obtained inconclusive results (Shannon, 1968; Fiorina, 1974). Results, however, have improved in those few cases in which several socioeconomic characteristics thought to be reflective of the aggregate party coalition have been grouped or combined and used to explore the relationship between constituency and party voting in general or overall terms (Flinn, 1964; Deckard, 1976). In the limited number of instances in which political indicators have been used to apply the degree of fit approach, results have been marred by conceptual deficiencies, ambiguous evidence, and substantive inconsistencies (Flinn and Wolman, 1966; LeBlanc, 1969; Weinbaum and Judd, 1970; Waldman, 1967; Markus, 1974).

The lack of success experienced by those who have emphasized the competitive or partisan aspects of party as an electoral force is not surprising. Such authors assume at least for heuristic purposes that electoral margins measure or reflect party strength at the electoral stage and therefore can be used to explain party voting at the legislative stage. However, margins of victory in particular constituencies do not measure party strength in any direct sense. They measure only the strength of the coalition within a constituency that elects a party member to office. Sound or valid measures rather must be based on the recognition that party is a phenomenon that is defined or takes shape at the aggregate level, and they accordingly must involve means of relating party at the aggregate and constituency levels. Given this need, results may well be expected to be confused and contradictory as long as the degree of fit between a particular constituency and the party as a whole is not taken into account. In short, the degree of safeness or marginality ought to be conceptualized and treated as a subsidiary and reinforcing element, not as a direct and primary determinant. Nor is it surprising that the relationship between the competitiveness of state party systems and overall levels of party voting is ambiguous. If party strength at the electoral level is, as we suggest in the first section of this article, a composite of interparty conflict and intraparty unity, then we might expect a variable that imperfectly measures one aspect of party strength and the other not at all to produce inconclusive results.

What merits greater attention is the fact that the substantive or aggregative approach to party as an electoral force has also produced a confusing and disappointing melange of results.

Here again the explanation lies in basic deficiencies of conceptualization and operationalization. To conceptualize the linkage between constituency and party voting correctly, it is essential both to focus on the legislative party and to avoid the pitfalls that stem from attempting either to wholly submerge party in or wholly distinguish party from its constituency base. The key to correct conceptualization is rather to approach party as a factor that both overlaps and conflicts with constituency, as a factor that arises and draws support from some elements of constituency while simultaneously excluding and drawing opposition from others. These constraints, in turn, can be satisfied if party is viewed as an entity that aggregates interests and viewpoints that crosscut particular constituencies and in so doing ties members and the political coalitions that elect them to a wider political coalition.

To approach party as an electoral force that unites members from particular constituencies by aggregating interests and views that crosscut their constituencies permits recognition of the overlap between party and constituency without reducing party to constituency. The degree of overlap rather becomes the prime question to be investigated at both the aggregate and constituency levels. At the aggregate level it may be assumed that the overall level of accommodation or harmony attained among the variety of interests and viewpoints that a party aggregates will vary over time. This is true not simply because history and considerations of electoral advantage shape the nature of political coalitions, but also because the interests and viewpoints that a party aggregates can be expected to vary in terms of their rational coherence and potential for mutually beneficial exchanges as cultural and economic conditions vary. At the individual or constitutency level it may be assumed that the fit between particular political coalitions within constituencies that elect party members to office and the overall aggregate of such coalitions that define the party as a whole at the legislative stage will also vary.

Similarly, to view party in aggregative and electoral terms avoids compartmentalizing party and constituency into distinct and rival determinants while still permitting recognition of party's ideological and organizational dimensions and its broader representative role.

If party is viewed as an entity that unites members from particular constituencies by aggregating interests and viewpoints that crosscut their constituencies, then the role of ideology in rationalizing and establishing points of concurrence among such interests and viewpoints can be recognized and assessed. In addition, since aggregation rests on exploiting communalities in discrete interests and viewpoints and since such communalities must be identified and maintained through active effort in the form of rational persuasion and bargaining, party does not simply record shared interests and viewpoints but serves as a mechanism for fashioning and sustaining them. Thus, the structured or organized facets of party and the range of impacts that result from them can also be acknowledged and assessed. In short, then, approached in this manner, both the ideological and organizational dimensions of party become matters for investigation rather than reasons for reifying party on the assumption that it somehow must be isolated from the contagion of constituency.

It follows as well that if party is seen as an entity that unites members from particular constituencies by aggregating interests and viewpoints that crosscut their constituencies, it does not have to be treated as distinct from constitutency to avoid doing violence to its broader representative character. As long as constituency is approached flexibly with attention to its segmented and political aspects, the ties that bind party to constitutency can be recognized without reducing it to some sum of local and parochial interests.

Measured in these terms, what we have called the degree of fit theory has a number of substantial strengths. To treat the linkage between constituency and party voting as a matter of the degree of fit between a particular constituency that elects a party member to office and the aggregate of constituencies that elect all party members to office assumes that party voting at the legislative stage depends on party strength at the electoral stage and that communalities in constituency interests and viewpoints provide the basis for such strength. It is thus to recognize that party is a phenomenon that is defined at the aggregate level, to view party and constituency as overlapping determinants that both support and conflict with each other, and to understand that the mix can vary in particular instances.

Nonetheless, the degree of fit theory also has significant weaknesses. Whatever its insights, it provides only vague and ambiguous guidelines for conceptualizing and operationalizing constituency and party as determinants and for treating their interaction. In the absence of such guidelines, the general tendency of authors who have applied the degree of fit approach has simply been to adopt common or familiar expedients in conceptualizing and operationalizing the primary variables. Though understandable, given the difficulties that exist, the result of such a strategy has been once again to discriminate against positive findings.

In most instances, adherents of the degree of fit theory have measured constituency in objective and overall terms and equated party with the socioeconomic characteristics that predominate among the constituencies that compose the party coalition. In so doing, they have transformed an approach that is conceptually sound at the highest level of generality into an approach that errs in ways that dual pressure theory, with all its problems, does not.

The reasons for error are, however, more complex than in the case of simple constituency pressure theory. They can best be understood if developed in terms of a point made earlier in this paper. That is, that party voting involves both intraparty unity and interparty difference. It follows that any attempt to link party strength at the constitutency level to party voting in the legislature—and this is what the fit hypothesis seeks to accomplish—must do justice to these two dimensions of party voting both individually and in terms of their interaction.

Objective indicators, however, are poorly suited to satisfy these needs. Though the fit hypothesis mitigates the effects of treating constituencies as wholes, reliance on objective measures of fit nonetheless leads to serious distortions in estimates of the overlap between particular constituencies and the overall party aggregate, in estimates of the potential for unity. At the individual or constituency level, objective measures obscure the critical and defining features of the political coalitions that actually elect party members to office. At the aggregate level, they obscure the contours and character of the actual or operative coalition not simply because they sum constituencies as locations but also because they cannot take account of the results of the political processes through which parties identify and develop communalities in interests and viewpoints that crosscut constituency boundaries. Nor for similar reasons can such measures provide anything but muddled reflections of the political differences that separate the parties.

Equally, if not more important, reliance on objective indicators produces unsatisfactory solutions to the problem of integrating unity and difference, to the problem of combining these dimensions so that estimates of overlap relate to actual areas of partisan conflict. Objective measures are blind to political factors and results. They thus can provide little or no guidance regarding the construction of a weighted index that would permit fit to be measured on the basis of a variety of indicators simultaneously. Hence, those who rely on such measures typically focus on particular socioeconomic characteristics that seem to qualify as both integral elements of a party aggregation and critical items of difference between party aggregations. Yet to measure fit on the basis of particular characteristics means predicating general estimates of party strength at the constituency level on isolated factors when the overlap between party coalitions at the constituency and aggregate levels is complex and variegated and when the differences between the parties are relative within policy areas and varying among them.

Given all this, it is hardly surprising that attempts to explain variation in party voting among individual members by operationalizing the degree of fit approach in objective terms have proved quite disappointing or that results have improved when constituencies have been grouped into broad categories on the basis of several characteristics and these categories related to party voting in a general or overall manner.

Nor in the limited number of instances in which political rather than objective measures of fit have been applied have authors transcended the difficulties posed by the theoretical gaps in the degree of fit approach. In truth, such measures have great potential since they seek by nature to isolate the actual party coalitions within constituencies and compare them to the aggregate party coalition. However, the task of conceptualizing and operationalizing party as a political coalition at the constituency and aggregate levels is far more difficult than it appears, and, in general, authors have not engaged in the type of extended and careful analysis that is needed to define sophisticated indicators and apply them with great success. Rather, here too they have tended to rely on broad and familiar indicators, such as the percentage of the party vote for President, either to confirm vague expectations of their utility or to attack some relatively concrete empirical relationship between certain political aspects of constituency and party voting. In addition, authors have tended to be overly facile or eclectic in defining their conceptual frameworks. In so doing, they have impeded decisive tests of the degree of fit approach even in those atypical cases in which the problem of estimating the political constituency has been approached in a direct and sophisticated manner.[9] Research has thus proceeded on the basis of general and impressionistic measures and within theoretical frameworks that confound basic issues or narrow and isolate topics of inquiry. As a consequence, here too positive results have been artificially restricted, though in this case by ambiguities and confusions in frameworks and measures rather than by anything inherently incorrect in the approach.

III. THE IMPORTANCE OF ELECTORAL FACTORS

We may conclude that the failure of current research to confirm a linkage between constituency and party voting in a clear and conclusive manner may be attributed to deficiencies in the approaches relied upon rather than to the absence of such a linkage. We may further conclude that, despite the attention that has been devoted to the influence of electoral determinants, the question of their importance remains unresolved and hence that it is necessary to improve conceptualization and operationalization of the problem and to subject it to further testing.

GUIDELINES FOR RESEARCH

The aim of this section of our article is accordingly to design and test a model that avoids the errors of conceptualization and operationalization that we have identified. In developing such a model the preceding sections of our article have much to contribute. The conclusions to be drawn from these sections are not merely negative in character. Rather, both our examination of the dimensions of party voting and our examination of current approaches to constituency impact suggest a number of guidelines for improving conceptualization and operationalization of the linkage between electoral determinants and party voting. These guidelines may be identified and summarized as follows:

1. Party should be conceptualized and measured in terms that recognize it as an entity that accommodates and aggregates interests and viewpoints that crosscut constituency boundaries. Hence, it should also be treated as a phenomenon that takes shape or is defined at the aggregate level.

2. The impact of electoral factors cannot be validly assessed without recognition of the role of constituency. Nonetheless, serious distortions can result if this variable is not conceived and measured in ways that are sound conceptually. The importance of constituencies derives from their status as the electoral units of legislative parties and from the impacts that this status has in shaping and constraining the accommodation and aggregation of interests and viewpoints within the overall party coalitions. Thus, it is not constituencies as geographic wholes that should be the focal points of conceptualization and measurement, but rather the political coalitions within them that elect partisans to office. In short, constituency should be

conceptualized and measured in terms that are consistent with the notion of party outlined above. It should be approached in subjective and segmented terms and treated as a variable that may have both positive and negative consequences for party voting.

3. The positive impact of constituency factors on party voting should be seen as mediated through party as an electoral force. It is the success that party has in accommodating and aggregating interests and viewpoints that crosscut constituencies, in providing grounds for cohesion among the representatives of diverse constituency coalitions, that promotes party voting at the legislative level. The basis of a positive relationship between electoral factors and legislative party voting thus inheres in the relationship between party strength at the electoral level and party strength at the legislative level.

4. Party strength at the legislative level should be seen as a composite or product of both intraparty unity and interparty difference. Thus, whether the problem is to explain variation in party voting among members or variation in overall levels of party voting through time, the measures that are employed must tap and integrate both dimensions.

5. Party strength at the electoral level involves the same two dimensions of unity and difference as party strength at the legislative level. Hence, to explain variation in party voting among members, the fit between political coalitions at the constituency level and the aggregate party coalition and the areas of conflict or difference between the two party aggregates must be measured and combined. Similarly, to explain variation in overall levels of party voting through time, the coherence of the sum of crosscutting constituency interests and viewpoints that the aggregate party coalition includes and the degree of difference or cleavage between the two party aggregates must be measured and combined.

6. At the electoral as well as the legislative level, reliance must be placed on political indicators to measure party strength. Whether the object is to explain variation in party voting among members or variation in overall levels of party voting through time, the crux of the problem is to measure the degree of coherence within and difference between actual party aggregates.

LINKAGE MODEL

In designing and testing a model based on these guidelines, our premise will be the traditional one that electoral factors are of great

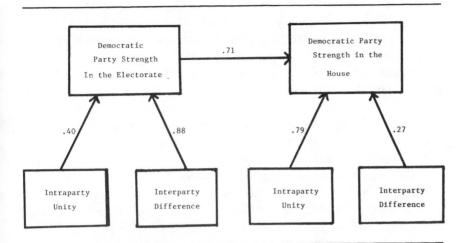

Figure 2: ELECTORAL IMPACT ON OVERALL PARTY VOTING:
HOUSE DEMOCRATS, 1887-1969

importance and have a substantial impact on party voting. Our choice of such a hypothesis derives both from the failure of past research to test this basic proposition adequately and from our own preconceptions. For purposes of brevity and simplicity, we shall, as previously noted, confine our model to the problem of explaining variation in overall levels of party voting in the House. Nonetheless, if we can demonstrate a strong causal relationship between electoral factors and legislative party voting, an important benchmark for future research will be established.

Figure 2 presents a model based on the guidelines that have emerged from our analysis. This model hypothesizes the existence of a causal relationship between party strength at the electoral level and party strength at the legislative level and tests this hypothesis for House Democrats in the 50th to the 90th Congresses (1887-1969).

In our model, party strength at both the electoral and legislative levels is conceptualized as a product of the degree of intraparty unity and interparty difference. So conceived, operationalizing party strength at the legislative level presents no great difficulties. The degree of interparty difference can easily and appropriately be measured by either a party vote score or the index of likeness. For reasons of aptness and simplicity, we shall use the 50% versus 50% party vote score (see Table 2). Similarly, the degree of intraparty unity can validly be measured by either the Rice index of cohesion or the party unity score. We shall use the party unity score (see Table

1). This score, as noted earlier, is more circumscribed than the Rice score. However, in the context of a model that seeks to test the joint effects of unity and difference, this is an advantage rather than a disadvantage. Thus, the limitations that the party unity score possesses as a measure that is insensitive to the extent of party voting are checked when it is combined with a party vote score. In contrast, the limitations that the Rice score possesses as a measure that cannot distinguish between partisan and bipartisan agreement retain their impact when it is combined with a party vote score.

Operationalizing the defining dimensions of party strength at the electoral level presents far greater problems. To pin down the degree of difference or conflict between the two party aggregates, we shall rely on Ginsberg's index of ideological conflict (1972) between the Democratic and Republican parties on the issue of capitalism. This index is derived from a content analysis of Democratic and Republican platforms from 1844 to 1968 and is chosen from a variety of indices provided by Ginsberg because of the salience of the capitalism issue during the period of our concern. To measure the degree of intraparty unity at the electoral level we shall assume that throughout the period from 1887 to 1969 the Democratic party in the House has been split into two primary factions—a Northern faction and a Southern and Border faction.[10] On the basis of this assumption we shall further assume that the political coalitions that dominate constituencies are more alike in interests and viewpoints within party factions than across party factions and hence that the greater the percentage of party members in the dominant faction of the House Democratic party the more homogeneous or coherent the party is as an electoral aggregate. In short, then, our measure of intraparty unity will be the percentage of party members in each Congress elected by the dominant faction of the Democratic party.

Having operationalized our model, we need only choose an appropriate and effective method of analyzing results to test it. Canonical correlation provides such a method (Cooley and Lohnes, 1971; Van de Geer, 1971). This technique measures the correlation between two concepts which are themselves defined by more than one variable. It can be seen as analogous to multiple regression with several dependent variables. In our model, two variables define each of the primary concepts, and the use of canonical correlation will give us both an overall measure of the causal relationship that exists between our primary concepts and individual measures of the relative contribution of each of the four variables to this relationship. The latter measures—i.e., the canonical variate loadings—are similar to standardized regression coefficients.

As Figure 2 indicates, canonical correlation analysis of the data secured by operationalizing our model confirms its basic assumptions. The canonical correlation between party strength at the electoral level and party strength at the legislative level is .71. The eigenvalue, or amount of shared variance, is 50%, and thus half the variation in overall levels of party voting among House Democrats in the period between 1887 and 1969 can be explained as a product of the degree of party unity and conflict at the electoral level. As for the canonical variate loadings, our findings indicate that at the electoral level interparty difference has more than twice as much impact on the causal relationship as intraparty unity. However, it is quite possible that this result is attributable to the crudeness of our measure of party homogeneity or coherence. In contrast, at the legislative level unity makes a far greater contribution to the hypothesized relationship than difference. Though this finding is in line with the judgments reached in the first section of this article, no firm conclusions can be drawn since the two variables as operationalized are intercorrelated at .71. Nonetheless, whatever their relative influence, the four canonical variate loadings we have obtained do indicate that unity and difference constitute important dimensions of party strength at both the electoral and legislative levels, and this result also provides important support for our model.[11]

IV. CONCLUSION

In closing this article, it is essential that we place our analysis and findings in proper perspective. Whatever the limitations of our measures and model, the fact that we can explain half the variation in House Democratic party voting over a period of nearly a century is quite significant. It highlights the critical nature of the tie between conceptualization and operationalization in all types of research and strongly suggests that electoral factors are, as they were traditionally thought to be, a highly influential determinant of party voting. To state this, however, is not to imply that electoral factors control or determine party unity in a highly mechanistic manner (Segal and Smith, 1972; Miller, 1970). Rather, we may continue to believe that legislators retain **considerable** freedom in making voting choices and that a major portion of the impact of electoral factors derives from the internalization of interests and viewpoints that characterize the most compatible and supportive portions of a member's constituency (Dexter, 1957; Fenno, 1975; Miller and Stokes, 1963; Sullivan and O'Connor, 1972). Nonetheless, the point remains that such internalization is just as much a medium of electoral impact as the discipline or control exerted by the formal process and thus that "personal attitudes" should not be treated in a manner that simply presumes them to be a nonelectoral determinant.

Similarly, to reaffirm the importance of electoral factors is not to argue that nonelectoral factors in the form of friendship cues, party caucuses, leadership skills, or presidential pressure are unimportant. As our model itself indicates, electoral factors per se do not explain a substantial portion of the variance. Nor do we wish to deny that operationalization of the key variables in terms that are correct conceptually is exceedingly difficult. Nonetheless, if this fact does much to explain the current tendency to make ease of operationalization the definitive criterion in the design of research, it cannot condone it. The results of such research are not necessarily reliable and can be quite deceptive. In short, then, what is needed now is both greater ingenuity in operationalizing the key variables in terms that fit conceptual guidelines and further exploration of the relative influence of electoral vis-à-vis nonelectoral determinants.

In pursuing these aims, our analysis and findings suggest three further hypotheses. The first is that the relative influence of electoral and nonelectoral factors on legislative party voting is not fixed or absolute, but rather varies with the strength of the electoral determinants. Thus, in periods or cases in which parties at the electoral level exhibit high degrees of unity and conflict, nonelectoral determinants will be less influential than in cases or periods in which the reverse is true. The second derives from the first. It is that, despite variations in their relative degrees of influence, electoral factors are the primary or more controlling determinant. Thus, though nonelectoral determinants may have a positive impact on party voting, they will not fully compensate for deficiencies in party unity and conflict at the electoral level nor sustain high levels of party voting when party unity and conflict at the electoral level are low.

Our final hypothesis also rests in large part on prior assumptions. It is that party strength at the legislative level has a substantial impact on organizational norms, structures, and behavior. Thus, though centralization of power in the formal and/or party structures of a legislature can contribute to party voting, the degree of such centralization will itself vary in relation to the potential for party voting that emerges from the electoral process (Cooper and Brady, 1973; Cooper, 1975). All these hypotheses have broad implications for understanding the House. If valid, the state of parties at the electoral level exists as a crucial factor in explaining both transitions in the institutional character of the House over time and the contours, politics, and problems of the modern House.

NOTES

1. Some prominent political scientists now believe that the proper way to study party voting is to disregard aggregate scores and analyze it instead in a segmented fashion in terms of discrete issue dimensions (Clausen, 1973). Nonetheless, our decision to rely on aggregate scores and focus on the overall level is quite deliberate. Though party strength of course varies from issue dimension to issue dimension, it is significant not simply in terms of its impact in structuring voting in specific policy domains but also in terms of its more general integrative effects in structuring voting across a variety of policy domains (Turner, 1951; Patterson, 1962; Broach, 1972; LeLoup, 1976). Similarly, party strength in a general or overall sense has important effects in structuring organizational and procedural decisions and in determining the level of centralization that will exist (Keefe and Ogul, 1973; Ripley, 1969; Cooper and Brady, 1973). Finally, for purposes of comparative analysis over long periods of time, the explanatory power of dimensional analysis is limited by changes in the character of issue dimensions and in overall levels of party strength. In short, then, the point is that the great utilities of dimensional analysis in terms of explaining individual or bloc voting, pinning down the precise contours of party strength, or identifying change in partisan issue dimensions should not be transformed into a rationale for denying the reality and importance of party and party strength as wholes or questioning the validity of approaching them in this manner. Method in other words should not be allowed to dictate to philosophy. A focus on the overall level is thus justifiable theoretically and in the case of this article more appropriate to our purposes. It should also be noted that the term "dimension" is frequently used in the text, but in a different sense than is understood or intended by those who engage in dimensional analysis.

2. The easiest way to obtain an index of cohesion score on a given motion is to take the absolute difference between the percentage of a bloc or group voting "aye" and the percentage voting "nay." This index is based on the realization that a 50% versus 50% voting break represents 0 cohesion, and it, in effect, treats raw scores so that they can be measured on a 0 = 100 scale (Rice, 1928; MacRae, 1970).

3. The party unity score is simply a raw cohesion score on party votes, i.e., the actual percentage of members voting with a majority of their fellow partisans on party votes (Turner and Schneier, 1970; Shannon, 1968).

4. On any given motion the index of likeness score is obtained by calculating the percentage of members from two separate blocs or groups that vote in the same direction and subtracting the difference from 100. Thus, the higher the score the greater the similarity or likeness (Rice, 1928; MacRae, 1970).

5. The party vote, cohesion, and likeness scores in Tables 1 and 2 have been calculated on all roll calls and thus may differ from reports in other published sources. Similarly, the

party unity scores in Table 1 have been calculated by averaging raw unity scores on party votes without reference to absences and thus are somewhat higher than party unity scores reported in recent decades by the *Congressional Quarterly*.

6. The text identifies four distinct approaches to the study of party voting. However, in distilling these approaches from the literature, we do not mean to imply that all individual authors can simply or neatly be placed within particular categories. Rather, the approaches represent basic modes of conceptualizing and operationalizing the problem, and individual authors often overlap the bounds of a particular category. To a large degree this occurs because researchers for heuristic reasons often apply more than one approach or seek to merge them. In part, however, it also occurs because researchers in their haste to operationalize variables and test them can be quite uncritical of the conceptual implications of the variables that they choose to operationalize and test. Finally, since the approaches that we identify are quite broad, it is also true that authors who explicitly or implicitly make similar basic assumptions can nonetheless differ in focus of attention and explanatory emphasis.

7. Given this fact, it is not surprising that the use of region as an explanatory variable produces better results than socioeconomic constituency characteristics (Deckard and Stanley, 1974; Clausen, 1973).

8. The method described and criticized in the text to test the impact of party as opposed to constituency is applied in the later work of Clausen (1973) and Stone (1965). In an earlier article Clausen and Cheney (1970) rely on a somewhat different technique to operationalize and confirm dual pressure theory. The general thrust of the criticism in the text nonetheless applies, since their operationalization of party in terms of the party identification of members and constituency in terms of socioeconomic variables commits the same basic error of attributing effects to party that may be constituency effects and vice versa.

9. John E. Jackson (1974) has done path-breaking work in this regard with respect to the relationship between constituency influence and the voting behavior of Senators. As yet, few students of party voting have followed his lead. For an example of one who has, however, see the work of Gregory Markus (1974).

10. Our definition of Southern and Border States follows that of the Survey Research Center. It thus includes the 11 states of the Confederacy plus Kentucky, Oklahoma, Maryland, and West Virginia.

11. We also subjected our data to multiple regression analysis. In doing so, we first averaged the party unity score and party vote score for each Congress in our time period in order to secure a legislative party strength score. This set of scores was then regressed on our measures of unity (% dominant faction) and difference (Ginsberg index of ideological conflict over capitalism) at the electoral level. The multiple R for this regression is .66, indicating that these two dimensions of electoral party strength explain 43% of the variance in our dependent variable. The standardized regression coefficients are .21 for our measure of electoral unity and .59 for our measure of electoral difference. In addition, we subjected our data for House Republicans to the same types of analysis. Here our multiple regression analysis yielded a multiple R of .61 and and R^2 of 38%. Similarly, canonical correlation analysis yielded an R of .62 and an eigenvalue of 38%. Thus, the results were quite positive but not as strong, owing to the greater limitations of the dominant faction approach as a measure of electoral unity in the case of House Republicans.

REFERENCES

BECKER, R.W., FOOTE, F.L., LUBEGA, M., and MONSMA, S.V. (1962). "Correlates of legislative voting: Michigan House of Representatives." Midwest Journal of Political Science, 6(November):384-397.

BRADY, D.W. (1973). Congressional voting in a partisan era. Lawrence: University of Kansas Press.

BROACH, G.T. (1972). "A comparative dimensional analysis of partisan and urban-rural voting in state legislatures." Journal of Politics, 34(August):905-924.

CLAUSEN, A.R. (1973). How Congressmen decide: A policy focus. New York: St. Martin's.

CLAUSEN, A.R., and CHENEY, R.B. (1970). "A comparative analysis of Senate-House voting on economic and welfare policy, 1953-1964." American Political Science Review, 64(March):138-153.

CNUDDE, C.F., and McCRONE, D.J. (1966). "The linkage between constituency attitudes and congressional voting behavior: A causal model." American Political Science Review, 50(March):66-72.

COOLEY, W.W., and LOHNES, P.R. (1971). Multivariate data analysis. New York: John Wiley.

COOPER, J. (1975). "Strengthening the Congress: An organizational approach." Harvard Journal On Legislation, (April):308-368.

COOPER, J., and BRADY, D. (1973). "Organization theory and congressional structure." Paper delivered at annual meeting of the American Political Science Association.

DECKARD, B. (1976). "Political upheaval and congressional voting: The effects of the 1960's on voting patterns in the House of Representatives." Journal of Politics, 38(May):326-346.

DECKARD, B., and STANLEY, J. (1974). "Party decomposition and region: The House of Representatives, 1945-1970." Western Political Quarterly, 27(June):249-265.

DERGE, D.R. (1958). "Metropolitan and outstate alignments in Illinois and Missouri legislative delegations." American Political Science Review, 52(December):1051-1065.

DEXTER, L.A. (1957). "The representative and his district." Human Organizations, 16(spring):2-13.

DYE, T.R. (1961). "A comparison of constituency influences in the upper and lower chambers of a state legislature." Western Political Quarterly, 14(June):473-480.

ERIKSON, R.S. (1971a). "The relationship between party control and civil rights legislation in the American states." Western Political Quarterly, 24(March):178-183.

——— (1971b). "The electoral impact of congressional roll call voting." American Political Science Review, 65(December):1018-1033.

FENNO, R.F. (1975). "Congressmen in their constituencies: An exploration." Paper delivered at the annual meeting of the American Political Science Association.

FIORINA, M.P. (1974). Representatives, roll calls, and constituencies. Lexington, Mass.: D.C. Heath.

FLINN, T.A. (1964). "Party responsibility in the states: Some causal factors." American Political Science Review, 58(March):60-71.

FLINN, T.A., and WOLMAN, H.L. (1966). "Constituency and roll call voting: The case of Southern Democratic congressmen." Midwest Journal of Political Science, 10(May): 192-200.

FROMAN, L.A. (1963). Congressmen and their constituencies. Chicago: Rand McNally.

GINSBERG, B. (1972). "Critical elections and the substance of party conflict: 1844-1968." Midwest Journal of Political Science, 16(November):603-626.

GRUMM, J.G. (1964). "The means of measuring conflict and cohesion in the legislature." Southwestern Social Science Quarterly, 44(March):377-388.

JACKSON, J.E. (1974). Constituencies and leaders in Congress: Their effects on Senate voting behavior. Cambridge, Mass.: Harvard University Press.

JEWELL, M.E. (1955). "Party voting in American state legislatures." American Political Science Review, 49(September):773-791.

JEWELL, M.E., and PATTERSON, S.C. (1973). The legislative process in the United States. New York: Random House.

KEEFE, W.J., and OGUL, M.S. (1973). The American legislative process. Englewood Cliffs, N.J.: Prentice-Hall.

KEY, V.O. (1961). Public opinion and American democracy. New York: Alfred A. Knopf.

KINGDOM, J.W. (1973). Congressional voting decisions. New York: Harper and Row.

LeBLANC, H.L. (1969). "Voting in state senates: Party and constituency influences." Midwest Journal of Political Science, 13(February):33-57.

LeLOUP, L.T. (1976). "Policy, party, and voting in U.S. state legislatures: A test of the content-process linkage." Legislative Studies Quarterly, 1(May):213-231.

LOWELL, A.A. (1902). "The influence of party upon legislation." Annual Report of the American Historical Association for 1901, 1:321-543.

MacRAE, D. (1952) "The relation between roll call votes and constituencies in the Massachusetts House of Representatives." American Political Science Review, 46(December):1046-1055.

——— (1958). Dimensions of congressional voting: A statistical study of the House of Representatives in the Eighty-First Congress. Berkeley: University of California Press.

——— (1970). Issues and parties in legislative voting: Methods of statistical analysis. New York: Harper and Row.

MARKUS, G.B. (1974). "Electoral coalitions and Senate roll call behavior: An ecological analysis." American Journal of Political Science, 18(August):595-607.

MATTHEWS, D.R., and STIMSON, J.A. (1975). Yeas and nays: Normal decision-making in the U.S. House of Representatives. New York: John Wiley.

MAYHEW, D.R. (1966). Party loyalty among Congressmen: The difference between Democrats and Republicans. Cambridge, Mass.: Harvard University Press.

McCALLY, S.P. (1966). "The governor and his legislative party." American Political Science Review, 60(December):923-942.

MELTZ, D.B. (1973). "Legislative party cohesion: A model of the bargaining process in state legislatures." Journal of Politics, 35(August):647-681.

MILLER, W. (1970). "Majority rule and the representative system of government." In E. Allardt and S. Rokkan (eds.), Mass politics. New York: Free Press.

MILLER, W., and STOKES, D.E. (1963). "Constituency influence in Congress." American Political Science Review, 57(March):45-56.

MOORE, D.W. (1969). "Legislative effectiveness and majority party size: A test in the Indiana House." Journal of Politics, 31(November):1063-1079.

PARSONS, M.B. (1962). "Quasi-partisan conflict in a one-party legislative system: The Florida Senate: 1947-1961." American Political Science Review, 56(September):605-615.

PATTERSON, S.C. (1961). "The role of the deviant in the state legislative system: The Wisconsin Assembly." Western Political Quarterly, 14(June):460-472.

——— (1962). "Dimensions of voting behavior in a one-party state legislature." Public Opinion Quarterly, 26(summer):185-200.

PESONEN, P. (1963). "Close and safe state elections in Massachusetts." Midwest Journal of Political Science, 7(February):54-70.

RICE, S.A. (1928). Quantitative methods in politics. New York: Alfred A. Knopf.

RIESELBACH, L.N. (1964). "The demography of the congressional vote on foreign aid, 1939-1958." American Political Science Review, 58(September):577-588.

RIPLEY, R.B. (1967). Party leaders in the House of Representatives. Washington, D.C.: Brookings Institution.

——— (1969). Majority party leadership in Congress. Boston: Little, Brown.

SEGAL, D.R., and SMITH, T.S. (1972). "Congressional responsibility and the organization of constituency attitudes." In D. Nimmo and C. Bonjean (eds.), Political attitudes and public opinion. New York: David McKay.

SHANNON, W.W. (1968). Party, constituency, and congressional voting. Baton Rouge: Louisiana State University Press.

SORAUF, F.J. (1963). Party and representation: Legislative politics in Pennsylvania. New York: Atherton.

STONE, C.N. (1965). "Issue cleavage between Democrats and Republicans in the U.S. House of Representatives." Journal of Public Law, 14(2):343-358.

SULLIVAN, J.L., and O'CONNOR, R.E. (1972). "Electoral choice and popular control of public policy." American Political Science Review, 66(December):1256-1269.

TRUMAN, D.B. (1959). The congressional party: A case study. New York: John Wiley.

TURNER, J. (1951). Party and constituency: Pressures on Congress. Baltimore: Johns Hopkins University Press.

TURNER, J., and SCHNEIER, E.V. (1970). Party and constituency: Pressures on Congress. Baltimore: Johns Hopkins University Press.

Van de GEER, J.P. (1971). Introduction to multivariate analysis for the social sciences. San Francisco: W.H. Freeman.

WAHLKE, J.C., EULAU, H., BUCHANAN, W., and FERGUSON, L.C. (1962). The legislative system: Explorations in legislative behavior. New York: John Wiley.

WALDMAN, L.K. (1967). "Liberalism of congressmen and the presidential vote in their districts." Midwest Journal of Political Science, 11(February):73-85.

WEINBAUM, M.G., and JUDD, D.R. (1970). "In search of a mandated Congress." Midwest Journal of Political Science, 14(May):276-303.

WIGGINS, C.W. (1967). "Party politics in the Iowa legislature." Midwest Journal of Political Science, 11(February):86-98.

Chapter 5

ELECTIONS, PARTIES, AND REPRESENTATION: THE U.S. HOUSE OF REPRESENTATIVES, 1952-1970

DAVID NEXON

Leading normative theories of representation assert that elected officials should advance the wishes of their constituents on important issues of public policy (Pitkin, 1967). Unfortunately, little is known about the conditions that make them more or less likely to perform this function. In this paper, I use a relatively new method of measuring constituency opinion to present data on representation in the U.S. House of Representatives for the period 1952-1970. The results of this longitudinal analysis are striking and consistent enough to suggest a general model of representation in the American electoral system. In part, this model is similar to what has sometimes been called responsible party government (Ranney, 1954).

I. METHODOLOGY

Data for the study were drawn from the election year polls of the Survey Research Center at the University of Michigan for the years 1952-1968, from roll call votes in the U.S. House of Representatives for each session 1953-1970, from the *Congressional District Data Book* based on the 1960 Census, and from a few miscellaneous sources. Two major methodological tasks had to be performed in order to use these data. The first task was to construct appropriate scales in each year—opinion scales for the mass public and parallel scales of legislative votes for the Congressmen. The two issue areas selected for examination were welfare policy and civil rights. The second and far knottier task was to estimate mean constituency opinion for each congressional district.

To construct opinion scales in the welfare policy area, generally representing New Deal, Fair Deal types of issues, three questions were used. One question dealt with government responsibility for jobs and housing, one with government responsibility for medical care, and one with government responsibility for education. The civil rights scale included two questions—one on federal responsibility to ensure school integration and one on governmental responsibility to ensure equal treatment in employment and housing. To make unidimensionality of the scales more likely, items were both inspected for face content and required to intercorrelate. The respondent's scale score on each scale was his average score on the items he answered. Each item was standardized through z-scoring before averaging. Scores on items were ordered so that the higher the score, the more liberal the respondent.[1]

A similar but slightly more complicated procedure was followed in scaling legislative roll calls. Descriptions of roll calls were examined in the *Congressional Quarterly Almanac* to see if their face content seemed to fit the general areas covered by the opinion scales. Selecting votes for the civil rights scale posed few problems. Items falling into the scale included such votes as those for the Civil Rights Act of 1957 and the Civil Rights Act of 1964. Selection of items for the welfare policy scale was somewhat more complex. In general, items were selected for preliminary inclusion if their face content seemed to involve use of federal resources to meet human needs. Bills that seemed to be primarily regulative in intent were not included. Votes falling into the scale for various years included such items as public housing authorizations, grants for hospital construction, the antipoverty bill, and medicare.

Once a vote was selected for possible inclusion in the scale because of its face content, it was subjected to several statistical tests before being included in the final scale. First, to make unidimensionality more likely, it had to correlate with all other items in the scale at a level of .3 (Pearson's r) or better. Second, it had to correlate at this level within each party as well as for the whole legislature. Finally, there had to be at least 15 dissenting votes within each party. The reason for the latter two requirements was to make sure that the scales were not tapping pure partisanship. Once votes were selected for inclusion, they were z-scored, and a mean score for each Congressman on all the votes in the scale was determined. Again, the higher the score, the more liberal the Congressman.[2]

Estimating a district's mean opinion was a much more difficult problem. Generating such estimates is essential if one wishes to consider the issue of representation in any empirical way. The most reliable way of getting such estimates would be to conduct respectably sized sample surveys in each congressional district. As the authors of one study point out, however, carrying out such a procedure would cost about as much as purchasing several nuclear reactors (Miller and Stokes, 1963). As an alternative, I used a regression procedure based on national polls and district character- istics analogous to the simulation of the opinions of state popula- tions carried out in several well-known studies.

The procedure employed was to use predictor variables available in the national polls to generate regression weights enabling the prediction of individual scores at the national level. These regression weights (after some statistical manipulation) were then applied to the predictor variables at the congressional district level to derive an estimate of mean opinion for each district on each scale.[3] The variables used at the district level were percent nonwhite, median income, median education, religion, percent in white-collar employ- ment, region (South or non-South), and vote for President.[4] Once an estimate of mean district opinion on each scale was derived for each congressional district for each Congress, the resulting estimate was standardized and used in the subsequent analysis.

This method of estimating district opinion obviously has a number of problems, and there is no denying the fact that a number of districts will be misplaced in their relative liberalism. This misplacing may arise from (1) idiosyncratic district characterisitcs (the presence of an unusually conservative or liberal newspaper for example), (2) sources of variance in opinion not represented by the predictor variables which may be distributed among districts in nonrandom ways, (3) the operation of the ecological fallacy. In spite of these sources of error, the method should provide estimates of district opinion that have a rough relationship to true opinion. Reasons for believing this to be the case, based on the evidence of other studies, are provided in the Appendix to this chapter.

In evaluating the relationships between district opinion and

Congressman's vote presented in this study, the reader should put the following limits on the interpretations:

(1) Where there is a consistently positive or consistently negative correlation between Congressman's vote and district opinion (either for the whole Congress or subgroups), the actual numerical value of the correlation probably understates the true degree of relationship. Where there is a consistently near zero relationship and especially where the relationship fluctuates between positive and negative, however, the true relationship will be near zero.

(2) Little faith can be put in exact statistical interpretation of the data—in the numerical value of the r or in terms of variance explained, for example.

(3) Confidence can be put in the rough rankings of relationships, strong versus weak, one group versus another, if these rankings are consistent over time and make theoretical sense. The relationships I emphasize in this paper fall in these categories.

II. PARTY POLARIZATION:
THE LEGISLATURE FOLLOWS THE PUBLIC

At the level of the mass public, the period 1952-1970 marked an increase in the degree to which adherents of each of the two parties could be described as a group of like-minded men. This increase dated relatively sharply from the 1964 election, but continued at least until the end of the period studied. Specifically, Democrats were more liberal than Republicans throughout the period in the welfare policy area, but the difference increased sharply in 1964. In fact, before 1964, one could make a better guess at an individual's attitudes on welfare policy by knowing his social class than by knowing his party affiliation. After 1964, the reverse was true. In the civil rights area the change was even more dramatic. Prior to 1964, there was little difference between adherents of the two parties in their liberalism on this issue. After 1964, the Democrats were consistently more liberal. Not only were adherents of the two parties more polarized in their opinions after 1964, but an independent investigation reveals that the mass public was much more likely to specify the Democrats as the more liberal party after 1964 (Pomper, 1972). Figure 1 displays the average liberalism of members of each party for the two issue areas in each year.

To what degree are these changes in the relationship of party to

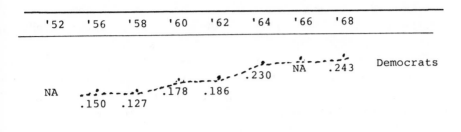

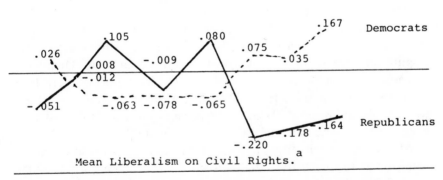

Mean Liberalism on Civil Rights.[a]

a. No scale could be constructed for welfare policy in '52 and '66. There was no appropriate poll in '54.

Figure 1: ATTITUDES OF THE GENERAL POPULATION, BY PARTY

opinion paralleled by changes in the relationship of party to legislative voting? This is clearly an important question. One might speculate that without such a parallelism, elections to the House will provide little opportunity for voters to influence public policy and little occasion for Congressmen to provide representation. Studies of these elections have indicated, without exception, that they are marked by extremely low levels of voter knowledge about both issues and candidates. Virtually the only factor systematically structuring the vote is party (Miller and Stokes, 1962; Arseneau and Wolfinger, 1973).[5] Hence, most of the votes cast in congressional elections can only be meaningful expressions of voters' opinions on the issues to the degree that party identification is related to issue position and to the degree that subsequent legislative votes on these issues are related to the party of Congressmen.

It is by no means obvious, however, that Congressmen will line up by party in their votes on issues in the same way that party identifiers do in their opinions on issues. After all, in this era of a highly "institutionalized" House and given the extremely low knowledge of Congressmen's behavior of most voters, why should Congressmen shift their behavior to conform to changes in attitude at the mass level? There is little likelihood that they will be punished at the polls for failure to do so.

In spite of the fact that there was no obvious reason for Congressmen's behavior to conform to mass opinion, there was in fact a rough parallelism during the period studied. In the welfare policy area, Democratic Congressman were consistently more liberal than Republican Congressmen 1953-1970 (although there was no marked increase in distance between the two parties after the 1964 election). In the civil rights area, the comparison to patterns among the electorate was even more striking. Before the 1964 election, the Republicans were, on the average, more liberal than the Democrats (because, as will be demonstrated, of the disproportionately large numbers of Southerners in the Democratic group). After 1964, there was an abrupt reversal. Democrats became more liberal, and by a wide margin. These patterns are shown in Figure 2.

What causal mechanisms produced this dramatic shift in legislative behavior at the same time that the shift was occurring for the mass public? The data do not permit a definitive answer to this question, but tentative hypotheses can be proposed and some accepted or rejected. Before explicating these hypotheses, it is necessary to recognize the impact of one very important variable affecting legislative voting during the period studied: region.

It has often been remarked that the Democrats in the Congress are not really representative of one party but rather of two parties, the South and the North. This is an exaggeration, but the impact on regionalism is nonetheless a very important one. Figure 3 compares mean scores of Southern Democrats on the two policy scales to

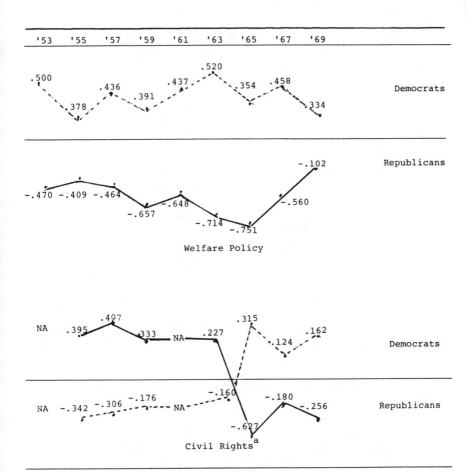

Figure 2: MEAN LIBERALISM OF VOTES IN THE HOUSE OF REPRESENTATIVES,
BY ISSUE AREA AND PARTY

[a]No scale could be constructed for civil rights in '53 and '61.
The headings for years refer to the first year of the relevant Congress.
Hence, '53 means the Congress meeting '53-'54.

Northern Democrats and Northern Republicans. For completeness, the very small group of Southern Republicans is also included.

It is clear from Figure 3 that region and party are both important variables on the welfare scale. The most liberal group, for the years examined, is the Northern Democrats. The Southern Democrats are, as a group, consistently more liberal than the Republicans, but consistently less liberal than the Northern Democrats. As examination of the figure indicates, the differences between these three groups are generally quite large.

In the area of civil rights policy, with the exception of the

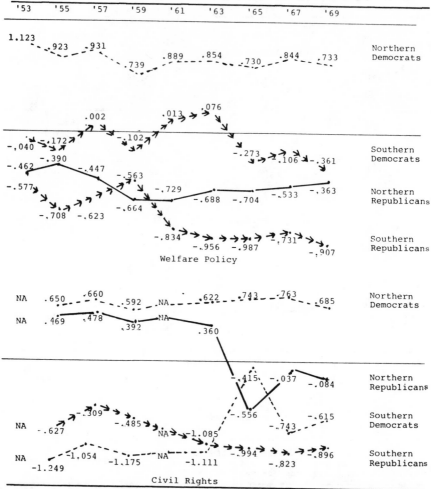

Figure 3: MEAN LIBERALISM OF VOTES IN CONGRESS, BY PARTY AND REGION

1965-1966 session, region is an even more important variable than party. Southern Congressmen from both parties are a substantially more conservative group than Northern Congressmen from either party. Within the Northern group, the findings reported earlier must be modified somewhat. In the years before 1964, Northern Democrats are slightly more liberal than Northern Republicans. The differences are not great, however, and they widen dramatically in the Congress elected in 1964.

In spite of these regional variations, the basic point still seems valid: a relationship between party and liberalism for votes in Congress is associated with the existence of such a relationship among the voters. There are several possible hypotheses to explain the 1964 shift in legislative party behavior. The first hypothesis to be explored is that the new men who entered the Congress in 1964 caused the shift. As individuals without established legislative records and as men nominated for office at the same time as the relatively ideological presidential candidates of 1964, new Congressmen might be presumed to gear their conceptions of themselves as legislators much more closely to the new images of the party enunciated by the presidential candidates and to influence the mass public more than the old hands. A look at Table 1 seems to support this idea. In the 1965-1966 session of the House, the first session to meet after the realigning election, the scores of the 57 Democrats new to the House in the civil rights issue area (the area where patterns of party voting undergo dramatic change) were substantially more liberal than the old hands in the House prior to the election (by a factor of better than two to one). Those Congressmen of the class of '64 who survived into the 1967-1968 and 1969-1970 sessions continued to be more liberal than their surviving pre-1964 colleagues, and by about the same ratio. The pattern among the Republicans had some similarities and some differences. The relatively small group from the GOP that bucked the Lyndon Johnson landslide and were newly elected in 1964 were markedly more conservative than the Republicans who welcomed them to Washington in 1965. They continued to be more conservative than their more senior colleagues in the 1967-1968 session, but by a smaller ratio. By the 1969-1970 session, the two groups of survivors were virtually identical in their voting records.

While Table 1 seems to substantiate the notion that the group of Congressmen first elected in 1964 accounted for a large part of the new relationship between party and vote on the civil rights issue area that occurred as a result of the election, it is still not clear what the operative mechanism involved is. I have suggested above that a kind of psychological variable was operative—greater perception of some kind of new party mandate by Congressmen elected in 1964. It may be, however, that the average new Congressman came from a different kind of district than the average old Congressman of his party.

Such an alteration in type of district would make sense in terms of the changes in mass political attitudes that occurred in 1964. To the degree that the new association between party identification and attitudes on civil rights was the result of party conversion by liberals

Table 1. COMPARISON OF THE MEAN LIBERALISM OF NEW AND OLD CONGRESSMEN ON CIVIL RIGHTS BY PARTY

	'65	'67	'69
Democrats: In the House before 1964	.238 (184)	.135 (151)	.181 (146)
Entered in 1964	.560 (56)	.291 (34)	.312 (36)
Republicans: In the House before 1964	-.565 (106)	-.166 (93)	-.189 (87)
Entered in 1964	-1.015 (17)	-.244 (17)	-.177 (15)

on civil rights, or to the degree that it was the result of a new basis for party choice by liberals on civil rights just entering the electorate, there should have been an increased probability that districts liberal on the civil rights issue would elect Democrats and districts conservative on the civil rights issue would elect Republicans. In fact, through a shift in the regional base of the two parties, this was one of the components of change in 1964.

Because of the continuous relationship of party to liberalism on welfare policy, individuals who were liberal (and districts disproportionately composed of liberal individuals) tended to vote for Democratic Congressmen throughout the period studied. Prior to 1964, however, liberals on the civil rights issue were about as likely to be found in the Republican party as in the Democratic party. Because of the South's strength on the Democratic side of the aisle in the House, there was actually a moderate tendency for districts that were more liberal than average on civil rights to elect Republicans rather than Democrats. But Barry Goldwater's decision to "go hunting where the ducks are" on the civil rights issue changed that. Goldwater's candidacy resulted in GOP gains in previously virginally Democratic Southern territory in 1964. Conversely, most of the Democrats' massive gain in the House seats in 1964 came from the North.

It was this regional variation in the origin of newcomers to the House that produced the pattern displayed in Table 1. Table 2 shows what happens when North and South are examined separately. The Northern Democrats first elected in 1964 were still somewhat more liberal than the old hands in each of the postrealignment sessions, but the differences were very slight. The small group of Northern Republicans were rather inconsistent: they were markedly more conservative in the 1965-1966 session, but were more liberal in the two subsequent sessions. The Southern Republicans elected in 1964 were moderately more conservative than the old hands in all three sessions; the new Southern Democrats showed no consistent pattern. Thus, the contribution of new Congressmen to polarization was not primarily due to a psychological sense of mandate but was rather a result of the regional shift within the two parties: a higher proportion of Democrats came from the North; a higher proportion of Republicans came from the South.

The notion that Congressmen elected in an election marking widespread changes in mass political attitudes will be more psychologically committed to the voters' new conception of party is still an

Table 2. COMPARISON OF MEAN LIBERALISM OF VOTES OF NEW AND OLD CONGRESSMEN
BY REGION AND PARTY ON CIVIL RIGHTS

	'65	'67	'69
North			
Democrats: In the House before 1964	.733 (107)	.767 (87)	.669 (88)
Entered in 1964	.766 (45)	.789 (24)	.718 (25)
Republicans: In the House before 1964	-.517 (93)	-.061 (80)	-.061 (75)
Entered in 1964	-.922 (10)	-.067 (12)	-.248 (10)
South			
Democrats: In the House before 1964	-.450 (77)	-.724 (64)	-.558 (58)
Entered in 1964	-.284 (11)	-.904 (10)	-.610 (11)
Republicans: In the House before 1964	-.911 (13)	-.812 (13)	-.990 (12)
Entered in 1964	-1.149 (7)	-.990 (5)	-1.028 (5)

Table 3. COMPARISON OF MEAN LIBERALISM OF DISTRICTS OF NEW AND OLD
NORTHERN DEMOCRATS AND SOUTHERN REPUBLICANS ON THE
CIVIL RIGHTS ISSUE, 1965

Northern Democrats:

    In the House before 1964   .756 (128)

    Entered in 1964   .462 (49)

Southern Republicans:

    In the house before 1964   -1.332 (13)

    Entered in 1964   -1.694 (9)

appealing one, however.[6] Perhaps we can find some support for it by looking at characteristics of the districts from which the new Congressmen came. While the direct relationship between constituency opinion and Congressman's vote is really a topic for the next section of this essay, assuming some relationship here for control purposes seems reasonable. As Table 3 demonstrates, the new Northern Democrats came from districts that were, on the average substantially more conservative than those of the old hands in their party. The new Southern Republicans also came from districts that were more conservative than those of the old hands in their party. Thus, constituency characteristics pushed the new Northern Democrats in one direction and our hypothesized sense of mandate pushed them in the other direction. For the Southern Republicans, on the other hand, both constituency characteristics and sense of mandate pushed in the same direction. That these characteristics seemed to be operating is demonstrated in Table 4, which shows the simple correlation between being a new Congressman and liberalism and the correlation after controlling for constituency opinion.

Thus, it seems fair to say that an enhanced sense of party differences among Congressmen elected as part of the realignment does contribute to the party polarization resulting from the realignment. It clearly does not produce the polarization; had the Congressmen who left office in 1964 not been replaced, the polarization would have been almost as large as it was. The enhanced

Table 4. CORRELATION BETWEEN LIBERALISM ON CIVIL RIGHTS AND BEING A NEW CONGRESSMAN IN 1964, CONTROLLING FOR CONSTITUENCY OPINION[a]

Northern Democrats

    simple r   .066

    controlled r   .123

Southern Republicans

    simple r   -.247

    controlled r   -.148

a. In all tables and figures, the correlation statistic used is Pearson's r.

sense of the issue-basis of realignment among new members, however, acted to keep constituency characteristics from pulling the polarization below what it would have been had no turnover in membership occurred.

Another way in which turnover in office might produce the polarization is if the members who leave office in the realigning year have vote profiles which would reduce polarization had they remained in office. Thus, if the most liberal Republicans and the most conservative Democrats disproportionately did not return after 1964, polarization would result. In fact, the characteristics of members who left office contributed little to polarization. The Northern Republicans for whom the 1963-1964 session is the last are more liberal on the average than their colleagues, but so are the Northern Democrats who leave. In the South, both Democratic and Republican leavers are more conservative than their colleagues.

The ideological distribution of people who do not return in the session after any given Congress can be quite accidental, of course, partly depending as it does on such nonpolitical vicisitudes of life as death, age, and illness. A more direct look at the effects that come from the electoral system can be gained if we examine the people whose seats were actually lost to the opposition party and those who entered by winning a new seat for their party.

Table 5. COMPARISON OF NEW SEATS TO OLD SEATS, NORTHERN DEMOCRATS
AND SOUTHERN REPUBLICANS, 1964

	Old Seats	New Seats
Northern Democrats:		
Mean Vote in Congress, civil rights	.735 (114)	.766 (38)
Mean Opinion of District, civil rights	.792 (137)	.274 (40)
Southern Republicans:		
Mean Vote in Congress, civil rights	-.938 (15)	-1.162 (5)
Mean Opinion of District, civil rights	-1.395 (15)	-1.662 (7)

Table 5 demonstrates that the pattern that we have noted does not change significantly if we look only at those who came to office by capturing seats previously held by the other party. The new Northern Democrats come from constituencies that are more conservative than those that their colleagues represent, but the Congressmen themselves are somewhat more liberal. The Southern Republicans who captured previously Democratic seats both vote more conservatively than their colleagues and come from somewhat more conservative constituencies.

Examining the group whose seats were lost to their party in 1964, then, does not alter the conclusion that the change in personnel that occurred in 1964, either the one that was electoral in origin or the one that occurred from other sources, did not fully explain the realignment of 1964. It does provide one interesting result, however. The Northern Republicans whose seats were lost in 1964 were an extremely conservative group in both the civil rights and welfare policy areas. Moreover, they came from constituencies that were relatively liberal for their party. Their scores are shown in Table 6 (there were no particularly interesting patterns for the other groups of lost seats). This pattern of extreme conservatism for Republicans who lost their seats in 1964, incidentally, makes the increase in interparty polarization even more striking and suggests the degree to which the Republican party in the House moved to the right after 1964.

Thus far, two sources of the new polarization have been noted.

Table 6. COMPARISON OF MEAN SCORES OF NORTHERN REPUBLICAN CONGRESS-
MEN WHO LOST THEIR SEATS IN 1964 TO THOSE WHO DID NOT,
1962-1963 SESSION

```
Votes in Congress on Civil Rights Issue

        Lost Seats                          .143 ( 43)

        Other Seats                         .443 (114)


District Opinion on Civil Rights Issue

        Lost Seats                          .512 ( 37)

        Other Seats                         .474 (111)
```

The most important source is a change in the regional base of the two parties as a result of the 1964 election. A subsidiary cause is a sense of mandate which seems to be felt especially strongly by new Congressmen. This sense of mandate does not really increase the polarization much, but it does keep the polarization from being reduced, by the fact that the new Democratic Congressmen come from districts that are, on the average, somewhat more conservative than those occupied by other Northern Democrats. Even with these two sources accounted for, however, a major part of the new polarization remains unexplained. Thus, even if attention is restricted to the North alone, the correlation between liberalism of Congressman's vote on civil rights and party goes from an average of only .193 for the 1953-1964 period to .626 for the 1965-1970 period. The mean scores presented in Figure 3 also demonstrate a dramatic new polarization even with region controlled.

What other variables might account for the remaining increase in polarization? Had there been a change in the party holding the Presidency, we might have looked to the influence of the President for an explanation. But no such change occurred. Another related possibility might be to attribute the change to the individual occupying the Presidency. Lyndon Johnson's superior legislative wizardry—so this argument might run—enabled him to make the legislative party more cohesive than John Kennedy could. It was the presidential influence of that particular President that produced the increased party polarization exhibited in 1965-1966. This argument

Table 7. CORRELATION OF LIBERALISM OF CONGRESSMAN'S VOTE WITH PARTY, CONTROLLING FOR PERCENT NONWHITE, NORTH ONLY[a]

	'53	'55	'57	'59	'61	'63	'65	'67	'69
Civil Rights vote with party									
simple r	–	.162	.192	.213	–	.206	.796	.498	.584
controlled r	–	.128	.159	.198	–·	.180	.781	.458	.555

a. Republicans were coded 1 on party, Democrats 3. Hence, a positive correlation means the Democrats are the more liberal party.

founders on several facts. First, both the votes in the 1963-1964 civil rights scale occurred after Johnson took office; yet, polarization in that session was far lower than in 1965-1966. Second, the polarization continued after Richard Nixon's election, when Johnson's influence clearly could not be a factor. Third, if Johnson's influence did make the Democrats more cohesive, it was certainly applied selectively: inspection of the standard deviation of Democratic votes indicates that cohesion in the welfare area was actually lower in 1965-1966 than in 1963-1964, although it did increase somewhat in the civil rights area.

Still another possibility is that the new polarization was a result of constituency pressure from a newly cohesive black population. Since blacks are disproportionately located in Democratic districts, this would have the effect of increasing party polarization. This hypothesis, too, seems invalid. Controlling for the size of the nonwhite population in congressional districts has little effect on the amount of party polarization that occurred, as Table 7 demonstrates.

A final way of accounting for the remaining variance in party polarization in the legislature would be to hypothesize that it is the result of growing within-party responsiveness to constituency opinion. The next section of the paper demonstrates that there is an increase in within-party responsiveness beginning in the 1965-1966 session of Congress. Since Democratic districts in the North have consistently tended to be somewhat more liberal than Republican districts, part of the polarization may be due to increased within-party responsiveness. Table 8 demonstrates that this hypothesis, while plausible, does not account for much of the new polarization.

The party polarization in the legislature that occurred in 1964 parallel to the shift in mass political attitudes, then, had at least three components. First, there was a regional shift growing out of the new

Table 8. CORRELATION BETWEEN LIBERALISM OF CIVIL RIGHTS VOTES CAST IN
CONGRESS AND PARTY, CONTROLLING FOR DISTRICT OPINION,
NORTH ONLY

	'53	'55	'57	'59	'61	'63	'65	'67	'69
simple r	–	.162	.192	.213	–	.206	.796	.498	.584
controlling opinion	–	.126	.155	.207	–	.172	.774	.482	.504

identification of the Democrats as the liberal party on civil rights.
Thus, the proportion of Democratic Congressmen coming from the
North was increased as was the proportion of Republican Congress-
men coming from the South.

Second, there was a very minor component of the shift that seems
to have been associated with a sense of psychological mandate felt
disproportionately by new Congressmen. This sense of mandate was
exhibited in the behavior of new Congressmen from both parties in
1965-1966, but seems to have been largely washed out for members
of the minority party by 1969-1970.

The remainder of the new polarization came from a source that
cannot be accounted for as readily. A variety of testable hypotheses
have made little contribution to explaining it. The most appropriate
explanation—although it is one that arises by default—is a sense of
party mandate experienced by most Congressmen. The images of
their parties enunciated in the presidential campaign seem to have
affected Congressmen just as they affected voters—by producing
greater polarization on the lines of the issues presented as party
differentiating during the campaigns.

III. PARTY POLARIZATION AND REPRESENTATION

I suggested earlier in the paper that a parallelism of this type
between divisions by party on legislative votes and divisions by party
in mass opinions might be the only way in which representation of
opinion could occur. My argument was that survey research shows
that the electorate has very little knowledge about the stands taken
by congressional candidates and even less about their actual
behavior: the most significant factor structuring the vote in elections
at this level is party identification. Elections, therefore, provide
Congressmen with little motivation to cause their legislative votes to

conform to public opinion in their districts on most issues and, in the absence of an association between party and opinion, give voters little opportunity to turn out Congressmen with whom they disagree. Thus, it seems reasonable to believe that representation of opinion will occur only when parties coincide with divisions of opinion in the electorate and when these divisions are mirrored by the lineup of parties on votes in Congress. It has just been demonstrated that both these conditions were met for the first time on the civil rights issue after the 1964 election. Did the association between district opinion and Congressman's vote increase as a result?

At first glance, the evidence for the hypothesis that representation is dependent on party parallelism is quite discouraging. If the hypothesis were correct, one would expect that there would be representation of opinion in the welfare policy issue area all during the period in question. Representation of opinion in the civil rights issue area should begin only in 1965, however. Figure 4 demonstrates a different pattern. There is representation of opinion in both issue areas throughout the period in question. Moreover, representation of opinion is consistently higher in the civil rights area—where there was no polarization prior to 1965—than it is in the welfare area. Finally, representation of opinion in the civil rights area actually drops in 1964 and remains consistently lower after this election than it was prior to the election.

A closer inspection indicates that these results are not as devastating to the preliminary hypothesis as they look at first, although they do lead to its modification. The apparently close fit between constituency opinion and representative's views on civil rights is largely a product of the Civil War. Examining the North and South separately leads to the results shown in Table 9. The correlation between opinions of constituency and vote of representative in the welfare policy area remains quite robust, particularly in the North, where the two-party system is most effective. In the civil rights area, however, the correlation drops to a very low level—until 1965.

The fact that the hypothesis works regionally suggests that it is not totally without merit. The fact that it does not work nationally—at least for civil rights—suggests that it needs modification. Table 9 essentially indicates that the relatively close fit between representative's votes and constituency opinion in the civil rights area prior to 1965 was almost entirely due to the fact that Southerners were much more conservative than Northerners and that

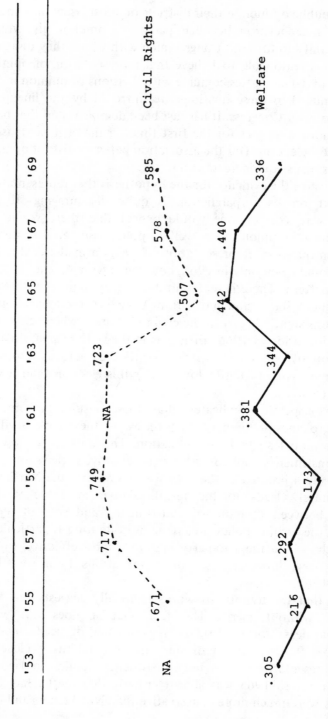

Figure 4: OPINION REPRESENTATION OVER TIME (WHOLE SAMPLE): CORRELATION BETWEEN VOTE OF CONGRESSMAN AND DISTRICT OPINION

Table 9. CORRELATION BETWEEN DISTRICT OPINION AND CONGRESSMAN'S VOTE, BY REGIONS

	'53	'55	'57	'59	'61	'63	'65	'67	'69
North									
welfare policy	.431	.391	.477	.286	.456	.395	.455	.495	.458
civil rights	–	.113	.135	.052	–	.135	.384	.207	.376
South									
welfare policy	.285	.279	.187	-.023	.212	.259	.473	.279	.100
civil rights	–	.052	.047	.162	–	.092	.190	.279	.394

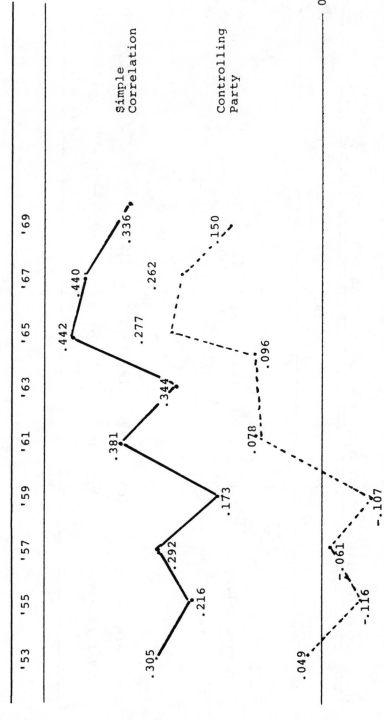

Figure 5: CORRELATION BETWEEN CONGRESSMAN'S VOTE AND DISTRICT OPINION IN THE WELFARE AREA, CONTROLLING FOR PARTY

their representatives voted much more conservatively. Votes in Congress, prior to 1965, reflect within-region variations in opinion scarcely at all. The modification in the hypothesis that seems most appropriate would be that issue-oriented parties are necessary to representation except where an issue is highly salient and consensual. In this latter case, opinions of constituents will be represented anyway, although any variation in the degree of consensus will not be picked up well in representatives' votes.

The fact that, with region controlled, there is a temporal connection between representation and changes in mass attitudes by party does not prove that party is the key link in the representative chain. The importance of party can be established more directly by examining what happens to representation when effect of party is removed. Figure 5 shows the correlation between district opinion and Congressman's vote in the welfare area first as a simple 0-order correlation and second after the effect of the party is removed from the relationship. Clearly, the relationship is almost entirely dependent on party until 1965, and even after 1965 the major part of the relationship is explained by the influence of party.

Figure 6 shows a similar approach to explaining representation on civil rights. In line with the modification in the hypothesis introduced above, the effect of party is removed only after the impact of region is controlled. This procedure demonstrates how much of the relationship is explained by party after the effect of the South's regional consensus is removed. In line with expectations, party explains none of the relationship until 1965, when its contribution becomes substantial.

IV. PARTY STRUCTURE AND REPRESENTATION

As Figures 5 and 6 indicate, there is some representation of opinion occurring (at least after 1965) that cannot be accounted for either by regional consensus or by the tendency of liberal districts to elect liberally voting Democrats and conservative districts to elect conservatively voting Republicans. The most obvious and time-honored way of accounting for this remaining segment of representation would simply be to assert, as generations of scholars have, that Congressmen vote both their party and their district. For a Congressman to vote his district is, in this formulation, essentially representation without parties. In point of fact, however, this

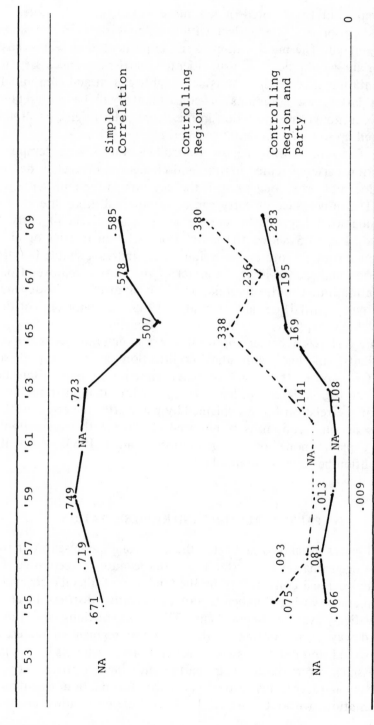

Figure 6: CORRELATION OF DISTRICT OPINION WITH CONGRESSMAN'S VOTE IN THE CIVIL RIGHTS AREA, CONTROLLING REGION AND PARTY

element of representation, too, may be a result of parties. Table 10 indicates the degree of within-party district representation exhibited by the three most important congressional groups—Northern Democrats, Northern Republicans, and Southern Democrats.

As Table 10 shows, the degree of within-party representativeness among the three groups is quite different. Specifically, until 1965, the Northern Democrats exhibited no relationship at all between the opinions of their constituencies and their votes in Congress. Indeed, the correlation was actually negative more often than not. After 1965, there is some relationship between constituency opinion and representative's vote, but it is not a very robust one. Both Southern Democrats and Northern Republicans, on the other hand, do exhibit fairly consistent positive correlations between their votes and opinion of their constituencies.[7] How might these intergroup differences be explained? Clearly, the fact that there is little or no within-party representation of constituency opinion among Northern Democrats indicates that the within-party representation that we do find is not simply a matter of Congressmen voting their constituencies.

One possible way of explaining at least the difference between Northern Democrats and Northern Republicans is to look at the differences in party organizational characteristics prevalent among these groups during the period under study. Research has indicated that the Republicans during this period, unlike the Democrats, were a high participation party relying on a corps of disproportionately conservative activists (Nexon, 1971; McCloskey et al., 1960; Verba and Nie, 1972; Nie et al., 1976).

How would this ideological, participant style of party organization lead to the results demonstrated in Table 10? The answer is that activist Republicans in each congressional district would exert continual pressure on their representative to respond to the views of at least the activist segment of the party. Unlike the ordinary citizen, a party activist—particularly one who becomes active in party affairs out of ideological motives—is likely to be fairly attentive to a Congressman's behavior in the Congress and engage in the kind of interactions with the Congressman that will make him aware of the feelings of at least the activist segment of the folks at home. Moreover, with a fairly large proportion of party identifiers active in party affairs, the man who is initially selected to carry the party banner in the congressional campaign is more likely to be ideologically representative of the activists than is a man who secures the

Table 10. WITHIN-PARTY RESPONSIVENESS: CORRELATION OF VOTE AND DISTRICT OPINION

Welfare Policy	Average	'53	'55	'57	'59	'61	'63	'65	'67	'69
Northern Republicans	.254	.164	.128	.192	.195	.319	.268	.392	.301	.331
Southern Democrats	.134	.217	.238	.060	-.158	.116	.172	.395	.158	.010
Northern Democrats	.072	.158	-.084	-.123	-.041	-.041	.151	.207	.248	.172
Civil Rights										
Northern Republicans	.225	–	.145	.201	.111	–	.162	.480	.132	.341
Southern Democrats	.245	–	.155	.160	.250	–	.081	.304	.335	.427
Northern Democrats	.094	–	.006	.004	-.068	–	.073	.317	.145	.195

nomination in a selection process where only a few people are involved. The Democratic Congressmen, on the other hand, are far less likely to be in contact with an attentive party elite.[8]

While this analysis seems reasonable, it is very difficult to test. No direct measure of party activism is available for congressional districts. Several variables that were thought to be possible surrogates for party activism were tried, but without success. Since their relationship to party activism was problematic to begin with, their failure to substantiate the hypothesis was not regarded as crushing. Still, it must be recognized that the inference that the highly participant structure of the Republican party causes the higher within-party responsiveness of Republican Congressmen to their districts cannot be definitely proven from the data presented in this paper.[9]

One competing hypothesis, however, could be disproven. It is well known that Republicans tend to come from districts of higher social status. It is also well known that people of higher social status are more active and knowledgeable politically. It may be, then, that Republicans are more in touch with their districts not because they receive lots of communications from activist elements in their highly participant parties but because they simply come from the kinds of districts where ordinary citizens tend to stay in touch with their Congressman. An examination of the data indicates that this is not the case. When districts were divided into thirds in terms of their socioeconomic status and the correlation between legislators' votes and constituency opinion within these socioeconomic groups was examined, there was no consistent tendency for the correlation to be larger in the higher socioeconomic groups of districts.

A hypothesis has now been presented to account for the surprising finding that Northern Republican Congressmen alter their voting in accord with the relative liberalism of their constituencies, while, for most of the period studied, relative constituency liberalism made not the slightest difference in the voting behavior of Northern Democratic Congressmen.

How about Southern Democrats? Primaries against incumbents are a far more frequent feature of Southern politics than Northern politics: indeed, there is no other way of taking office away from an incumbent in a one-party situation. While V.O. Key, Jr. (1949), among others, has argued that the Democratic primary is no true substitute for two-party politics, it may be that its widespread prevalence does promote more intraparty representativeness in the

Table 11. FREQUENCY OF PRIMARIES AGAINST INCUMBENTS AND PERCENT OF THE VOTE RECEIVED BY INCUMBENTS IN PRIMARIES, BY REGION AND PARTY

	'53	'55	'57	'59	'61	'63	'65	'67	'69
Average Number of primaries per election[a]									
Southern Democrats	.353	.409	.425	.411	.394	.392	.364	.380	.344
Northern Democrats	.293	.355	.355	.327	.323	.322	.274	.309	.314
Northern Republicans	.214	.256	.154	.213	.197	.138	.108	.094	.091
Average per cent of the vote received by incumbents when primaries occur[a]									
Southern Democrats	.677	.680	.691	.699	.705	.712	.704	.721	.726
Northern Democrats	.690	.703	.706	.727	.731	.744	.754	.756	.757
Northern Republicans	.715	.718	.724	.736	.753	.761	.789	.779	.787

a. These figures are based on primaries occurring from 1956 on and they represent averages for the incumbent's whole time in the House (after '56), not the average for the particular year.

South—even though the total amount of representativeness achieved may be inferior.

It is unquestionably true that there are more primaries in the South than in the North and that, on the average, incumbents do not do as well as they do in the North. Table 11 shows the average number of times per election that incumbents had to face primary opposition in the three party groups and the average percent of the vote that they got on the occasions that they were challenged.

The contrast is even more dramatic if we look at the number of incumbents defeated in primaries. During the period from 1954 to 1968, 24 Southern Democrats were defeated in primaries, as compared with 11 Northern Democrats and 5 Northern Republicans. This numerical discrepancy exists in spite of the fact that there were more Northern Republicans in the House than Southern Democrats in every year of the series and more Northern Democrats in every year after the 1958 elections.

It is clear, then, that the primary is alive and well in Southern Democratic districts. Fear of the primary may cause Southern Democrats to modify their stands to fit their districts more than Northern Democrats do, even if, as V.O. Key contended, there is a persistently conservative tilt to the positions taken. If this fear does exist and does explain the greater within-party representativeness of Southern Democrats, does it have any basis in reality? Do the exceptionally discrepant Congressmen really get punished? The answer is a qualified "yes."

If we use a discrepancy variable created by standardizing the representative's voting scale score and measuring the difference between that score and the district's opinion score, we can seek to answer this question. Table 12 shows that those who are defeated in primaries are consistently more distant from their district than those who are not, at least in the welfare area. The fact that the civil rights issue area behaves differently is probably a result of the fact that in districts where civil rights is likely to be an issue, gradations of opinion are likely to be masked by the extremely negative nature of opinions. Thus, civil rights as an issue in campaigns is likely to revolve around things less tangible than the Congressman's voting record. It seems reasonable to believe, then, that the Southern primary does indeed provide an explanation for the greater tendency of Southern Democratic Congressmen to vary their voting behavior with their district's opinion preferences.

Table 12. MEAN DISCREPANCY OF THOSE DEFEATED IN PRIMARIES DURING PERIOD STUDIED COMPARED TO THOSE NOT DEFEATED, SOUTHERN DEMOCRATS ONLY

	'53	'55	'57	'59	'61	'63	'65	'67	'69
Welfare Policy[a]									
1) Defeated	1.008(12)	1.33(13)	1.25(7)	1.52(8)	.982(8)	1.216(3)	1.898(2)	.406(1)	–
2) Not defeated	1.082	1.16	1.09	1.08	.939	.928	.881	.940	–
Civil Rights[a]									
1) Defeated	–	.375(13)	.474(11)	.410(10)	–	.225(7)	.413(2)	–	–
2) Not defeated	–	.529	.554	.610	–	.526	.909	–	–

a. Figures are for all Congressmen in the House in the specified year *ultimately* defeated in a primary, not just for those defeated in the specified year.

V. DIRECT REPRESENTATION

There is still a correlation between district opinion and vote of the representative that has not been explained: the relationship that occurs among Northern Democrats after the 1964 election. There is no evidence that the Democratic party took on the high-partici-pation, ideological, Republican-style structure at this point in time (although I think that did occur by 1972).[10] Moreover, although the rise is not fully uniform within all groups on both scales, there does seem to be a general tendency for within-party responsiveness to leap upward in all regional party groups about this time. This may truly be some evidence of representation without parties. I can think of two possible explanations for this phenomenon, neither of which can be definitively established or refuted with the data at hand. First, several studies have established that there was a marked increase in political interest and ideological thinking, though not in partisan activity, around this time (Nie, 1974; Bennet, 1973). This change may have produced more contacts between representative and represented and have given the representative a greater sense of being watched by his constituents. The effect of these two phenomena would, if the argument earlier in this section is valid, cause Congressmen as a group to have a relationship with their general constituency more like that typical of Republican Congressmen's relationship with party activists.

A second possibility is that this rise in representation without parties was a result of the new campaign techniques that were coming into wider vogue during this period.[11] The most important feature of the new technique is the use of polls to find out the policy preferences and interests of segments of the electorate and then the sending out of messages by the candidate that speak to segments of the electorate individually rather than to the electorate as a whole. The result of such techniques, if funded adequately and used by both candidates, is that each member of the electorate has a far better perception of the views of the candidates on issues of concern to each particular voter. This growth in information may make it less necessary for voters to rely on parties in making election choices and it may also make the representative more cognizant and careful of the views of his constituency before he casts his vote. Either effect could produce an increase in nonparty forms of representation.

Whatever the explanation of this phenomenon, we have now identified four sources of opinion representation by legislators: (1)

representation by party selection on the part of the voters (the portion of representation created by associations between opinion and party at the mass level and paralleled by party voting in the legislature), (2) representation through party structures (a highly participant, ideologically organized party in the case of the Republicans, a tradition of primaries in the case of the Southern Democrats), (3) representation through a salient consensus (the representation of Southern views on civil rights issues), and (4) at least a trace of representation without parties after 1964.

VI. SUMMARY AND CONCLUSION

The doctrine of responsible party government asserts that political parties at their mass base should consist of a group of like-minded men on major public issues, that parties in the legislature should vote cohesively and consistently in support of the views of their partisans in the electorate, and that party organizations should be democratically governed and operated by a broad group of ideologically motivated activists. Partisans of responsible party government have always contended that one of the primary virtues of this form of governmental organization would be the promotion of representation. The analysis presented in this paper demonstrates that two of the major sources of representation present in the United States from 1952 to 1970 were conditions roughly approximating the model of responsible party government—a parallelism between ideological divisions in the mass parties and legislative parties and a democratic, participant, ideological party structure.

The changes occurring during the period also make it possible to infer the causal factors producing at least the first two characteristics of responsible party government. The separation of party adherents into groups of like-minded men seems to arise from electoral campaigns in which the parties take clear and sharply opposed stands on salient issues. The parties took exactly this kind of stand in 1964 during the Goldwater-Johnson contest. By this action, they seem to have created a division between adherents of the two parties on civil rights issues and deepened the previously existing division on welfare issues. The latter division probably arose from the New Deal elections when similarly clear divisions between the parties were presented to the electorate on welfare policy. In general, this kind of clash of issues seems to be characteristic of realigning elections and, according to one theory, typically has this sort of impact on the mass of party identifiers (Sundquist, 1973).

When ordinary adherents of the two parties divide on the issues as the result of an electoral campaign that clearly indicates differences between party programs on salient issues, the legislative party also divides in a similar way. The principle mechanisms operating in 1964 to polarize the legislative party along the lines of the mass public were three. The first was the new tendency of more liberal districts on civil rights to elect Democrats; this tendency was represented by the change in the regional base of the two parties and, given the importance of party identification for voting decisions in congressional elections, was a logical outgrowth of the shift in the correlates of party identification in the mass public. The second mechanism was a mild tendency (with region and constituency opinion controlled) for newly elected legislators to be more extreme in their votes than other members of their party. This was interpreted as a more sharply felt sense of mandate by new Congressmen. The third mechanism could not be explained as readily as the first two, but was speculatively identified with a general sense of party mandate felt by Congressmen. The generality of these mechanisms are suggested by other studies of realigning elections which have found that they are consistently associated with greater legislative polarization on the issues associated with the election campaigns (Nexon, 1976) and that the three mechanisms noted above seem to explain much of the polarization (Brady, 1975).

While the approximation of responsible party government revealed in this data creates representation at least on the issues that are the focus of interparty polarization, it is not the only source of representation. A salient consensus, such as the South's hostility to civil rights assures some representation of opinion. Moreover, after 1965, there is at least a trace of representation unrelated to party polarization, party structure, or a salient consensus. Given the conventional wisdom that representatives vote both their party and their district, however, the weakness of this mode of representation is striking.

The fact that the picture of representation presented here is valid for 1952-1970 does not, of course, mean that it will always be valid. The recent transformation of the Democratic party into something approximating the highly participant, ideological, Republican model will presumably increase the amount of representation received by districts electing Northern Democrats (Nie et al., 1976). Recent moves toward public financing of elections may increase candidates' ability to utilize the new campaign techniques and thus increase the importance of representation occurring independent of issue polarization of parties and party structures. The data provided in this paper, however, provides a baseline for measuring future changes in representation and a causal model that should contribute to our assessment of the likely impact on representation of reforms in the political process.

APPENDIX

A key question in evaluating the research reported in the second half of this paper—the section describing the relationships between constituency opinion and representative's vote—is the accuracy of the estimates of mean constituency opinion derived from the regression procedure. (The description of changes in the national electorate and of the relationship of party to votes in the U.S. House of Representatives is, of course, unrelated to the validity of these estimates.) If one does not put much weight on exact numerical interpretations of the estimates and focuses instead on rough orders of magnitude and comparisons between groups, the estimates of constituency opinion do not have to be fully accurate for the findings to be valuable and valid; the estimates must, however, have at least a moderate relationship to the true values for the districts. What evidence is there that such a moderate relationship exists?

Conceptually, the problem is really the so-called "ecological fallacy" in reverse (Robinson, 1950). In the ecological fallacy, the investigator attempts to infer causal models of individual behavior from aggregate data: for example, he may wish to infer the characteristics of the voting behavior of American blacks by looking at the correlation between percent black in each county and vote for President. In the case of this article, the procedure is reversed: I have tried to estimate the opinion characteristics of ecological units —congressional districts—from the characteristics of the individuals making up the units. The potential sources for error are virtually identical in either method.

What are these possible sources of error? A recent article makes a persuasive argument that the debilitating effects for theory of the ecological fallacy are often overstated (Hanushek, 1974). The essence of the argument is that the sources of error in going from the behavior of groups (aggregate data) to the behavior of individuals (and, by implication, vice versa) are identical to the sources of error in inferring the causes of the behavior of individuals from individual-level data: the principal source in both cases is inadequate model specification. Specifically, if one wishes to explain the voting behavior of blacks, for example, from a limited number of predictor variables, one will draw erroneous conclusions about the impact of ·the predictor variables if there are major variables outside the model (contained in the residual) that are correlated with the variables in the model. The problem is particularly acute if the variables outside the model are inversely correlated with the variables in the model: in such a case one risks not merely misjudging the size of the impact of variables in the model but the actual direction of causality.

Since one can never know for sure that he has included all the relevant variables in his model, how can one be sure that the ecological fallacy has been avoided or minimized? One easy way is if the variables in the model account for a very high proportion of the variance in the dependent variable. If there is no residual to speak of, a correlation between the residual and variables in the model can hardly be distorting the results. Unfortunately, social science models are rarely this accurate, and the estimating equations used in this article are no exception: variance explained in opinion at the individual level by the variables available at the congressional district level typically hovers around 25%.

Since the amount of variance explained by the estimating equations used in the article offers no quick and easy validation of the method, two other types of evidence were relied on. The first type of evidence is other studies that have used a similar set of predictor variables and have come up with what the authors consider satisfactory levels of validation; the second is a direct comparison of the estimates derived from my method to those used in the one other study that has attempted a direct estimate of district opinion (Miller and Stokes, 1963). Neither type of evidence offers unambiguous support for the method, but the results are positive enough to support the limited scope of interpretation suggested above.

There are three major studies that have attempted to estimate either opinion or variables similar to opinion for ecological units from poll data for general populations. The first was the Pool et al. (1965) simulation of the 1960 and 1964 presidential elections. The authors divided the national survey population into 480 "voter types" based on a cross-tabulation of a limited number of variables thought to be important in opinion and vote determination. Their variables were quite similar to the ones used in my estimation equation and included socioeconomic status, region, size of place, religion, race, and sex. These variables were related to attitudes drawn from a large variety of polls. Opinions and vote in each state were assumed to be determined entirely by the composition of voter types in each state: that is, it was assumed that unspecified variables and local factors introduced only minimal inaccuracies into the model. By making some limited assumptions about the impact of certain types of opinion on the vote, the authors were able to produce a correlation of .82 between the actual state-by-state vote for John Kennedy and their predicted vote. This is an especially impressive correlation because there were two potential sources of inaccuracy—the assumptions about the impact of opinion and the "ecological fallacy." In 1964, the authors were able to achieve a correlation of .90.

The "population type" method of estimation is not identical to the regression equations used in my procedure, although there is little conceptual difference. The advantage that the population type model has is that any curvilinearities in relationship will be picked up in the estimates; regression weights, which are averages across the whole population, will not reflect such curvilinearities. The disadvantage of the population type model is that the likelihood of mistakes in estimate for particular voter types due to sampling error is fairly high because of the large number of cells into which the population must be divided. In general, the methods should not yield markedly different levels of accuracy, and a satisfactory level of result for one should be evidence for a satisfactory level of result for the other.

The second study was an attempt to estimate opinion at the state level from national opinion polls (Weber et al., 1973). The variables used in the estimation procedure were quite similar to mine and to the Pool et al. (1965) study. Like the earlier study, state populations were constructed from a cross-tabulation "population type" procedure rather than from regression weights. As in the earlier study, the authors did not test their estimates of state-by-state opinion against an independent measure of opinion. Rather, they used the procedure to estimate two other variables independently available —vote for President and mean years of school completed. They were able to explain about 50% of the variance in their dependent variables, a level they felt was satisfactory enough to give them confidence in their state-by-state estimates of opinion. A number of articles have since been published using these state-by-state estimates of opinion as causal variables.

A final study used Texas polls to estimate intrastate variance in opinion toward school integration (Pettigrew, 1970). Only three predictor variables were used (one of which was similar to variables used in my study), but, unlike the other two studies, a direct comparison was made to poll data. The comparison indicated that statewide data could be used very effectively to predict intrastate variance of opinion (r of .92).

These three studies, in spite of their fairly good level of prediction, are obviously not conclusive proof of the validity of the method used in this article. Two of the studies did not test their predictions against opinion directly (although one would think that vote for President would be subject to many of the same sources of variation as opinion). None of the studies used exactly the same predictor variables that were used in my estimation equations. Moreover, the opinions that the other studies sought to estimate were not identical to those used in my study and the time frame was not exactly the same. On the other hand, one cannot but be encouraged by the fact that all three studies found satisfactory levels of validation for their estimation procedure in spite of the fact that all three made the basic assumption present in my estimation procedure: there are no unspecified variables in the residual of the estimation equation that are correlated with the specified variables in such a major and perverse way as to drastically mistake the character of opinion in small geographic units.

A direct comparison to an estimation of opinion for congressional districts by a sample survey method is also moderately encouraging for the validity of my estimation procedure. In the Miller and Stokes study (1963) previously cited in this article, a sample of 116 congressional districts was employed and interviews from a national sample that fell in those districts were used to estimate mean opinion for each district. This sample survey method, too, had serious problems—the very small numbers of interviews for each district and the fact that the sampling framework was not designed in such a way that the interviews taken were a probability sample of each district. Nonetheless, correspondence between the estimates developed by Miller and Stokes and the estimates developed by my regression method were reasonably good. Using the estimates of opinion kindly supplied by Miller and Stokes for civil rights attitudes in 1960 as the test variable, the Pearson product-moment correlation between the two estimates for the 79 districts that were not missing in either estimation procedure was .47. While a higher correlation would, of course, have been even more encouraging, .47 is a respectable level of correlation, particularly given the nonparametric nature of the opinion scales employed and the likelihood of very marginal real differences in opinion between many districts.

An interesting result of the two estimating procedures is that the levels of gross correlation reported between Congressmen's vote and constituency opinion for the two issue domains considered in both articles (civil rights and welfare policy) are about the same for each estimation procedure. This correspondence suggests that, to the degree the two procedures misestimate true district opinion, they do so to about the same degree.

In evaluating the findings of this paper, the conclusions must be balanced against the previous state of knowledge. Conclusions based on imperfect data are better than conclusions based on no data at all. While the results reported here must remain tentative and subject to disproof by better estimating procedures, unless and until such procedures are developed and actually disprove these findings, the data reported here must be considered the best current level of knowledge of the phenomena studied.

NOTES

1. Exact question-wording in the scales varied somewhat from year to year and may be found in the SRC codebooks. Not all questions were available in all years; in these cases questions from the group that were present were used to make up the scales. Using Pearson's r as the correlation statistic, items on the welfare scale intercorrelated at levels ranging from .29 to .47, with an average intercorrelation of .38. Items on the civil rights scale intercorrelated at levels ranging from .33 to .51 with an average intercorrelation of .44. Respondents were scored as missing on the scale if they failed to answer enough questions. The standard of enough questions varied from year to year and was set up to require as many answers as possible without excluding more than one quarter of the respondents. Characteristics of the z score are such that the mean for respondents on each scale approximated 0 and the standard deviation approximated 1.

2. For purposes of score assignment, a Congressman's announcement of a position on the *Congressional Quarterly* questionnaire was treated as a vote, as was a pair. For the 15 dissenting votes criterion, however, only actual votes were used. The necessity of distinguishing partisanship from ideology is emphasized in MacRae (1970). Congressmen were assigned missing scores on the same basis that was used for the opinion items.

3. The necessity for manipulation arose from the fact that some of the variables were categorical at the individual level (Catholic or not Catholic) but expressed as percentages at the district level. The procedure used is described in Melichar (1965).

4. One additional alteration was made in the data before estimates of mean opinion were carried out. It seemed unreasonable to include blacks as part of the constituency in areas where they were prevented from voting. Accordingly, for the Southern states, percent nonwhite was multiplied by the ratio of percent blacks registered to percent whites registered in the relevant year for the state in which the district was located, and the result was used in estimating constituency opinion.

5. Miller and Stokes found name recognition also affects the vote, but it does so in a way unrelated to issues.

6. Using a selection of "key votes" and looking at switched seats only, a recent article found new Congressmen to be more loyal to party than other Congressmen after both the 1964 and the 1896 elections (Brady and Lynn, 1973). An additional article reports similar findings for 1932 (Brady, 1975).

7. It is striking that an independent investigation of roll call voting in the Senate finds this same pattern in these three groups (Jackson, 1974).

8. At least inferential evidence in support of this contention is provided by a study of congressional challengers in the 1964 election. Republicans were far more likely to have been recruited into candidacy by local party leaders than were Democrats (Fishel, 1973).

9. The variables that were used as surrogates were primaries against Congressmen unrepresentative of their districts and turnout.

10. Evidence to this effect is provided by Nie et al. (1976).

11. The literature on the new technology is a growing but still inadequate one. The best single book is a reader edited by Agranoff (1972); also excellent is DeVries and Tarrance (1972). Other works of interest include Maisel (1976), Nimmo (1970), and Napolitan (1972).

REFERENCES

AGRANOFF, R. (1972). The new style in election campaigns. Boston: Holbrook.

ARSENEAU, R., and WOLFINGER, R. (1973). "Voting behavior in congressional elections." Paper presented at the annual meeting of the Political Science Association.

BENNETT, S. (1973). "Consistency among the public's social welfare policy attitudes in the 1960's." American Journal of Political Science, 17(August):544-570.

BRADY, D. (1975). "Critical elections, congressional parties and clusters of policy changes: A comparison of the 1896 and 1932 realignment eras." Paper presented at the convention of the American Political Science Association, September.

BRADY, D., and LYNN, N. (1973). "Switched seat congressional districts: Their effect on party voting and public policy." American Journal of Political Science, 17(August): 528-543.

DeVRIES, W., and TARRANCE, V.L. (1972). The ticket-splitter. Grand Rapids, Mich.: William B. Eerdmans.

FISHEL, J. (1973). Party and opposition. New York: David McKay.

HANUSHEK, E. (1974). "Model specification, use of aggregate data, and the ecological correlation fallacy." Political Methodology, Winter.

JACKSON, J. (1974). Constituencies and leaders in Congress. Cambridge, Mass.: Harvard University Press.

KEY, V.O. (1949). Southern politics in state and nation. New York: Alfred A. Knopf.

MacRAE, D. (1970). Issues and parties in legislative voting. New York: Harper and Row.

MAISEL, L. (ed., 1976). Changing campaign techniques: Elections and values in contemporary democracies (Sage electoral studies yearbook, vol. 2). Beverly Hills, Calif.: Sage.

McCLOSKY, H., HOFFMAN, P., and O'HARA, R. (1960). "Issue conflict and consensus among party leaders and followers." American Political Science Review, 54(June): 406-427.

MELICHAR, E. (1965). "Least squares analysis of economic survey data." Proceedings of the American Statistical Association 60:373-385.

MILLER, W., and STOKES, D. (1962). "Party government and the saliency of Congress." Public Opinion Quarterly, 26(Winter):531-546.

——— (1963). "Constituency influence in Congress." American Political Science Review, 57(March):45-66.

NAPOLITAN, J. (1972). The election game and how to win it. Garden City, N.Y.: Doubleday.

NEXON, D. (1971). "Asymmetry in the political system: Occasional activists in the Republican and Democratic parties, 1956-1964." American Political Science Review, 65(September):716-730.

——— (1976). "The impact of realigning elections on congressional voting." Paper presented at the annual meeting of the Southwestern Political Science Association, April.

NIE, N. (1974). "Mass belief systems revisited: Political change and attitude structure." Journal of Politics, 36(September):541-591.

NIE, N., VERBA, S., and PETROCIK, J. (1976). The changing American voter. Cambridge, Mass.: Harvard University Press.

NIMMO, D. (1970). The political persuaders. Englewood Cliffs, N.J.: Prentice-Hall.

PITKIN, H. (1967). The concept of representation. Berkeley: University of California Press.

PETTIGREW, T. (1970). "A study of social integration" (Microfilm ED 044468). Cambridge, Mass.: Eric.

POMPER, G. (1972). "From confusion to clarity: Issues and American voters, 1956-1968." American Political Science Review, (June):415-428.

POOL, I., ABELSON, R., and POPKIN, S. (1965). Candidates, issues and strategies. Cambridge, Mass.: Massachusetts Institute of Technology Press.

RANNEY, A. (1954). The doctrine of responsible party government. Urbana: University of Illinois Press.

ROBINSON, W. (1950). "Ecological correlation and the behavior of individuals." American Sociological Review, 15(June):351-357.

SUNDQUIST, J. (1973). Dynamics of the party system. Washington, D.C.: Brookings Institution.

VERBA, S., and NIE, N. (1972). Participation in America. New York: Harper and Row.

WEBER, R., HOPKINS, A., MEZEY, M., and MUNGER, F. (1973). "Computer simulation of state electorates." Public Opinion Quarterly, 36(Winter):549-565.

Chapter 6

THE MEDIA AND THE PRESIDENTIAL SELECTION PROCESS

HERBERT B. ASHER

I. INTRODUCTION

The institutional context within which political behavior occurs has once again become the focus of much social science investigation. Unlike earlier institutional analyses which often emphasized formal governmental structures and statutes, attention has currently turned to nongovernmental features of the institutional environment, foremost among these being the mass media. Investigators have come to recognize the relevance of the media, especially television, to many of the central political concerns confronting social scientists. For example, in the area of political socialization, more and more questions are being raised about the effects of television on a generation of children who experienced the violence of Vietnam (not to mention standard television fare) and the scandals of the Nixon administration almost directly (Kraus, 1973; Comstock et al., 1972). Likewise, analyses of the sources of the political agenda have increasingly stressed the role of the media in identifying and publicizing issues and structuring the alternatives (Weaver et al., 1975; McCombs and Shaw, 1972, 1976; Funkhouser, 1973; Shafer and Larson, 1972; McClure and Patterson, 1976; Robinson and Zukin, 1976). Finally, the increased levels of cynicism and distrust in the United States have in part been attributed to the media, particularly television, which have made graphic the shortcomings of political leaders and institutions (Wamsley and Pride, 1972; Robinson, 1976).

The list of areas in which media effects appear pronounced can be expanded greatly. I propose in this paper to focus on one specific class of consequences: the effects of the media, especially television and newspapers, on the presidential selection process. Presidential selection is viewed herein as a three-step process consisting of the primary season, the national nominating conventions, and the general election campaign. The greatest attention will be given to the preconvention period, for it is here that the media's impact is most substantial for reasons to be detailed later. In fact, one argument to be made in this paper is that, in covering the primaries, the media are not neutral but actually affect the outcome of the process. This intrusiveness of the media is not attributed to any systematic bias or conspiracy on the part of reporters and television commentators, but instead reflects structural aspects of the news reporting enterprise as well as ambiguities and complexities inherent in the primary season. The strongest charge leveled herein against the media is an occasional lapse into incompetence, but, as the examples to be presented suggest, these lapses do not represent any deliberate partisan or incumbent bias.

I am emphasizing primary elections as opposed to district and state caucuses and conventions in the first stage of the selection process because they seem to be the major site of political activity, as evidenced by the proliferation of presidential primaries in 1976 which selected about three-fourths of the delegates to the nominating conventions. Television and newspapers are stressed over radio and magazines, since numerous surveys have indicated that the former media are more often relied upon for political and campaign (especially general election) information (Asher, 1976:222-227).

My emphasis on the preconvention period should not be construed as indicating that we know all or most of what we should know about the impact of the media in the latter two stages of the presidential selection process. In fact, there is reason to believe that much of our now classical lore about the weak effects of the media during the general election campaign is in need of substantial revision, a point developed later. Nevertheless, there is a paradox as we try to analyze media effects across the three steps of presidential selection. If it is indeed the case that media impact is greatest in the primary season, it is also the case that the empirical evidence relevant to this first phase is weaker than the information on the latter stages, especially the general election. This means that the portion of this paper devoted to the primaries must of necessity take on a more speculative tone.

There are a number of difficulties in studying media effects that should be identified to give the reader some sense of the problems involved in replacing speculation with solid empirical evidence. First, many of the effects of the media are subtle and cumulative and perhaps affect only indirectly such classic dependent variables as vote choice. If media effects are indeed cumulative, a longitudinal design such as a panel survey would be the best approach to assess such impacts. Yet over-time designs can be very costly and, more importantly, can produce severe reactivity effects. For example, understanding the process by which a candidate develops name recognition would be facilitated by interviewing the same voters over time. Yet one can hardly imagine a more reactive situation in which respondents' recognition of a candidate at later waves is a function of interviewer mention of that candidate at an earlier wave.

The subtlety of media effects raises the classic question about the optimal research design to use in isolating media impact (Hovland, 1959; Converse, 1970). Given the presence of sampling and measurement errors as well as the problems in controlling for relevant other variables and in measuring media effects at optimal time points, the sample survey may be less than satisfactory for estimating media consequences, especially where such effects might be weak. Certainly one need in much survey research is to develop better measures of media usage and better ways of ascertaining what people actually get from the media. This is both a methodological and a substantive problem since the measures that one constructs must emerge from some theoretical perspective or substantive concern. At the least, one must be clear about which media effects are being investigated: is it the impact of the media on vote choice, candidate image, level of political information, or what? Furthermore, one should not talk about television or newspaper effects in general, but rather should distinguish between different television programming such as news shows versus political commercials or between different newspaper content such as front page campaign coverage versus editorials. No matter how sophisticated the measures, one problem that seems likely to remain in survey studies is that respondents will have to report on and reconstruct behaviors, often at some time after their actual occurrence, when such behaviors were not all that conscious and purposive in the first place. Perhaps Nielsen-style viewing and reading logs could be used more frequently to better monitor media behavior, although this places a greater burden on respondents.

Experimental designs may be helpful with respect to controlling for other variables and assessing media effects at more meaningful time intervals, but they suffer from the obvious problem of external validity: to what other groups or populations can the findings of our experiment be generalized? Sometimes we will be in the fortunate position of being able to do quasi-experimental work in the natural setting and then external validity will be less worrisome, but these opportunities are infrequent (Simon and Stern, 1955; Robinson and Burgess, 1970; Nimmo and Savage, 1976:161-183).

While the above discussion deals with problems of obtaining reliable and valid information from individuals, there is another problem involved in dealing with the veritable mountain of data obtained from such sources as the nightly television news broadcasts and newspapers. One can content-analyze such information, but then one must decide how to relate the results of the content analysis to individual political behavior. This brings us back to the need to develop more sophisticated measures of media attentiveness and use. And it also raises questions about appropriate statistical techniques to analyze media effects. Are media impacts to be treated as residual influences or are their effects viewed as primary as individual level background and attitudinal variables? Finally, it becomes clear that as one tries to relate individual behavior to the media environment, national studies may provide insufficient information (cases) to study important local level phenomena such as distinctive patterns of media availability. With local level studies, however, one must be on the alert for possible factors that might upset their generalizability. Likewise, one should be careful that national level results are not simply an artificial and misleading aggregation of distinctive sub-national patterns.

Lest the reader come away from the above discussion despairing of the possibility of systematically analyzing media effects, it should be noted that in recent years ambitious research efforts have been carried out, mainly on the general election, and that major research programs are currently under way to monitor the media throughout the entire 1976 presidential selection process. The results of this more recent research will be reported in the subsequent pages and should suggest that, while much remains to be learned about the impact of the media in presidential politics, an impressive start has been made.

II. THE PRIMARY SEASON

It seems on a priori grounds that the impact of the media should be greatest during the primary election phase of the presidential selection process. This is so because of the ambiguity and complexity inherent in the primaries which facilitate media influences and intrusiveness. For example, primary elections are often multiple candidate contests so that standards of victory may not be as clear as they are in the general election and the nominating conventions. Unlike the general election, the structure of competition shifts over the primary season, with candidates declaring themselves in and dropping out, thereby making the comparative interpretation of a series of elections more problematic. Furthermore, despite the apparent confusion that the Electoral College adds to the general election, the variety of primary arrangements—binding versus non-binding, delegate versus beauty contests, winner-take-all versus proportional allocation of delegates, popular vote versus delegates won, and so on—represents a level of complexity that literally invites media interpretation and misinterpretation. Finally, the amount of information available about the candidates is low, especially early in the primary season, so that what the media chooses to emphasize can be very consequential for the candidate's fate, particularly since party identification cannot serve as a cue for candidate choice in a partisan primary.

Some theoretical perspectives on mass communications also argue for the greater impact of the media during the primaries as opposed to the later stages. There is an ongoing debate as to whether candidate images are perceiver-determined or stimulus-determined (e.g., through television). The former view (Sigel, 1964) argues that one's candidate images are filtered by one's own predispositions such as party identification and that selective processes help maintain cognitive consistency. The stimulus-determined position (McGrath and McGrath, 1962; Baskin, 1976) asserts that citizens' images of candidates are more directly a function of what they actually see or read about the contenders. Although there is evidence supporting both sides, it is certainly the case that one's perceptual defenses are lower during the primaries than during the general election, and hence images of the candidates formed during the primary season, especially early on, are more likely to be stimulus-determined. In the general election, as people have more information about the candidates and as the perceptual screen function of party identification comes into play, images may be less stimulus-determined. In a related vein, given the low information levels characteristic of primaries, the media, even if they do not create or alter attitudes directly, can determine the grounds (e.g., issues, personality) on which people choose between the candidates, an agenda-setting effect.

In summary, primary elections tend to be less well-defined phenomena, thereby allowing substantial leeway in media reporting and interpretation. This is not to say that media coverage of primary election outcomes and of opinion poll presidential preferences necessarily advantages or disadvantages candidates or ˉgenerates bandwagons. Recent empirical studies of presidential nominations indicate that poll and primary results produce weak bandwagon effects at best. Beniger (1976) found that a candidate's standing in the preference polls had little or no effect on changes in his standing in subsequent polls, although preference poll position contributed directly to primary election success. His results also indicated that primary election success led to an improvement in a candidate's poll standing, especially for Democratic candidates in the early primaries, a finding supported by Collat et al. (1976). A more intriguing aspect of this research is the suggestive evidence it presents that recent primary election campaigns have differed from the traditional patterns. Writing about nomination contests between 1936 and 1972, Beniger (1976) identifies only three genuine horse races—the Democratic contests in 1960 and 1972 and the Republican race in 1964. Likewise, Lucy (1973) has observed that between 1936 and 1972, only once—in 1972—in 20 cases has the presidential contender leading in the last preprimary Gallup poll lost primaries and permanently lost the poll lead. Although this occurred only once in 36 years, it happened again in 1976 when Jimmy Carter overcame an initial low standing in the polls to capture the Democratic nomination. The question arises as to why the traditional pattern of open-and-shut nomination campaigns in which the early leaders ultimately emerged victorious has been broken twice in the last few years. One answer is certainly the proliferation of primaries, which has resulted in the overwhelming majority of delegates being popularly elected. But to the proliferation of primaries must be added the manner in which the media cover the primaries, and it is to this concern that we now turn. The following discussion will show by example how the media can affect the course of the primary process. A list of examples obviously does not constitute compelling proof of the intrusiveness of the media, but the cases to be discussed are thought-provoking. The discussion will focus on three interrelated themes: the complexity of the primaries, the games that candidates play, and the emphases of the news-reporting enterprise.

THE COMPLEXITY OF THE PRIMARIES

The primaries are complex in many ways, one being that they are often multiple candidate contests. At times the field of declared candidates is only a small subset of the total number of prospective nominees. The media play a very prominent role here in determining which of all the potential candidates are serious and viable. David Broder (1976:215-217) cites one role of reporters in presidential politics as being that of the talent scouts who decide which candidates merit genuine consideration as presidential aspirants. The power of this screening function is detailed very insightfully by Timothy Crouse (1973:39, 194-199) who describes how the press gave careful scrutiny to George Romney in 1968, ultimately overplaying his "brainwashed" comment and destroying his credibility as a candidate. Whether Romney merited such treatment is not central here. What is crucial is that, in the same period when Romney was undergoing intensive scrutiny, Richard Nixon was enjoying a free ride from the press since he was maintaining a low profile. After the press was through with Romney, Nixon's path to the White House was made easier.

A more important aspect of the presence of multiple entrants in primaries is that standards of victory are less obvious. Where more than two candidates are vying, the simple majority criterion may have little utility, and the media may establish their own tests of candidate performance. Passage of these tests may indicate that a candidate is running strongly, but the question arises as to why one test is chosen and not others. For example, the Florida primary in 1976 was deemed crucial to Jimmy Carter's hopes. It was argued that, in order for Carter to establish himself as a serious contender, he had to defeat George Wallace. But why did Carter have to win, particularly since the Henry Jackson candidacy in Florida was likely to hurt Carter more than Wallace? As an alternative test, how about simply a strong showing by Carter in Florida, especially since Wallace had swept the Florida primary in 1972?

The standards that the media establish allow for interpretation of events at some variance from what actually occurred. The classic example of this occurred in 1972 in the New Hampshire Democratic primary in which Edmund Muskie "failed" to get the magic 50% of the vote needed to give his candidacy a boost, even though he defeated his chief rival George McGovern by a margin of 46% to 37%. James Perry explained how the 50% standard gradually emerged as the media consensus beginning with a story by David Broder on January 9 (nearly *two* months before the primary) in which Broder wrote, "As the acknowledged front-runner and a resident of the neighboring state, Muskie will have to win the support of at least half the New Hampshire Democrats in order to claim a victory" (Perry, 1973:85). Perry claimed that television newsmen picked up the 50% figure and thereby managed to infuse drama in a race in which the outcome was largely a foregone conclusion. Perry (1973:86) attributed part of Muskie's problem to a preprimary poll showing Muskie with 65% of the vote. Despite the instability and unreliability of many preprimary polls (Roper, 1975), the 65% and later the 50% mark became an albatross on the Muskie candidacy.

The interpretation of the New Hampshire primary in 1972 was also flawed by the failure of the media to provide the context of the famous Muskie crying incident (Witcover, 1972). William Loeb, publisher of the *Manchester Union Leader,* New Hampshire's largest paper, conducted a vendetta against Muskie that included attacks on his wife and the publication of phony letters accusing Muskie of ethnic prejudice against Franco-Americans, an important voting bloc in New Hampshire. In the first four primaries in 1972, Muskie won New Hampshire with 46% of the vote and Illinois with 63%, while Wallace carried Florida with 42% and George McGovern Wisconsin with 30%. Yet it was the McGovern candidacy that was building and Muskie's that was collapsing when Wisconsin voted. Certainly media coverage of the New Hampshire primary hastened the downfall of the Muskie candidacy.

Burns Roper (1975) has called for reform of media coverage of primaries, but his message has not been heeded. On the day before the 1976 New Hampshire primary, Walter Cronkite opined on the evening news that anything less than 55% of the Republican vote for Gerald Ford should be construed as a setback for the incumbent

President. Luckily for Ford, this standard was not universally adopted. (In fact, other standards more favorable to Ford were—a point elaborated in our later discussion of the games that candidates play.)

The point is that primary success, poll standing, and the ability to raise money and attract volunteers are all interrelated. The quest for the presidential nomination is in part a psychological battle, and the media can be very influential in unwittingly creating a psychological climate beneficial to one candidate. Morris Udall complained in April of 1976 that Jimmy Carter had profited from an "orgy of publicity." Although Udall's complaint must be taken with a grain of salt given his own aspirations, his comments (Cannon, 1976) nevertheless get to the heart of the issue:

> Never underestimate the importance of momentum in these presidential elections. We all said we weren't going to let New Hampshire do it to us again, and New Hampshire did do it. We all said that the Iowa caucus was not that important, and the press made it that important. . . . Once that avalanche starts down the ski slope, get out of the way.
>
> . . . The people want winners and losers and if you make 27 points in a football game and I make 26, you're called a winner and I'm called a loser.

Udall's comments reflect the tendency of the media to make the primaries a sporting contest, most often a horse race, where winners and losers must be identified even if there are no clear victors. Given the emphasis on outcomes, the question still remains how to define winning and losing. If the media had decided on delegates won as the standard instead of popular vote pluralities, then the early Democratic primaries in 1976 would not have seemed so definitive and certainly would not have given the Carter candidacy as much of an impetus. As it is, it seems that the media began to emphasize delegates won in coverage of the later primaries so that even as Carter began to lose elections to his late-entering opponents, his losses were offset by news reports emphasizing his delegate gains and his inexorable march to a delegate majority.

The notion that the media needs to identify winners and losers can be extended to say that winners and losers must be individuals and not such undefined entities as "uncommitteds." In fact, throughout 1976, beginning with the precinct caucuses in Iowa in January and culminating with the New Jersey primary in June, the performance of the uncommitteds was reported in at best questionable ways. Even though the uncommitteds won in Iowa with 37% of the vote compared to 28% for Carter and 13% for Birch Bayh, press attention focused on Carter. Elizabeth Drew (1976a:133) reported that as a result of his Iowa "victory," Carter was interviewed on the CBS Morning News, while NBC's Today Show and ABC's Good Morning America also ran segments on Carter. On the CBS Evening News, Walter Cronkite said that Iowa voters have spoken, "and for the Democrats what they said was 'Jimmy Carter.'" Yet given the amount of time that Carter spent in Iowa, his performance might have been portrayed as less impressive. It may be that there was no significant political interpretation to be given by the media to the victory of the uncommitted in Iowa beyond being a function of oddities in the delegate selection rules, but the victory of the uncommitted in New Jersey is a far different matter, a point to be developed shortly.

Given the sharp increase in the number of primaries between 1968 and 1976, an additional problem that media interpretations must address is which primaries are to be stressed. Rick Stearns, deputy campaign manager for McGovern in 1972, claimed that the McGovern strategy was formulated on the assumption that the primaries that had been significant in the past would continue to be so viewed by the press in 1972 (May and Fraser, 1973:97). Hence, the McGovern camp stressed the Wisconsin primary and won it, but, as Stearns himself said (May and Fraser, 1973:97), there was no reason other than press inertia that "Wisconsin should have been the watershed for the McGovern campaign that it was; the Wisconsin primary fundamentally was not that important."

An additional complication associated with the increased number of primaries was the fact that in 1976 more than one major primary occurred on the same day whereas in previous years the major primaries unfolded in a nice temporal and geographic sequence starting in New Hampshire, moving to Wisconsin, and concluding with Oregon and California. In 1976, the media had more difficult decisions to make about which primaries to stress, and it is not entirely clear that they made the right choices. For example, the Wisconsin and New York primaries occurred on the same day, and it appears that the Wisconsin contest, despite allocating many fewer delegates than New York (68 versus 274), received the lion's share of media attention. This may have been due to Wisconsin's traditional importance or to the widespread feeling that Henry Jackson was expected to win in New York, which therefore made that race less exciting and hence less newsworthy, or to the fact that Wisconsin was a simpler story to report since it entailed only two major candidates *and* a straightforward popular vote contest. Likewise, the Oregon primary was held on the same day as five other primaries in 1976. Oregon became the featured primary because it was deemed the most competitive race; Kentucky, Arkansas, and Tennessee were conceded to Southerner Jimmy Carter; Idaho to native son Frank Church; and Nevada to neighboring California Governor Edmund G. Brown. But even though Oregon was the most competitive race between Carter, Church, and Brown (as a write-in) it is arguable whether this made it more newsworthy, except that it more resembled the horse race that the media seem wont to emphasize. The mentality underlying this view of news is illustrated by *Washington Post* columnist Ed Walsh (1976:A6), who wrote about the California primary that it "appeared to lose some of its luster as polls continued to show Reagan a solid favorite to take the state's 167 delegates." With this kind of reporting, a victorious candidate will gain greater mileage by defeating a rival in a hotly contested race in doubt to the end rather than in a convincing victory evident some time prior to the actual voting.

The problem that multiple and complex primaries on the same day pose for the media is best illustrated by "Super Tuesday" of the 1976 primary season. On June 8, California, New Jersey, and Ohio all held primaries which on the Democratic side selected 540 delegates, more than a third of the total needed for nomination. The question was: how would these primary results be interpreted? Which state outcome would be viewed as most significant? In retrospect, it was Ohio—not California and New Jersey—that proved critical. Carter's smashing victory in Ohio was widely seen as locking up the nomination for him. But why Ohio? Was "Super Tuesday" such an unqualified success for the former governor of Georgia?

The *New York Times* front page story about New Jersey on the day before the primary read "Carter Victory is Forecast in Jersey Vote Tomorrow." On primary day, R.W. Apple's front page story was entitled "Carter Appears Near Goal in Last 3 Primaries Today." On Wednesday the *Times* headline was "Ford and Carter Lead in Votes in Jersey and Ohio; California Leaning to Brown and Reagan." The front page headline in the *Times* on Thursday proclaimed "Carter Seems Due to Win on First Ballot," while on page 43 was a story entitled "Humphrey-Brown Victory in Jersey is Called Futile."

The question becomes how an anticipated Carter victory in New

Jersey which turned into an overwhelming delegate loss (83 for uncommitted, 25 for Carter) could be given so little attention. At one level, the New Jersey story did deserve less attention, since the fact that Carter picked up over 200 delegates on "Super Tuesday" even while being thumped in California and New Jersey may have been the major story of the day, because it put Carter so much closer to the nomination. But in terms of the popular appeal of the candidates, the Ohio results should have been balanced by the New Jersey and California outcomes, yet they were not. The question is why.

A part of the answer is the inability or unwillingness of the media to handle complexity. An NBC television reporter argued that Ohio was the real test since there was a native son on the California ballot and in New Jersey there were uncommitted delegates which made interpretation difficult and confused the issue. This, however, is no explanation, but simply an admission that Ohio was more congenial to media coverage. One could convincingly argue that front-runner Carter's loss to an uncommitted delegate slate widely advertised as supporting Hubert Humphrey and Jerry Brown was truly the significant outcome of the day. Yet evidently this was too complicated to explain to readers and viewers. New Jersey was further complicated by a nonbinding beauty contest as well as the delegate selection vote. The fact that Carter won the former easily against token opposition and lost the latter decisively would have made the New Jersey story even more difficult to report. The lesson of all this is that the media seek excitement and simplicity, a point developed more later.

GAMES CANDIDATES PLAY

While the media may inadvertently misinterpret primary results because of reasons inherent in media coverage, it is also the case that politicians try to manipulate the media to further their own ends. As Elizabeth Drew notes (1976b:89), "A classic problem for candidates is how to inflate their prospects in order to attract allies and followers without creating a standard against which they can be measured unfavorably." This helps explain how the front-runner status hurt Muskie, but not Carter. Muskie was a strong front-runner expected to do well, but Carter was a weak one who, each time he ran well, surprised observers with his strength. By the time Carter started to lose primaries to Jerry Brown and Frank Church, he was so far out in front that it did not matter much. As Roper (1975:29) notes, a candidate's goal is to run better than expected and hence the incentive, especially for underdog candidates, is to poor-mouth their own prospects so that the eventual results appear more promising.

An excellent example of successful media manipulation was Gerald Ford's quest for the Republican nomination in 1976. Despite the bungling attributed to the Ford campaign staff, one can argue that the Ford operatives were more skillful than the Ronald Reagan camp in manipulating the media to their own ends. Late in the New Hampshire primary race, the Reagan forces leaked a poll showing their candidate eight percentage points ahead. This was a tactical mistake since it created expectations of a Reagan win against which Ford's narrow victory was seen as impressive; Ford's 51% of the vote was not interpreted as a weak showing for an incumbent President despite Cronkite's aforementioned judgment that an incumbent President should be able to get at least 55%. Clearly the Reagan strategy should have been one of publicly hoping for 40% of the vote, and then New Hampshire might have served as Reagan's springboard to the nomination. Thus, Reagan's 48% of the New Hampshire vote in 1976 did him less good than McGovern's 37% in 1972.

The Ford partisans skillfully manipulated the New Hampshire results in subsequent primaries. In Florida, they were aided by Reagan's campaign manager, who had predicted a two to one Reagan victory (Rosenbaum, 1976). After New Hampshire, the campaign manager lowered his estimate to a 55% Reagan win. This allowed the Ford forces to claim a 12% gain and the ever-important momentum while at the same time preserving their underdog status, a tactic that almost perfectly follows Drew's advice cited above. Had the President lost narrowly in Florida, the Ford people might have been successful in portraying this as a moral victory even as the Reagan camp was unsuccessful in claiming New Hampshire as a moral victory.

After Reagan's string of primary successes in Texas, Indiana, Nebraska, and elsewhere, one can argue that the Ford campaign was very skillful in setting up the Michigan primary as one that the President might lose. It is hard to demonstrate that Ford was ever in any serious trouble in Michigan, yet the successful conveying of that impression served to inflate the significance of his Michigan win and thereby put his campaign on the right track again. In retrospect, it is interesting to note that an incumbent President's victory in his own home state was accorded so much more importance than his challenger's victory in his own home state.

A final example of successful game playing is Chicago Mayor Richard J. Daley's claim that a Carter victory in Ohio would mean that Carter "will walk in [to the nomination] under his own power." Daley had picked Ohio as decisive and it was. The question is: which came first? Was Ohio always crucial, and Daley simply recognized a fact? Or was Ohio crucial because Daley said so? If the latter, then this helps explain why Ohio and not California and New Jersey received the most attention on "Super Tuesday." The preprimary polls in Ohio indicated that a substantial Carter victory was in the making. Thus, it appears that Daley ably manipulated the media to put himself in the position of kingmaker.

Media manipulation by candidates can affect the outcome of the primary process. Imagine if the Reagan people in New Hampshire had been more savvy and understated their expectations. Likewise, one can only speculate about what would have happened had Mayor Daley said that New Jersey and not Ohio was the ball game. Had California and New Jersey been described as major Carter setbacks instead of second-place finishes, would people have been so eager to jump on the Carter bandwagon the next day? Again, the point is that politics is in part a psychological game and the side that can set the standard of performance adopted by the media has a tremendous advantage. To the extent that the media are successfully manipulated by the candidates, they are playing an intrusive role in presidential politics.

THE NEWS REPORTING EMPHASIS

How the media report the primaries can be very consequential for their outcome. As mentioned above, the dominant perspective that news reporting takes on the primaries is that of the horse race with emphasis on who's winning and losing, who's closing fast, and who's fading. Perry (1973:10) blames the "who's ahead" mentality in part on Theodore White's books on presidential elections. White, of course, had the advantage of writing after the winner's identity was already known. Newsmen following the primaries as they occur do not have this luxury, yet they may get so hooked on the importance of proclaiming "who's ahead" that they put themselves in untenable positions such as awarding the nomination to Muskie before any of the primaries had been held in 1972. As Broder observes (1976:217), the handicapper role of reporters may mislead readers into believing that a candidate's current standing necessarily predicts accurately his final standing.

The horse race mentality is, of course, encouraged by the need to attract readers and viewers. A horse race is by definition an exciting event with identifiable winners and losers. And as Collat et al. (1976:34) point out, newsmen tend to agree in their judgment of who is ahead since "they see the same polls, read the same things, and talk to the same people." This results in a certain homogeneity in news reporting about the viability of candidates and can make the media more influential in the winnowing out of candidates. The focus on who is winning even shows up on election night coverage of the primaries when the networks often seem to be in a race among themselves to be the first to call the outcome of each primary. It should be noted that the networks in 1976 commissioned major surveys in order to determine *why* the primaries turned out as they did.

It has also been argued that the horse race emphasis reflects the competence of political reporters to cover politics and their inability to cover government. Charles Peters (1976:56) described political reporters as knowing "much about the process of being elected and little about what the government does or how it could be improved." This means that coverage of what the candidates actually stand for and what they plan to do often gets overwhelmed by the concern for winning and losing, a phenomenon which also occurs in the general election campaign. The policy positions of candidates are often inadequately reported.

There are times when the political acumen of reporters may fail them and they fall back on standard operating procedures. The occurrence of major, multiple primaries on the same day in 1976 was probably a situation for which newsmen lacked clear guidelines as to which races merited major coverage; hence, reporters fell back on the criterion of competition—the horse race—in order to identify the critical primary.

At other times, reporters may simply not know what sort of focus should be given to a story and may therefore follow the lead of an influential journalist. The classic example of this occurred in 1972 when newsmen were perplexed about the significance of the Iowa precinct caucus results. According to Crouse (1973:85), when R.W. Apple wrote as his lead for Iowa that McGovern had made a surprisingly strong showing, the other newsmen picked up the story and reported the same theme back to their papers. Drew (1976a: 127) reports a similar occurrence in Iowa in 1976. Apple had written a story that Carter was doing well in Iowa, and this story itself became a political event "prompting other newspaper stories that Carter was doing well in Iowa, and then more newspaper, magazine, and television coverage for Carter than might otherwise have been his share."

The horse race mentality can be very intrusive. Few people would want to bet on a candidate identified in the media as a loser. The interaction between media coverage, poll results, and primary outcomes can generate interpretation and prophecies that assume a life of their own and act to promote the prospects of one candidate over another.

III. THE CONVENTIONS

In discussing the effect of the media, especially television, on the nominating conventions, one can identify three targets of impact: the procedural and structural arrangements of the convention, the delegates to the conventions, and the home viewers of the conventions. With respect to the first, conventions today are events staged for television. Since 1952, conventions have been streamlined to be more attractive to the television audience. For example, Judith Parris reports (1972:150) that the 1952 Democratic convention totaled 10 sessions that lasted over 47 hours, while the 1968 convention consisted of just 5 sessions that ran less than 29 hours. Despite McGovern giving his acceptance speech at 3 o'clock in the morning Eastern time, convention activities such as the nominee's speeches are scheduled to reach the largest possible audience.

If the effect of television on conventions was simply one of streamlining and scheduling, then it would be difficult to argue that television was intrusive in any negative or harmful sense. Unfortunately, television's effects go beyond routine shaping of the convention. For example, the Democrats in 1976 were very concerned that their convention be perceived by the American public as a harmonious and orderly affair. They believed that their raucus and conflictual conventions of 1968 and 1972 as portrayed to the American public via television were major contributing factors to Humphrey's and McGovern's defeats. Hence, the 1976 Democratic convention adopted a rule that minority reports on the platform, rules, and credentials had to have the support of 25% of the members of the appropriate committee in order to be brought before the full convention; only 10% had been required in the past. Certainly this rule change was an attempt to avoid televised divisiveness, to minimize the prominence of fringe elements, and to keep the convention on schedule.

Although making minority reports more difficult may not be the optimal way to achieve full airing of issues, one can sympathize with party professionals who are concerned with what the citizen at home sees of the conventions on television. The Republicans in 1964 and the Democrats in 1968 and 1972 left stormy conventions as seriously divided parties, and all three lost in November. It is an empirical generalization that the nominee selected at the convention should gain ground in the polls right after the convention, yet McGovern actually lost ground in the postconvention polls conducted *before* the Thomas Eagleton affair. It appears that the vast majority of Americans are not enthralled by conventions characterized by conflict and rancor nor are they sympathetic to parties and candidates whose conventions appear dominated by groups alien and threatening to the average citizen.

Paletz and Elson (1976) have presented one of the few systematic analyses of what aspects of the conventions television actually emphasizes. Their quantitative analysis of NBC's coverage of the 1972 Democratic convention demonstrated that violence and fringe elements were not given undue coverage nor was there any bias for or against McGovern. In their qualitative analysis of NBC coverage, however, Paletz and Elson came to a different conclusion. They argued that the predominant impression left by television of the Democratic convention was one of conflict and disorder. They attributed this not to any deliberate bias on the part of newsmen, but to the norms and procedures of television news reporting. For example, they argued that the media interpret fairness to mean getting all sides. But, as Paletz and Elson point out (1976:122), getting all sides

> can make the "Stop McGovern Movement" seem as strong as the "Elect McGovern Movement" whether it is or not. Moreover the technique may actually create the impression of sides that do not really exist to a substantial degree among the delegates as a whole. It certainly increases the elements of conflict and drama.

Furthermore, when reporters do portray divisiveness, they do not do so in ways to suggest that it represents a healthy discussion of issues, but instead that it symbolizes bitterness and hostility.

What Paletz and Elson are saying is that television distorts the conventions for reasons inherent in the news reporting enterprise. Warren Weaver (1976) points out that in a dull convention, television, unlike newspapers which can cut back convention column space, must fill the time and, to accomplish this, may seize upon an inconsequential story and blow it out of proportion. Weaver asserts that reports of anti-Carter dissension at the Democratic convention received much more attention than they deserved, for just this reason.

The networks are in competition to attract viewers and this seems to be reflected in their readiness to push any story. The problem is that, if substantial coverage is given to an inconsequential story, it may be elevated to a matter of genuine importance. This is reflected in the eagerness with which the networks seized upon the alleged bribing of two Ford delegates from Illinois; the television coverage was replete with interviews with representatives on both sides, the reporting of heated charges and denials, and the like. On the CBS convention coverage, Walter Cronkite himself said very dramatically that this might be the kind of issue that could shake delegates loose. It seems that the direct effect of this kind of reporting is to generate excitement and the indirect effect is to increase the level of conflict and make party unity more difficult to achieve. The CBS preconvention program on the GOP gathering was entitled "Kansas City Showdown" which captures the media emphasis well. Just as the primaries are infused with drama, so are the conventions.

At times, the networks themselves are skillfully manipulated by groups seeking to use the convention and the concomitant television coverage to promote their own causes. The networks, of course, must be the final arbiters of which groups and issues merit coverage. But if the definition of news is "outstanding deviation from civil norms" rather than "events of importance to sizeable number of viewers" (Shafer and Larson, 1972:16), then the networks may unwittingly serve to increase the appearance of discord.

Thus, the intrusiveness of television on the conventions is in large part a function of the nature and incentives of television news reporting. But sometimes television simply blows it, as evidenced by the misinterpretation of the South Carolina delegation challenge at the 1972 Democratic convetion which led some people to believe that the McGovern candidacy was in trouble when just the opposite was the case. At the 1968 Democratic convention, newsmen Sander Vanocur and John Chancellor were responsible for a Kennedy-for-President boom that electrified the convention, but was simply not accurate (Perry, 1973:171).

One can speculate how intrusive the media might be at a deadlocked or close convention in which events are unfolding rapidly and television is the major source of information for the delegates. On the second night of the Republican convention in 1976 before the test vote on the critical rule 16-C (on vice-presidential selection) had occurred, there was an uproar fanned by the television networks over alleged comments in an Alabama newspaper by Ford campaign manager Rogers Morton that the "Cotton South" would be written off by Ford. Morton claimed to have said that certain Southern states would be difficult for Ford to carry because of Southerner Carter heading the Democratic ticket, but he denied that these states had been written off. Nevertheless, newsmen confronted the Mississippi delegation with the "fact" that Ford was writing off the South. Earlier in the day the Mississippi delegation had invoked the unit rule by a very narrow margin of 31-28 to support Ford's position on 16-C and thereby cast all 30 votes against the rule. When Morton's alleged comments became known, the Reagan forces wanted the Mississippi delegation to caucus again in the hope of changing two votes and breaking the unit rule and perhaps converting some Ford supporters. The intrusiveness of the media became absurd here. Newsman Dan Rather offered to lead Rogers Morton across the convention floor so that he might meet with the Mississippi delegation. Newsman Mike Wallace provided the Mississippi Reagan delegates with a CBS trailer in which to caucus. No votes were changed as a result of all this, but it should suggest how the media can sometimes forget that they are there to report the news and not play an active part in generating it.

IV. THE GENERAL ELECTION

Unlike the situation for the primaries and nominating conventions, there is a substantial body of empirical materials on the impact of the media in the general election campaign. Much of this work is of recent vintage, with two studies in particular meriting attention because of the comprehensiveness of their coverage. The first, by

Patterson and McClure (1976), included a three-wave panel survey in 1972 of a sample of respondents from a medium-size metropolitan area and a content analysis of all weeknight ABC, CBS, and NBC evening news broadcasts between September 18 and November 6, 1972, and of all televised McGovern and Nixon political commercials in that same period. The second study, conducted by Hofstetter in 1972, consisted of a pre- and postelection national level mass survey (Hofstetter et al., 1976), interviews with county level McGovern and Nixon campaign activists (Howell, 1976) designed to mesh with the primary sampling units of the mass survey, and a survey of news personnel from local television stations that broadcast in the primary sampling units. Hofstetter's study also entailed content analysis of the network evening news shows between July 10 (the first day of the Democratic convention) and November 6, 1972 (Hofstetter, 1967a), the Democratic, Republican, and minor party political advertising, the Associated Press wire coverage from August 8 to November 6, and the campaign coverage of the *Washington Post* and the *Chicago Tribune*. Particularly impressive about the Hofstetter and Patterson and McClure projects was the care given to identifying types of television political programming, such as nightly news and political advertising, and to analyzing distinct dependent variables, such as candidate image and information level. Hence, the first part of our discussion of the media in the general election will be a straightforward report of some of the empirical findings about television and newspaper effects. Then our attention will turn to more speculative concerns with emphasis on those features of general election media coverage that facilitate manipulation and game playing on the part of candidates and hence media intrusiveness.

EMPIRICAL STUDIES OF MEDIA EFFECTS IN THE GENERAL ELECTION

The classic studies (Berelson et al., 1954; Lazarsfeld et al., 1968) of the impact of the campaign and the mass media found only weak effects on vote intentions, the major impact being the reinforcement of the voter's initial predispositions rather than attitude change. These studies left the impression of minimal media effects, but a number of qualifying points must be made. First, these early works predate the major entry of television into presidential politics. Second, they focused mainly on the dependent variable of vote choice. Third, a part of the explanation given for the primacy of reinforcement effects was the tendency of people to expose themselves mainly to communications sympathetic to their existing beliefs. One might question, however, whether such predispositions as party identification are as strong today; if not, the opportunities for reinforcement will be less.

Like their precursors, the recent studies also do not indicate any great effect of the media on vote preference. Moreover, Patterson and McClure (1976:49, 116) found that regular viewing of network news had no effect on the voter's issue awareness, but that viewing of political commercials was associated with higher voter awareness of candidates' issue stances. The simple explanation for this was that political advertising actually had more issue and information content to it than did the nightly network news shows. Hofstetter et al. (1976:11) support this finding somewhat; they found that exposure to network election specials and to political advertising was more highly correlated with richness of issue perceptions than was exposure to network news programs. O'Keefe and Sheinkopf (1974) dispute the information-producing effects of political advertising. They argued that, even though the political use of television in 1972 involved longer and more informative ads than the short ads used in previous elections, the television ads were not seen by viewers as important information sources. Moreover, O'Keefe and Sheinkopf concluded that, no matter what their length, television ads served mainly as image builders rather than information sources. The contradiction between their findings and those of Patterson and McClure can be reconciled by the notion of the inadvertent audience. While it may be true that O'Keefe and Sheinkopf's respondents did not consciously view political commercials as important information sources, they were nevertheless acquiring information from then unknowingly. Spot commercials come on during regular programming, so that many viewers who might not ordinarily tune in political programming accidently end up watching political commercials and learning from them. A study (Bowen et al., 1972) of spot commercials in the Wisconsin and Colorado gubernatorial races in 1970 supports this notion; the authors found that specific information, such as candidates' qualifications and issues stands, rather than more general images were learned from the ads.

Patterson and McClure (1976:67-68) uncovered no effect of television news shows on the candidate images of committed voters. Among the undecided voters exposed to television, images of Nixon and McGovern changed very little until *after* the decision was made about which candidate to support. Hofstetter et al. (1976:10) agreed with this finding in part, claiming that exposure to news programming "appeared to have increased the total amount of imagery about the candidates, but failed to influence the nature of this imagery."

The content analyses of the network evening news shows indicate that the issue stands and qualifications of the candidates receive very little attention. Instead, it is the hoopla, the rallies, the noise and excitement that are covered; network news treats the general election campaign like a horse race. For example, Patterson and McClure (1976:31) reported that about 60% of the time that a presidential candidate was shown on camera in 1972, he was shown in a crowd scene. They charge (p. 144) that the networks maintain the charade of the horse race with the active cooperation of the candidates who gear their campaigns to this kind of media coverage. Obviously, campaigns are media oriented: rallies are scheduled early so that television reports will be ready for the nightly news shows; speeches are designed to provide headlines for news broadcasts; and rallies themselves are arranged with the television image of enthusiastic support in mind. This emphasis on how the campaign will look on television leads Mendelsohn and Crespi (1970:281-282) to employ the term pseudocampaign.

With respect to newspapers, recent studies have identified surprisingly strong effects on information levels and vote choice. Patterson and McClure (1976:51) discovered that people who read the newspaper regularly became much better informed about the campaign. Three studies have indicated that newspaper endorsements have a direct effect on vote choice. Erikson (1976:217-218) analyzed the effect of newspaper shifts in partisan endorsements between 1960 and 1964 on the Democratic presidential vote. Among other things, he found that in single major newspaper counties the 1964 vote was 5% more Democratic if the paper supported Lyndon Johnson over Barry Goldwater. He speculated (p. 220) about the long term impact of the Republican press, arguing that the cumulative effect of newspaper endorsements over time may be important. Two studies by John Robinson also demonstrate the importance of newspaper endorsements on vote choice. In one study (1972), Robinson found that the perception that a newspaper supported one candidate over the other was assoicated with about a 6% vote advantage for the preferred candidate, an effect most pronounced among respondents with weaker party loyalties. In the other study (1974), Robinson found that there was a correlation across five presidential elections between presidential endorsements made by newspapers and the vote choice made by readers of these newspapers, controlling for relevant other variables.

MANIPULATION AND GAME PLAYING IN THE GENERAL ELECTION

If the media generally have weak effects, particularly on vote choice, as the empirical studies seem to indicate, then one might ask why one should worry about the potential manipulation of the media by candidates. One response to this question is that the empirical studies have only scratched the surface in assessing media effects. For example, more powerful independent variables that measure the content of (as opposed to simple exposure to) media coverage may indicate greater media impact on attitudes (Miller et al., 1976). Another response more relevant to our discussion is that successful manipulation of the media by a candidate may serve to alter the course of politics in ways not readily amenable to quantitative verification. This can be illustrated by reference to Richard Nixon's reelection campaign in 1972. The Nixon camp recognized the structural aspects of news reporting and ran a campaign designed to take advantage of these features. Nixon campaigned as President from the White House while surrogate campaigners carried the Republican message on the stump. As Jules Witcover notes (1973:24-25), the absence of Nixon from the campaign trail resulted in intensive scrutiny of McGovern. Every little flaw in the campaign, every squabble among his advisors received substantial media attention because of the availability of the McGovern camp to the media. McGovern was covered as a candidate striving for office, while Nixon was treated as the incumbent President above the political fray. Witcover argues (1973:26) that, even had Nixon campaigned more, he would likely have kept himself insulated from press questioning with the result that the accessible McGovern campaign would still have been subjected to intensive and critical scrutiny.

Ben Bagdikian (1973) points out that the Nixon campaign strategy led to news coverage that effectively served as Nixon propaganda in many instances. One procedure that contributed to this was "twinning"—giving both sides of a story equal coverage even when they did not deserve such comparable treatment. McGovern himself complained about this (Ryan, 1976:8):

Let me register one beef from my own campaign. There were times when we would have a great rally where local leaders would tell us, "This is the biggest crowd we've ever seen at Cleveland Airport!" Or: "This is the biggest crowd we've ever had at Post Office Square in Boston!" I would turn on the television set later to see the enormous throng, and well, there *would* be a 15-second spot of me addressing this crowd. Then, under some kind of curious interpretation of the equal-time rule, since Nixon was not campaigning, they would pick up some guy along the fence who would say, "I think McGovern stinks."

And this would be the way the program would end—or "McGovern said this, but a disgruntled former Democrat interviewed by our roving reporter said this." And then they had some jerk get up and say that I was too radical for him or that I couldn't make up my mind on the issues. What the viewer was left with was a final negative image. It happened repeatedly during the campaign.

Bagdikian (1973:11) did not blame Nixon for adopting the strategy that he did, arguing that this was standard behavior for a heavily favored incumbent. Instead, he criticized editors and publishers who allowed the Nixon camp to get away with such conduct. The point, however, is that a candidate could count on the networks and newspapers to try to present balanced coverage even when only one candidate was actively campaigning. Perhaps given the lesson of 1972, the media will be more alert to the problem and devise appropriate responses. This of course raises the question of the proper role of reporters and journalists. Is it simply to record the campaign? If so, then the media may be the vehicle of skillful candidates. Or should media personnel evaluate as well as record? This latter role is certainly controversial, opening up news organizations to charges of bias and threats of political and economic reprisals.

Candidates are also skillful in recognizing that news personnel need to file stories even when little hard news exists. Candidates can then construct media events that project desired images without much hard content. Buchanan (1976) described an excellent example of this phenomenon with respect to how the media covered Jimmy Carter's extended stay in Plains, Georgia, after winning the Democratic nomination. Each day reporters would issue a report from Plains on who visited the candidate or how the softball game went. The television viewer was treated to pictures of Carter greeting fellow Democrats, Carter playing softball, Carter going to church, and the like. The question, of course, is whether this merits coverage. It is not the fault of the Carter camp that this occurred; its contribution was simply to recognize that the media need "news" and to provide tidbits and scenes designed to show the candidate in his best light. There is an obvious response available to the media to counter such behavior, and that is simply not to report such activities. But this would require a redefinition of what constitutes news as well as a restructuring of media incentives that encourage this type of news coverage. Unfortunately, it seems that the candidates have the upper hand. It is hard to imagine the media ignoring a speech designated by the President as major which in fact turns out to be a rehashing of existing policy. But the media can do much more in providing context and background.

V. CONCLUSION

A recurrent theme of this paper has been that the media treat the presidential selection process like a horse race with emphasis on who's ahead rather than what a candidate stands for. Paul Weaver (1976) has described television network coverage of the 1976 primary season as a melodrama complete with plot, cast of characters, peril, the intervention of outside forces, and the ultimate denouement. While this type of coverage may foster viewer interest, it also encourages media intrusiveness, especially during the primary season, since judgments must be made about candidates' performance and these judgments, whether appropriate or not, can serve to promote or hinder a candidacy. The intrusiveness of the media was not attributed to any deliberate partisan or candidate bias (although at times news personnel may harbor dislikes for candidates) but, instead, to characteristics of the news reporting enterprise, the shortcomings of reporters, and the skill of candidates in exploiting media coverage.

Although a plausible case has been made for the intrusive impact of the media, it is difficult to demonstrate such effects empirically, particularly those occurring during the primary season. For example, it is impossible to reconstruct what would have happened had Muskie's New Hampshire performance been interpreted as impressive rather than weak or had Reagan's New Hampshire showing been viewed as a moral victory rather than a defeat. It seems intuitively plausible that the course of politics might have been changed dramatically given different news emphases on the New Hampshire primary. Yet in order to assess the effects of New Hampshire reportage on, for example, the Ford-Reagan Florida race, one would have to know how Florida vote intentions as well as the enthusiasm of campaign workers were affected by the New Hampshire coverage, a very costly and complex enterprise.

There is an ongoing program of research described by Chisman (1976) on the effects of the media throughout the entire presidential selection period. This research appears to have tremendous potential payoffs, for it entails not only longitudinal mass surveys and content analyses but also investigations of how media and campaign elites interact, of how media decisions are made to handle major campaign events, and of how the behavior of news organizations is affected by their organizational and interpersonal dynamics. The enormity of the task suggests that no single program of research will yield definitive answers, but hopefully the results will provide some supporting or disconfirming evidence of the intrusive effects of the media discussed herein.

REFERENCES

ASHER, H. (1976). Presidential elections and American politics. Homewood, Ill.: Dorsey.

BAGDIKIAN, B.H. (1973). "The fruits of Agnewism." Columbia Journalism Review, 11(January/February):9-21.

BASKIN, O. (1976). "The effects of television political advertisements on candidate image." Paper presented at the annual meeting of the International Communication Association, Portland, Ore., April 14-17.

BENIGER, J.R. (1976). "Winning the presidential nomination: National polls and state primary elections, 1936-1972." Public Opinion Quarterly, 40(spring):22-38.

BERELSON, B., LAZARSFELD, P., and McPHEE, W. (1954). Voting. Chicago: University of Chicago Press.

BOWEN, L., ATKIN, C.K., NAYMAN, O.B., and SHEINKOPF, K.G. (1972). "Quality vs. quantity in televised political ads." Public Opinion Quarterly, 37(summer):209-224.

BRODER, D.S. (1976). "Political reporters in presidential politics." Pp. 217-222 in C. Peters and J. Fallows (eds.), Inside the system (3rd ed.). New York: Praeger.

BUCHANAN, P. (1976). "How the networks fall easy prey to political manipulation." TV Guide, 24(August 14):A-3.

CAMPBELL, D.T., and STANLEY, J.C. (1963). Experimental and quasiexperimental designs for research. Chicago: Rand McNally.

CANNON, L. (1976). "Udall complains 'orgy of publicity' benefits Carter drive." Washington Post, April 17, p. A-4.

CHISMAN, F.P. (1976). "New directions and developments." Journal of Communication, 26(spring):91-94.

COLLAT, D., KELLEY, S., and ROGOWSKI, R. (1976). "Presidential bandwagons." Paper presented at the annual meeting of the American Political Science Association, Chicago, September 2-5.

COMSTOCK, G.A., RUBENSTEIN, E.A., and MURRAY, J.P. (eds., 1972). Television and social behavior. Rockville, Md.: National Institute of Mental Health.

CONVERSE, P.E. (1970). "Attitudes and non-attitudes: Continuation of a dialogue." Pp. 168-189 in E.R. Tufte (ed.), The quantitative analysis of social problems. Reading, Mass.: Addison-Wesley.

CROUSE, T. (1973). The boys on the bus: Riding with the campaign press corps. New York: Ballantine.

DREW, E. (1976a). "A reporter in Washington, D.C.: Winter notes—I." The New Yorker, May 17, pp. 126-156.

——— (1976b). "A reporter in Washington, D.C.: Winter notes—II." The New Yorker, May 31, pp. 54-99.

ERIKSON, R.S. (1976). "The influence of newspaper endorsements in presidential elections: The case of 1964." American Journal of Political Science, 20(May):207-233.

FUNKHOUSER, G.R. (1973). "The issues of the sixties: An exploratory study in the dynamics of public opinion." Public Opinion Quarterly, 37(spring):62-75.

HOFSTETTER, C.R. (1976a). Bias in the news. Columbus: Ohio State University Press.

——— (1976b). "Biased news in the 1972 campaign: A multimedia analysis." Paper presented at the International Communication Association Convention, Division VI, Political Communication, Portland, Ore., April 14-17.

HOFSTETTER, C.R., ZUKIN, C., and BUSS, T.F. (1976). "Political imagery in an age of television: The 1972 campaign." Paper presented at the annual meeting of the American Political Science Association, Chicago, September 2-5.

HOVLAND, C.I. (1959). "Reconciling conflicting results derived from experimental and survey studies of attitude change." American Psychologist, 14:8-17.

HOWELL, S.R. (1976). American political parties in a presidential campaign: A study of the 1972 local campaign activists. Unpublished Ph.D. dissertation, Ohio State University.

KRAUS, S. (1973). "Mass communication and political socialization: A re-assessment of two decades of research." Quarterly Journal of Speech, 59:390-400.

LAZARSFELD, P., BERELSON, B., and GAUDET, H. (1968). The people's choice (3rd ed.). New York and London: Columbia University Press.

LUCY, W.H. (1973). "Polls, primaries, and presidential nominations." Journal of Politics, 35(November):830-848.

MAY, E.R., and FRASER, J. (eds., 1973). Campaign '72: The managers speak. Cambridge, Mass.: Harvard University Press.

McCLURE, R.D., and PATTERSON, T.E. (1976). "Print vs. network news." Journal of Communication, 26(spring):23-28.

McCOMBS, M.E., and SHAW, D.L. (1972). "The agenda setting function of the mass media." Public Opinion Quarterly, 36(summer):176-187.

——— (1976). "Structuring the 'unseen environment.'" Journal of Communication, 26(spring):18-22.

McGRATH, J.E., and McGRATH, M.F. (1962). "Effects of partisanship on perceptions of political figures." Public Opinion Quarterly, 26:236-248.

MENDELSOHN, H., and CRESPI, I. (1970). Polls, television and the new politics. Scranton, Pa.: Chandler.

MILLER, A.H., ERBRING, L., and GOLDENBERG, E. (1976). "Type-set politics: Impact of newspapers on issue salience and public confidence." Paper presented at the annual meeting of the American Political Science Association, Chicago, September 2-5.

NIMMO, D., and SAVAGE, R.L. (1976). Candidates and their images: Concepts, methods, and findings. Pacific Palisades, Calif.: Goodyear.

O'KEEFE, M.T., and SHEINKOPF, K.G. (1974). "The voter decides: Candidate image or campaign issue?" Journal of Broadcasting, 18(fall):403-411.

PALETZ, D.L., and ELSON, M. (1976). "Television coverage of presidential conventions: Now you see it, now you don't." Political Science Quarterly, 91(spring):109-131.

PARRIS, J.H. (1972). The convention problem. Washington, D.C.: Brookings Institution.

PATTERSON, T.E., and McCLURE, R.D. (1976). The unseeing eye: The myth of television power in national elections. New York: G.P. Putnam's Sons.

PERRY, J.M. (1973). Us and them: How the press covered the 1972 election. New York: Clarkson N. Potter.

PETERS, C. (1976). "The ignorant press." Washington Monthly, 8(May):55-57.

ROBINSON, J.P. (1972). "Perceived media bias and the 1968 vote: Can the media affect behavior after all?" Journalism Quarterly, (summer):239-246.

——— (1974). "The press as king-maker: What surveys from the last five campaigns show." Journalism Quaterly, (winter):587-594.

ROBINSON, M.J. (1976). "Public affairs television and the growth of political malaise." American Political Science Review, 70(June):409-432.

ROBINSON, M.J., and BURGESS, P. (1970). "The Edward M. Kennedy speech: The impact of prime time television appeal." Television Quarterly, 9(winter):29-39.

ROBINSON, M.J., and ZUKIN, C. (1976). "Television and the Wallace vote." Journal of Communication, 26(spring):79-83.

ROPER, B.W. (1975). "Distorting the voice of the people." Columbia Journalism Review, 14(November/December):28-32.

ROSENBAUM, R. (1976). "A Ford not an Edsel." New Times, March, pp. 39-44.

RYAN, M. (1976). "View from the losing side." TV Guide, 24(June 12):8.

SHAFER, B., and LARSON, R. (1972). "Did TV create the 'social issue'?" Columbia Journalism Review, 11(September/October):10-17.

SIGEL, R.A. (1964). "Effects of partisanship on the perception of political candidates." Public Opinion Quarterly, 28:483-496.

SIMON, H.A., and STERN, F. (1955). "The effect of television upon voting behavior in Iowa in the 1952 presidential election." American Political Science Review, 49(June):470-477.

WALSH, E. (1976). "President hopes to offset likely California loss." Washington Post, June 9, p. A-1.

WAMSLEY, G.L., and PRIDE, R.A. (1972). "Television network news: Rethinking the iceberg problem." Western Political Quarterly, 25(September):434-450.

WEAVER, D.H., McCOMBS, M.E., and SPELLMAN, C. (1975). "Watergate and the media: A case study of agenda-setting." American Politics Quarterly, 3(October):458-472.

WEAVER, P. (1976). "Captives of melodrama." New York Times Magazine, August 29, pp. 6-7, 48, 50-51, 54, 56-57.

WEAVER, W. (1976). "Television and politics: A mixed effect." New York Times, July 18, p. E-1.

WITCOVER, J. (1972). "William Loeb and the New Hampshire primary: A question of ethics." Columbia Journalism Review, 11(May/June):14-25.

——— (1973). "The trials of a one-candidate campaign." Columbia Journalism Review, 11(January/February):24-28.

Chapter 7

DIRECT DEMOCRACY AND POLITICAL DEVELOPMENT:
LONGITUDINAL REFERENDA VOTING PATTERNS
IN AN AMERICAN STATE

DAVID R. MORGAN
SAMUEL A. KIRKPATRICK
MICHAEL R. FITZGERALD
WILLIAM LYONS

Policy making by plebiscite is a widespread political phenomenon in the United States. Nineteen states permit their constitution to be amended through the use of initiative petition, while 40 states have provisions for referenda voting by petition and/or legislative submission (Council of State Governments, 1974:22, 48). In recent years referenda were placed before the electorate in over three-fourths of the American states on such varied topics as gambling, mass transit, energy, aid to private schools, sex discrimination, and modernized government (State Government News, 1974:2). With all this electoral activity, in many cases involving important changes in the fundamental law of a state or embracing controversial, far-reaching measures, we have very little understanding of the process by which these issues reach the public and how and why the electorate responds as it does. This direct electorate-policy linkage represented by referenda voting has been seriously slighted in favor of an almost exclusive focus on popular voting for political parties and candidates. Furthermore, referenda are significant not only for

AUTHORS' NOTE: A number of people have contributed to this project over a period of time. In particular, we wish to acknowledge the assistance of C. Kenneth Meyer, James R. Bohland, and James L. Regens.

policy making but also for the extent to which they represent citizen response to issues and developmental processes in an electorate over time.

An argument has appeared recently suggesting that referenda voting does not adequately represent the policy views of the average citizen. Scott and Nathan (1970), for example, insist that referenda run the risk of being dominated by special interests who use them as a veto mechanism to protect the status quo. Even if true, many of the measures offered the electorate are important, are contested vigorously, and may have far-reaching policy consequences. For instance, between 1963 and 1968, the state of California and 10 of its cities conducted open housing referenda, all of which were initiated by those who sought to cancel such legislation by an appeal to the sovereign electorate (Hamilton, 1970:125). Even though this fundamental question was eventually settled by a U.S. Supreme Court decision, the open housing issue provides only one illustration of how direct democracy has played a crucial part in highly controversial policy matters. And while Wolfinger and Greenstein (1968:767-768) are critical of the referendum, they nonetheless admit that the legislature in California has persistently failed to reflect the wishes of the voters of that state (also see Bone and Benedict, 1975). Despite the skepticism among some political scientists concerning the value of this form of direct democracy, there is certainly no indication that the use of referenda as a means of expressing the popular will on public policies is lessening. To the contrary, its growing importance suggests an even greater need for a more complete understanding of what this process represents in the political life of a state or community.

Although studies of statewide referenda voting are scarce, elements of direct democracy have been rather thoroughly examined at the local level where such matters as fluoridation of water, mass transit, and a variety of bond issue elections for schools and municipal facilities have been analyzed.[1] Much less is known about the plebiscite process at the state level, however. Most research, largely of the descriptive variety, has been concerned with the use of referenda voting to amend state constitutions (Radabaugh, 1961; Sturm, 1970). Recently, more systematic studies of factors associated with referenda success have begun to emerge. Evidence is accumulating to show that voting on state propositions may be even more closely associated with income, education, and subjective social status than is voting in partisan races (Clubb and Traugott, 1972). In addition, there appears to be some association between Republican voting and support for certain state questions (Mueller, 1969). Thus, while the findings are limited, state referenda outcomes are apparently responsive to variations in individual life-styles and political orientations.

Longitudinal referenda voting patterns may also capture issue-oriented[2] and developmental aspects of a state's political culture (Almond and Verba, 1965; Patterson, 1968; Devine, 1972) and represent trends in the institutionalization of the electoral system. Voting on state questions may reflect fundamental changes in the mass electorate which are obscured by analyses of partisan voting. Rather than focusing attention on the development of the *party system* (Chambers, 1967; Burnham, 1970; Sundquist, 1973), historical referenda analysis more uniquely treats the development of the *electorate* and the nature of the issue space[3] which defines policy controversy. Such concepts as institutionalization, stability, and continuity are vital components of "political development" (Huntington, 1968; Przeworski, 1975), yet the plethora of crucial state referenda have never been examined from a developmental or historical process perspective.

I. RESEARCH DESIGN

In order to address both the static and process issues implied above, the following analysis incorporates all state questions submitted to the electorate of a state which has a rich history of direct democracy—Oklahoma. Our research questions address both the descriptive and analytical patterns of relationships at various times, as well as the historical process of development and change:

1. What is the general nature of referenda voting patterns in Oklahoma over time, especially with regard to patterns of rejection and acceptance by the electorate? Many referenda measures are of quite low salience and might be substantially affected by certain institutional arrangements such as the mode of referral (referenda or initiative petition) or the type of election in which the question is presented (general, primary, or special). Therefore, referenda success and failure are examined across structural categories in order to assess the impact of institutional arrangements.

2. To what extent may distinct patterns of relationships be delineated from among the series of phenomena (state question

votes) that are expected to be substantially interrelated? That is, is it possible to discern separate issue or temporal patterns within referenda voting behavior?

3. To what extent are the underlying characteristics of state question voting patterns associated with socioeconomic and political patterns within the state over time? Drawing on previous research, we would hypothesize that such characteristics as education, income, urbanization, industrialization, race, and population changes will affect support for or opposition to political issues represented by referenda propositions.

While there is a time dimension implied in each of the preceding questions, we are especially interested in addressing long-term processes of development. Developed political systems are most frequently characterized by stability of patterns of behavior over time, by a convergence of demographic cleavages, and by the appearance of more explicit value preferences on the part of the electorate (Riggs, 1967; Ilchman and Uphoff, 1971). In particular, if the political system within a state matures over time, we would expect that referenda voting might be reflective of that process.

In this regard, we assume that an institutionally mature and developed political culture will be characterized by increasing demographic diffusion, greater substantive issue differentiation, increasing stability and decreasing critical disturbances, and the emergence of relatively fewer' underlying dimensions of voting relative to the size of the issue space as defined by referenda.

The basic unit of analysis for which data are gathered in this study is the Oklahoma county (N = 77).[4] Data (percent "yes") are included on every state question to appear on the ballot since statehood—261 separate referenda items between 1907 and 1974. To facilitate comparisons with other measures and lend structure to time-bound analysis, these state questions are separated into seven 10-year periods. The socioeconomic and other political data are also used for the final three 10-year periods for which substantial and common observations are available, i.e., since 1945. The post-World War II era thus becomes the focus for the major portion of the analysis to follow, both for ease of analysis and for comparability.

The set of independent variables are of two types: socioeconomic characteristics and partisan voting patterns. The following socio-economic characteristics are employed for each Oklahoma county for three separate periods (1950, 1960, 1970)—roughly comparable to the latest three state question periods (1946-1955, 1956-1965,

1966-1974): percent urban, percent rural farm, percent manufacturing, percent nonwhite, median school years, median age, percent population increase, and percent owner occupied dwellings. Eventually these separate socioeconomic variables are factor-analyzed within each 10-year period, and county factor scores consolidating their basic socioeconomic patterns are generated. These scores become the socioeconomic independent variables with which state question voting patterns are subsequently analyzed. The partisan voting trends are measured as the mean percentage within any given period voting Republican in gubernatorial elections.

II. THE EFFECTS OF INSTITUTIONAL ARRANGEMENTS

The Oklahoma Constitution provides three basic methods for the exercise of direct democracy—the legislative referendum, the referendum (petition), and the initiative (petition). Since most legislative enactments bear the emergency clause, which places the law in effect immediately, the referendum by petition is seldom used. And, even in a state with around 2.5 million population, securing signatures of qualified voters on an initiative or referendum petition of either 8% (for a law) or 15% (for a constitutional amendment) is a sizable undertaking. For this reason, most plebiscite voting in the past 30 years in Oklahoma has been the result of legislative referenda. For the first postwar period (1946-1955) referenda propositions constituted 63% of all such measures. This increased to 73% for 1956-1965; and, for the last period (1966-1974), 90% of all state questions were placed on the ballot by legislative action. During this same 30-year span, most direct legislation occurred in primary elections (46%), although in recent years greater use has been made of special elections.

Since statehood (1907), 38% of all state questions have been approved by the Oklahoma electorate. Since World War II, however, the rate of success has increased to 47%. For this same period (1946-1974), constitutional amendments (N = 118), with a rate of passage of 53%, have fared somewhat better than statutory enactments (N = 20), which have had only a 10% success rate. The mode of referral also appears to affect the outcome: 55% of all legislative referenda were adopted, compared with only 20% for those proposals emanating from the petition process (initiative and referenda). The type of election likewise has an impact on state question success or failure. Those propositions offered at general elections do quite poorly (only 18% passed), while those referred at special elections and primaries fare much better—49% and 61% adopted respectively.[5]

Table 1 reports the rate of success for all state questions for 1946 to 1974 when both mode of referral and type of election are taken into account. The cell reflecting the highest adoption level is the primary election with legislative referral (63% success) closely followed by the special election-legislative referendum category (56% adopted). Rejection was most frequent for those issues brought to the ballot by legislative resolution at general elections (only 14% passed).

There may also be a relationship between institutional arrangements and the substance of state questions. For this analysis, referenda votes have been divided into seven basic categories —education; revenue and expenditure; electoral structure and reform; regulation of business and property; state government organization, structure and reform; local government; and social issues and benefits. For the entire postwar period those questions devoted to state organization and reform clearly were most dominant (32.6%). As far as mode of referral is concerned, electoral structure and regulation matters virtually always appeared on the ballot by way of legislative referenda. But popular action played a key role for many education and social issues; almost one-third of those questions found their way to the ballot as a result of initiative petition. This indicates that the initiative, and especially the referenda petition, may be used as protest devices—either to circumvent a recalcitrant legislature or to veto its action. These steps were most likely to be taken in the areas of education (most of these questions involved

Table 1. STATE QUESTION OUTCOMES BY MODE OF REFERRAL AND ELECTION TYPE: 1946-1974

| | Election Type | | | | | |
| | Special | | Primary | | General | |
	I*	R	I*	R	I*	R
Adopted	22.2%	56.3%	0.0%	62.9%	21.1%	14.3%
	(2)	(18)	(0)	(39)	(4)	(2)
Rejected	77.8	43.7	100.0	37.1	77.9	85.7
	(7)	(14)	(2)	(23)	(15)	(12)
Total	100.0	100.0	100.0	100.0	100.0	100.0
	(9)	(32)	(2)	(62)	(19)	(14)

*Includes both initiative petition (n = 23) and referenda petition (n = 7) questions.

school finance) or in the social area where such issues were more likely to evoke emotional, ideological, or group conflict.

Certain questions were more likely to appear at particular types of elections. Until very recently, because of the "silent vote,"[6] the "deck was stacked" against referenda items placed on the general election ballot. As noted earlier, state questions voted on at special elections or primary ballots have a higher rate of success. In most cases, this election decision is made by the governor in Oklahoma. Since 1946, an unusually large proportion of education issues were voted on in general elections (45% compared to local government's 15%, for example). On the other hand, referenda votes on most other matters were taken at special or primary elections over 80% of the time. No precise explanation for the deviant position of education issues comes to mind. It could be that it reflects the continuing tension between educational interest groups (particularly the Oklahoma Education Association) and state officials who may, at times, resent the pressure from this powerful lobby.

With regard to success or failure since World War II, a considerable difference is found by substantive area. The easiest questions to get passed were those pertaining to the regulation of business and property (80% succeeded). Social issues had the lowest rate of passage (23%). Despite their frequent placement on general election ballots, education issues succeeded 60% of the time. Revenue and expenditure matters were not as fortunate, winning voter approval only 47% of the time.

Finally, when one considers the substance of the questions by mode of referral, election type, and rate of success, several patterns emerge. First, all revenue-expenditure and electoral structure matters were successful when they resulted from legislative referral and were placed on a nongeneral election ballot. At the other extreme, no social issue questions were approved that were initiated, irrespective of election type (N = 5). The only such questions that have been successful since 1946 (N = 3) were those referred by the legislature and voted on at nongeneral elections. Type of election was especially crucial in three issue areas. All revenue and expenditure measures voted on at primary or special elections were approved (N = 8). Electoral structure questions and those regulating business and property had a success rate of 88% when they were placed on nongeneral election ballots (N = 8 in both categories).

Institutional structure does make a difference, but it surely is not the whole story. Other considerations may be equally or more

Table 2. FACTOR ANALYSIS (ORTHOGONAL ROTATION) OF STATE QUESTIONS FOR 1946-1955

State Question	Year	Factor 1 1946 (Education)	Factor 2 1950	Factor 3 1952 (Revenue)	Factor 4 1954 (Toll Road)	h^2
Tax Separate Schools (RPAC)	1946	.79	.06	.37	−.03	.76
Incr. School Revenue (IGAC)		.89	.23	.06	.07	.86
School Aid (IGAC)		.90	.21	.11	.06	.86
Tax for Segregation (IGAC)		.90	.21	.10	.05	.87
Free Textbooks (IGAC)		.88	.22	.20	.05	.87
School Tax Levy (RPAC)	1948	.78	.20	.26	.12	.73
St. Coll. Bd. of Reg. (RPAC)		.74	.34	.34	.12	.79
Leg. Pay Raise (RPAC)		.66	.34	.40	.13	.73
Repeal Prohibition (ISFC)	1949	.08	.82	−.07	.08	.70
Cig. Tax.-Cap. Impr. (RSAC)		.19	.64	−.22	.05	.51
Wkmns. Comp. (RPAC)	1950	.54	.21	.43	.33	.62
Estab. Hwy. Comm. (IGFC)		.22	.93	.09	.15	.94
Hwy. User's Tax (IGFC)		.20	.94	.01	.12	.94
Endorse U.N. (RGFS)		.15	.69	.51	.04	.76
Okla. Mil. Acad. (RGFC)		.24	.94	.03	.13	.96
St. Constit. Conv. (RGFS)		.27	.92	−.01	.20	.96
Amend. St. Constit. (RPAC)	1952	.67	.53	.02	.14	.75
End All-Male Gr. Jur. (RPAC)		.54	.60	−.24	.17	.74
Mil. Comp. (RGFC)		.24	−.05	.93	.01	.93
Voting Age (RGFC)		.21	−.18	.89	−.02	.87
Incr. Sales Tax (IGFS)		.23	−.05	.94	.03	.94
Tnpk. Authority (RSAS)	1954	.14	.25	.00	.94	.96
Est. Tnpk. Auth. (RSAS)		.14	.26	.00	.94	.96
Corp. Real Estate (RPAC)		.65	.43	.39	.26	.83
St. Vet. Benefits (RPAC)		.52	−.04	.59	−.02	.62
Real Estate Tax (RGAC)		.50	−.03	.28	.33	.43
School Revenue (RSAC)	1955	.52	.30	.46	.20	.60
Eigenvalue		8.13	6.63	4.45	2.30	21.5
% of Total Variance		30.1	24.6	16.5	8.5	79.7

Table 2 (continued)

*LEGEND:	1st column (Mode of Referral)	R = Legislative Referendum I = Initiative Petition P = Referendum Petition
	2nd column (Type of Election)	S = Special P = Primary (and Runoff Primaries) G = General
	3rd column (Outcome)	A = Adopted F = Failed
	4th column	C = Constitutional Amendment S = Statutory Enactment

important in explaining levels of support for various propositions. Certain social, economic, and political forces must be explored to provide a more complete understanding of the referenda phenomena. For this purpose, an analysis by county using multivariate statistical techniques is undertaken in the following section.

III. PATTERNS OF COUNTY REFERENDA VOTING

In order to assess the underlying dimensions of referenda voting behavior, a factor analysis[7] was performed using all state questions occurring during each of the three 10-year periods since World War II. The resulting factor solutions (Tables 2, 3, and 4) lack distinctive patterns of a substantive nature, yet it appears that referenda voting is not random and that factor patterns are capturing meaningful common variance among most of the variables. These factor patterns are sufficiently complex, however, to warrant a more extended discussion of their interpretation before an effort is made to account for variation in each of the factors.

PERIOD 1 (1946-1955)

In the first period the factor patterns appear to be primarily election-specific. The four state questions most closely related to factor 1 (those with the highest loadings), for example, all appeared on the 1946 general election ballot, and all were adopted. These four propositions reflected various educational issues, but in our judgment the most critical influence in producing the clustering pattern was the appearance of each together at the same election. Thus we named factor 1 "1946 (Education)" with the name in parentheses indicating a secondary influence. This same situation apparently prevailed with

Table 3. FACTOR ANALYSIS (ORTHOGONAL ROTATION) OF STATE QUESTIONS FOR 1956-1965

State Question	Year	Factor 1 1956	Factor 2 (Governmental Reorganization)	Factor 3 1964 (Educational Reorganization)	Factor 4 1963 (Term of Office)	Factor 5 1965 (Revenue)	h^2
Vets Loan Org. (RPFC)*	1956	.79	-.47	.14	.08	-.05	.88
Vets Benefits (RPFC)		.83	-.13	.27	.09	.19	.82
Create New Bd. Reg. (RPFC)		.76	.14	.34	.05	.38	.86
Bd. Reg.-Ok. Mil. Acad. (RPFC)		.80	.17	.32	.08	.36	.90
Water Supply Indebt. (RPFC)		.74	.21	.23	-.20	.32	.79
Create Wildlife Comm. (RPFC)		.67	.25	.33	.30	.32	.82
Corp. Stock Ownership (PRFC)		.83	.18	.22	.10	.27	.85
Congressional Redist. (IGFS)		-.34	.63	.21	.22	.41	.76
Create Cnty. Office (IGFC)		-.57	.23	.20	.30	.35	.63
Cnty. Op.-Prohib. (ISFC)	1957	.01	-.84	.07	-.19	.12	.76
Ad Valor. Tax. (RSAC)	1958	.51	.37	.15	-.01	.40	.58
City Water Facil. (RSAC)		.56	.43	.03	-.07	.39	.65
Repeal Prohibition (RSAC)	1959	.12	.39	-.19	.10	.12	.23
Cnty. Opt.-Prohib. (RSFC)		.09	-.83	.19	-.10	.07	.75
Nom. of Candidate (RSAC)	1960	.60	.47	.24	.10	.45	.86
Leg. Pay Raise (RPFC)		.64	.26	.34	.19	.41	.80
Dept. of Health (RPAC)		.74	.16	.21	.06	.35	.74
Cap. Improvement (RPAC)		.44	.21	.38	.18	.47	.64
Indus. Fin. Auth. (RPAC)		.58	.47	.17	.17	.30	.71
Multi-Cnty. Libs. (RPAC)		.47	.54	.23	.16	.34	.70
State Highway Comm. (ISFC)		.11	.89	.15	-.07	.24	.88
Leg. Apportionment (ISFC)		.09	.89	.15	-.08	.23	.88
Control Cnty. Rds. (ISFS)		.10	.89	.15	-.07	.23	.88
Leg. Special Sess. (RGFC)		.37	.22	.45	.05	.53	.67
State Income Taxes (RGFS)	1961	.43	.57	.17	.31	.32	.73
Criminal Prosecution (RSAC)		-.22	.30	.02	-.40	.12	.31

[244]

Variable	Year						
House Apport. for Census (RSFC)	1962	−.03	−.50	−.13	−.33	−.24	.43
Industrial Bonds (RPAC)		.67	−.01	.21	.19	.28	.61
Leg. Sess. and Pay (RPFC)		.29	.03	.28	.40	.45	.52
Local Emergency Juris. (RPAC)		.31	.36	.23	.18	.61	.69
Repeal Prohibition (RGFC)		.39	.72	.12	.01	.01	.69
Leg. Apportionment Comm. (ISFC)	1963	.35	.81	.11	−.17	.26	.88
Cap. Improvement (RSAC)		.50	.43	.45	−.10	.50	.45
Incr. Cnty. Off. Term (RSFS)		.11	.17	.07	.90	.09	.86
Cnty. Jdg. Off. Term (RSFC)		−.06	.32	.02	.78	.04	.71
Incr. St. Off. Terms (RSFC)		.16	−.10	.11	.88	.02	.82
Right to Work (IPFC)	1964	−.87	−.20	.11	−.12	−.06	.82
Elector Resid. (RPAC)		−.84	.14	.29	−.04	.23	.86
Legis. Comp. (RPFC)		.07	−.44	.63	.13	.16	.63
Leg. Reappor. (RPAC)		−.14	−.87	−.16	−.07	−.21	.85
Leg. Pay Raise (RGFC)		.40	.02	.85	.08	.15	.91
Create Judic. Court (RGFC)		−.02	.51	.77	−.03	.25	.92
Special Election Vacancy (RGFS)		.06	−.03	.95	.09	.14	.94
School Support Levy (IGFC)		.07	.25	.93	.03	.12	.95
State Aid to Schools (IGFS)	1964	.22	.04	.95	.10	.08	.96
Sch. Consolid. (IGFS)		.13	.26	.92	−.04	.10	.93
Cnty. Sch. Superdent. (IGFS)		.26	−.03	.94	.05	.01	.95
Incr. Sales Tax (RSFS)	1965	.30	−.13	.24	−.06	.70	.66
Cap. Improvement (RSFC)		.35	.35	.12	−.02	.73	.79
Cap. Improvement (RSFS)		.30	.42	.03	.02	.73	.80
School Rev. (RSAC)		−.11	.53	.14	.11	.27	.40
Cap. Improvement (RSAC)		.22	.28	−.04	.14	.44	.35
Eigenvalue		10.8	10.4	8.0	3.4	5.9	38.5
% of Total Variance		20.8	20.0	15.4	6.6	11.3	74.0

*For Legend see Table 2.

respect to the relationship among many of the measures appearing later in this 10-year period, so that in each similar case we have designated the factor by the year of the election. Where some substantive interpretation seemed appropriate (as for factors 1, 3, and 4), we also provided a brief name in parentheses. This indicates that *some* of the state questions with high loadings on that factor appeared to at least partially represent such a substantive issue. Factor 3, for instance, contained important revenue measures and has been named "1952 (Revenue)"; factor 4 had two toll road questions with very high loadings and was designated "1954 (Toll road)." In some cases, as with factor 2, no meaningful name seemed suitable, and the factor is labeled only as to election date, e.g., "1950."

PERIOD 2 (1956-1965)

Again in this period, four of the five factors seem to result primarily from clustering among state questions that appeared on the same ballot. Thus factor 1 has been named "1956." Factor 2, however, does not appear to be election-related, as evidenced by high loadings across time (down the factor). Those propositions with high loadings suggest a governmental reorganization dimension (three votes on legislative apportionment load high). The third factor, "1964 (Education Reorganization)," is not only election-specific but also reflects high loadings on several propositions dealing with educational reform (state aid to schools, school consolidation, and compensation for county superintendents). Factor 4 has been named "1963 (Term of Office)." As before, certain high loadings appear for measures affecting government officials, this time increasing their terms of office, but these questions all appeared at the same time. It is difficult to determine precisely which influence is most dominant —the substantive issues or their joint occurrence at the same election. Finally, factor 5 is revenue-related, yet it is primarily the result of state questions with high loadings which were voted upon at the 1965 special election and has thus been termed "1965 (Revenue)."

PERIOD 3 (1966-1974)

During the final period under examination, the election-bound nature of the factor solutions begins to disintegrate. With the exception of factor 5, the dimensions are more substantive than time-specific. Although factor 1 has been named "Miscellaneous Change (1968-1969)," since no other designation seemed appropriate given the diverse nature of those issues with high loadings, factor 2 appears to represent primarily a government and more general reform dimension. High loadings are reflected on matters relating to school segregation, impeachment of certain state officers, a second term for the governor, and several tax issues. The third factor represents a "Revenue" dimension since several questions load here having to do with raising revenue for state or local governments. A combination of certain moral issues (liquor-by-the-drink and pari-mutuel betting) and government reform questions load highly on factor 4 ("Moral/ Government Reform"). Factor 5 seems to make little sense substantively and has been labeled merely "1971." The final factor seems to reflect issues relating to local control of government activities and has been named "Local Control."

In general, a number of state questions in Oklahoma over the past 30 years are interrelated primarily in time or election-bound patterns. Yet the irregularities of elite agenda-setting[8] are given some structure by the electorate; complete randomness obviously does not exist. As a result, time-bound elements and substantive issue dimensions are meshed together. In addition, structure is evident in patterns of yea-saying and nay-saying. As Mueller (1969:1198) suggests concerning the vote on noncontroversial referenda in California, "It is difficult to avoid the conclusion that there exists an underlying mood of favorableness or unfavorableness toward the propositions which forms a background from which specific propositions, due to reasonable or capricious circumstances, may deviate." We, too, observed a phenomenon not unlike this in which important measures appearing at the same election succeed or fail together. In some cases this undoubtedly occurs as a result of a particularly controversial issue that has attracted considerable attention and serves as a point of issue centrality governing passage *or* failure for an entire set.

There is evidence, however, that the extent of yea/nay-saying in Oklahoma has decreased somewhat over the years. For the postwar era, for example, all of the factor clusters (enclosed in boxes) are completely homogeneous in acceptance and failure patterns for 1946-1955, but by the 1956-1965 period two of the five factors shown in Table 3 represent clusters of issues where 78% and 88% failed (compared to 100% passage or failure earlier). The most recent period contains two factors where only 67% failed and 80% were

Table 4. FACTOR ANALYSIS (ORTHOGONAL ROTATION) OF STATE QUESTIONS FOR 1966-1974

State Question	Year	Factor 1 Miscellaneous Change (1968-1969)	Factor 2 Governmental/ General Reform	Factor 3 Revenue	Factor 4 Moral/ Governmental Reform	Factor 5 1971	Factor 6 Local Control	h^2
End School Seg (RPAC)*	1966	-.15	-.93	.17	.01	.12	-.03	.92
St. Off. Impeach (RPAC)		.07	-.93	-.01	.08	.16	.14	.92
Court of Judic. (RPAC)		.58	-.45	-.01	.39	.36	.15	.85
Pres. Electors (RPAC)		.74	-.22	-.20	.30	.30	.21	.86
Re-elec. of Governor (RPAC)		.13	-.74	.27	.43	.06	-.23	.88
Vocational Ed. Prgm. (RPAC)		.70	.28	.24	.31	.06	.01	.73
Limit Leg. Sess. (RPAC)		.30	-.45	.47	.34	-.12	-.04	.65
Fix Congrsnl. Bound. (RGFS)		.25	.54	.33	-.40	.26	-.21	.74
Jud. Nom. (RSAC)	1967	.36	-.48	-.22	.32	.46	-.07	.72
Jud. Department (RSAC)		.28	-.59	-.17	.30	.44	-.10	.75
Cng. in Est. Rev. (RSAC)	1968	.08	-.83	.05	.09	.19	-.09	.75
Invest. Sch. Funds. (RPAC)		.25	-.88	.04	.21	.06	.09	.89
Leg. Reg. of Tax (RPAC)		.73	.11	-.07	.46	.20	.18	.84
Pdn. and Prl. Bd. (RPFC)		.58	-.37	.26	.18	.08	.32	.68
Salaries Elec. Off. (RPFC)		.64	-.20	.16	.49	.28	.07	.81
Petition Gr. Jurs. (RPAC)		.28	-.71	.24	.41	.21	-.16	.88
Intang. Prop. Tax (RPAC)		.19	-.84	-.06	.17	-.07	.14	.81
Cong. Est. Revs. (RPFC)		.49	-.36	.52	-.12	.02	-.22	.71
Conf. of Int. (RPAC)		.80	.11	.23	.28	.21	-.06	.83
Jud. Reform (IPFC)		.58	.20	-.11	.16	.50	.19	.69
Taxtn. Transit. Prop. (RPAC)		.54	-.31	-.33	.34	.38	.35	.88
Fix Max. Int. Rate (RPAC)		-.03	-.87	-.07	.16	.18	.20	.87
Corp. Reports (RPAC)		.45	-.51	-.27	.30	.30	.41	.88
Issue Corp. Stock (RPAC)		.50	-.46	-.26	.34	.28	.39	.88
Jury Trials (RPAC)		.56	-.42	-.23	.35	.29	.38	.90
Repeal Oath (RGFC)		.47	-.23	.25	.30	.54	-.07	.72
Cap. Improv. Auth. (RSAC)		.50	.04	.27	-.04	.36	-.12	.47
Require Oath (RSAC)	1969	.65	-.23	.21	-.02	.11	.06	.53

Measure	Year							h^2
Finance Bonds (RSFC)		.64	-.19	.22	-.10	.11	.12	.54
Constit. Conv. (RSFC)	1970	.40	-.32	-.18	.50	.56	.02	.88
Mode of Amend. (RSFC)		.48	-.32	-.15	.47	.52	.12	.87
St. Fin. Bonds (RSFC)		.58	-.30	-.06	.25	.43	.08	.68
Reapportionment (RPFC)		.24	-.11	.65	.18	.44	.03	.72
End Segregation (RPFC)		.36	-.22	.29	.22	.59	.30	.75
Estab. Hospt. Dist. (RPFC)		.07	-.12	.68	.04	.28	.12	.58
Non-Part. Elec. (RGFS)		.38	-.30	.31	.60	.29	-.06	.78
Dpst. St. Funds.(RGFS)		.26	-.08	[.70]	.20	.22	-.05	.66
No Sunday Sales (ISFS)	1971	.22	-.06	.14	.10	.58	.13	.44
Bond Elector (RSFC)		.20	-.28	.26	.30	[.75]	.01	.84
Student Loans (RSAC)		.00	.06	.11	.17	[.71]	-.01	.55
Immun. Law-Stns. (RSAC)		.24	-.30	.15	.41	[.70]	-.06	.83
Grand Jury Rev. (RSAC)		.26	-.29	.11	.42	[.73]	.10	.89
Voting Age (RSAC)		.26	-.19	-.01	.20	[.71]	.23	.70
Raise Hwy. Funds (RSFC)	1972	-.01	.18	[.73]	-.02	-.02	-.10	.57
Municp. Elctrte. (RPFC)		.15	-.11	.50	.15	.53	-.08	.60
10% Debt Limit (RPAC)		.03	-.68	.33	.08	.46	.15	.80
70% Value Invst. (RPFC)	1972	.24	-.09	.07	-.17	.36	.59	.58
Liquor by Drink (IGFC)		.20	-.23	.00	[.82]	.27	-.10	.85
Ad Valor. Tax (RGAC)		.13	-.12	-.20	.07	-.41	.64	.66
Emgcy. Sch. Levies (RGFC)		.32	-.33	.30	.43	-.03	.32	.59
Elim. Slnt. Vote (RPAC)	1974	.14	-.20	.27	[.79]	.29	.23	.90
Elim. Slnt. Vote (RPAC)		.24	-.26	.14	[.81]	.29	.18	.92
Cnty. Revenue (RPFC)		-.21	.06	.60	.17	.01	.41	.61
Parimutl. Bet. (RPFC)		-.04	-.12	-.12	[.80]	.16	-.00	.71
Res. Vot. Reqs. (RPFC)		.22	-.18	.37	.67	.41	.18	.86
Exec. Reorg. (RPFC)		.21	-.20	.33	[.78]	.34	.03	.92
Pdn. and Prl. Bd. (RPFC)		.36	-.19	.07	.70	.21	.26	.76
Emer. Med. Dist. (RPFC)		.11	.05	.12	.22	.24	[.69]	.61
Labor Comm. Apt. (RGFC)		.25	-.15	.38	.36	.52	-.03	.64
Eigenvalue		8.9	10.1	5.3	8.6	8.3	3.1	44.4
% of Total Variance		15.1	17.1	8.9	14.5	14.1	5.3	75.1

*For Legend see Table 2.

Table 5. FACTOR ANALYSIS* OF COUNTY DEMOGRAPHIC CHARACTERISTICS IN OKLAHOMA: 1950, 1960, 1970

Characteristic	1950 Factors			1960 Factors			1970 Factors		
	Urban-Industrial	Cultural Deprivation	Population Stability	Urban-Industrial	Cultural Deprivation	Population Growth	Affluence	Population Stability	Urban-Industrial
Percent urban	.92	-.17	-.11	.83	-.25	.04	.55	-.50	.45
Percent rural farm	-.89	.28	.11	-.91	-.03	-.01	-.24	.56	-.66
Percent manufacturing	.75	.30	.27	.63	.36	-.48	-.24	-.01	.78
Percent nonwhite	.20	.82	-.08	.31	.82	.14	.14	.02	.75
Median income	.43	-.75	.05	.40	-.83	-.10	.93	-.09	.09
Median school years	.54	-.70	-.18	.26	-.83	.13	.96	-.04	-.11
Median age	.01	-.57	.49	-.69	.24	-.28	-.25	.80	-.21
Percent population increase	-.18	-.05	-.83	-.11	.19	.72	.03	-.43	-.13
Percent owner occupied dwelling	-.41	-.17	.70	-.40	.12	-.80	.07	.88	-.13
Percent total variance	32.5	25.4	17.2	32.2	26.1	16.7	25.4	24.3	21.2

*Varimax rotation; Kaiser's criterion for the number of factors; fourth factor (1970) eigenvalue = 1.02. The three reported factors explain the following percent of total variance: 1950 (75.2%), 1960 (75.0%), 1970 (70.9%).

rejected. While there is substantial clustering around acceptance-failure patterns, such patterns appear to be eroding for the more recent periods.

IV. SOCIOECONOMIC AND POLITICAL CORRELATES
OF STATE QUESTION DIMENSIONS

Before attempting to account for variations in referenda dimensions with demographic and political characteristics, it is important to describe the underlying socioeconomic milieu in postwar Oklahoma.

Table 5 reveals the results of factor-analyzing nine fundamental demographic characteristics for the 77 counties of the state for the three recent time periods. While some shifting of variables among factors occurs across time periods, three essentially similar dimensions can be identified for each 10-year period—Urban-Industrial, Affluence (or Cultural Deprivation), and Population Stability (or Growth). As suggested by the name reversals in parentheses, the signs changed on certain factors between periods, e.g., Population Stability for 1950 becomes Population Growth in 1960 but returns to Stability in 1970. A somewhat similar situation occurs for Affluence, yet the underlying patterns remain quite similar. The Urban-Industrial factor accounts for the most variance in the 1950 and 1960 solutions but is displaced by the other two factors for 1970. Percent of work force in manufacturing loads on this factor in each period as does percent rural farm (negative loading). Percent urban also appears prominently on this factor during the two early periods but is split almost evenly between all three factors for 1970 (with slightly higher loading on Affluence). The second basic socioeconomic factor, designated as Cultural Deprivation (1950 and 1960) and Affluence (1970), has high loadings on median income, median school years, and percent nonwhite (first two periods only). Finally, Table 5 reveals a third demographic dimension with high loadings on percent population increase and percent owner-occupied dwellings that has been named Population Stability (1950, 1970) and Population Growth for 1960.

The regression analysis to follow includes as independent variables the three basic socioeconomic dimensions of the counties for each time period plus the average Republican vote for governor during the same span of time. Table 6 reports the results of these regression

Table 6. STATE QUESTION REGRESSION ANALYSIS WITH STANDARDIZED COEFFICIENTS FOR THREE TIME PERIODS

Period 1 (1946-1955)	State Question Factors			
Demographic and Political Characteristics	1946 (Education)	1950	1952 (Revenue)	1954 (Toll road)
Urban-Industrial (1950)	.60	.50	−.20	.23
Cultural Deprivation (1950)	−.10	.25	.65	.04
Population Stability (1950)	−.08	−.19	.04	−.15
Percent Rep., Gov. (1950)	−.64	.50	−.27	.07
R^2	.63	.53	.69	.08

Period 2 (1956-1965)	State Question Factors				
Demographic and Political Characteristics	1956	Govt. Reorg.	1964 (Educ. Reorg.)	1963 (Term of Office	1965 (Revenue)
Urban-Industrial (1960)	.21	.67	.23	.13	.43
Cultural Deprivation (1960)	.49	.02	−.30	.21	−.20
Population Growth (1960)	−.15	.03	.18	−.06	.07
Percent Rep., Gov. (1960)	−.47	.40	−.37	.26	−.14
R^2	.79	.49	.26	.07	.25

Period 3 (1966-1974)	State Question Factors					
Demographic and Political Characteristics	Change (1968-1969)	General Reform	Revenue	Moral/ Govt. Reform (1974)	1971	Local Control
Affluence (1970)	.41	.07	.29	.25	.37	.06
Pop. Stability (1970)	.26	−.32	−.12	−.16	.26	.32
Urban-Industrial (1970)	.20	−.30	.15	.36	.18	−.35
Percent Rep., Gov. (1970)	.06	−.05	−.51	.59	−.19	.05
R^2	.29	.22	.54	.36	.23	.26

equations including the standardized partial regression coefficients (Beta weights) and the percentage of explained variance (R^2).

Three of the four state question factors for the first period (1946-1955) bear a reasonably close relationship to the socio-economic and political variables as revealed in Table 6. In particular, Urban-Industrial and percent Republican are consistently associated with variation in most of the factors. In the case of the "1946 (Education)" factor, the more industrial and urban counties supported education-related measures, while those areas voting strongly Republican were generally opposed (R^2 = .63). The "1950" factor is also prominently related to industrialization and Republican vote, but this time both exert a positive influence (R^2 = .53). The "1952 (Revenue)" factor is most closely linked to Cultural Deprivation

(.64), which means that the less affluent counties actually provided greater levels of support for these measures than their richer counterparts. While Urban-Industrial (−.20) and percent Republican (−.27) are only modestly related to factor 3, the total R^2 (.69) is the highest achieved for the period. The final factor, "1954 (Toll road)," is almost totally unresponsive to the particular socioeconomic and political measures employed in the analysis (R^2 = .08). In sum, with the exception of the fourth factor, considerable variation among the state question dimensions for the first period can be accounted for by a limited number of demographic and political variables. In particular, counties with more urban-industrial characteristics frequently tend to vote in a similar way. The same is true with respect to partisan voting among counties. To a lesser extent, levels of wealth also seem to influence referenda voting.

Using multiple regression, reasonably good statistical explanation is achieved for only two state question factors for time period two (1956-1965), as revealed in Table 6. Seventy-nine percent of the variance can be accounted for in the "1956" factor using the four independent variables. Cultural Deprivation (.49) and percent Republican (−.47) have the strongest impact on this first factor. The next dimension, "Government Reorganization," with R^2 = .49, is most affected by Urban-Industrial (.67) and percent Republican (.40). This means that issues promoting governmental change (three well-publicized reform measures pushed by a new governor) were supported primarily by the more urban areas within the state and those counties that tend to vote Republican (the governor in this case was a Democrat but widely perceived as a young, urban-oriented reformer). Although only two factors in this period are primarily determined by the specific variables employed in the regression analysis, it again appears that the urban-industrial character of a county and its partisan predisposition do have important consequences for county referenda voting.

In the final period (1966-1974), when the state question factors are least time-related and more differentiating, regression equations produce relatively low levels of explained variance (see Table 6). Only in the case of the "Revenue" factor (R^2 = .54) can as much as half the variation in a factor pattern be accounted for by the effects of the four independent variables. In this instance, percent Republican (−.51) has the greatest effect, with some contribution also occurring from Affluence (.29). These regression coefficients suggest that the more Republican the county the less likely it was to support certain revenue-related propositions while, at the same time, the more well-to-do counties tended to support such measures.[9] Table 6 also reveals that each of the four independent variables makes important contributions to certain of the state question factors despite the relatively low level of overall explanation achieved for the six factor patterns for this period.

In summary, of the six equations over the total period when explained variance was about 50% or more, four of the state question factors had identifiable issue substance. Two were revenue-related, one had an education orientation, and one appeared to be primarily a government reorganization dimension. The most consistently potent independent variable in these four equations was percent Republican vote for governor. The urban-industrial nature of a county and its level of wealth were also important in most of these four cases. Unfortunately the direction of these effects was not consistent for every cluster of issues. In most cases, the urban-industrial counties tended to support these referenda measures. Republican-leaning counties were not congruent, however. Such areas generally were opposed to revenue-related measures but were otherwise not uniform in their support or opposition. This suggests that referenda voting is somewhat regularly affected by certain structural cleavages within the state and by partisan voting trends.

V. DEVELOPMENTAL ASPECTS OF ELECTORAL RESPONSE

As indicated earlier, we suspect that patterns of referenda voting and associated environmental characteristics are keys to understanding the electoral aspects of political development. While Table 5 reveals relatively comparable, independent socioeconomic factors for each of the three postwar periods, this was accompanied by an equalization of variance caught by each factor. This is largely a reflection of the diffusion of urban-industrialization components and a weakening of cleavages along that structural dimension. These demographic shifts over time are more precisely reflected in the standard deviations of the various demographic variables with the means taken into account. This is measured by the coefficient of variation, which is the ratio of the standard deviation to the mean (Blalock, 1972:88). Table 7 presents the coefficients of variation for each demographic variable in each postwar period. With regard to most structural variables, especially urbanism, manufacturing, and

Table 7. COEFFICIENTS OF VARIATION FOR COUNTY DEMOGRAPHIC
CHARACTERISTICS IN OKLAHOMA: 1950, 1960, 1970

Characteristic	1950	1960	1970
Percent population increase	.51	.69	1.08
Percent urban	.71	.72	.67
Percent rural farm	.40	.53	.55
Median age	.08	.12	.14
Percent nonwhite	.84	.80	.57
Median school years	.11	.16	.09
Percent manufacturing	.81	.68	.56
Percent owner occupied dwelling	.07	.08	.06
Median income	.30	.27	.20

income, and to some extent patterns of ownership, education, and racial distribution, there is a decrease in the variability of each element by county across time. That is, there is movement toward greater homogeneity and intercounty similarity in the last decennial period. Much of this reflects a meshing of center and periphery cleavages and a spread of urbanism, industrialization, and income throughout the state.

Previous data in Table 6 suggest that linkages between subjective (as reflected in referenda voting) and structural features of political culture are becoming slightly weaker and more diffuse. The environmental *political* variable employed in the analysis (percent Republican for governor), however, tends to increase in its relevance on a selective basis. Yet for the most part, the entire environmental set of demographic and political variables is able to explain less variance in the dependent referenda variables over time; for example, the mean multiple coefficient of determination (R^2) decreases from .48 in 1946-1955 to .37 and .32 in the more recent periods. Any demographic bases for issue reorientations are becoming less clear over time and less reflective of underlying structural cleavages in the social system. In sum, social and economic diffusion is occurring so as to lessen traditional demographic cleavages; yet we note a slight rise in the relevance of partisan cleavages. Although Republican voting has increased in Oklahoma since the mid-fifties, it seems unlikely that such partisan shifts will be sufficiently powerful to interrupt the trend toward a more consensual political culture as exemplified by the weakening of demographic ties to referenda voting.

The above trends are accompanied by a considerable expansion in the size of the electoral space as defined by the number of ballot issues and by a tendency for the electorate to exhibit greater substantive issue differentiation (versus time or election-bound dimensions) in recent periods (Tables 2, 3, and 4). While the policy agenda is becoming more diverse, the electorate appears to be increasingly capable of reacting selectively to substantive issues.

A related developmental question suggested earlier draws attention to long-term tendencies in the stability and continuity of electoral patterns. In addition to the previously suggested trends, a developing polity and an electorate characterized by increasing institutionalization of behavior patterns should exhibit increasingly fewer random electoral disturbances and more prominent signs of continuity. In order to test for this effect, a "critical elections" analysis (Key, 1955; MacRae and Meldrum, 1960) was performed to isolate any apparent divergence from established referenda voting patterns that could signal a long-term reorientation of county behavior or other forms of discontinuity. Toward that end, all of the state questions appearing on the ballot since statehood were divided into seven periods at approximately 10-year intervals. Every state question appearing within a 10-year period was then entered into a principal component factor analysis.[10] The factor loadings for the initial principal component were selected as the single best measure of the basic period voting pattern because, as Harman (1967:136) has observed, "The first principal component is the linear combination of the original variables which contributes a maximum to their total variance." The larger this loading the closer the given referendum item is related to the basic county voting pattern within the period. State questions that deviate from the basic pattern of any given period will have factor loadings approaching zero; i.e., deviation is apparent when nonsuccessive issues (elections) load on the same factor. In those instances when all of the state questions present in an election do not fit the overall period pattern, that election will be considered a "deviating" election.[11] If subsequent elections do not similarly reflect such low loadings, but instead return to the basic period pattern, no fundamental reorientation in county voting behavior will be considered to have occurred. In such cases the "deviating" election will not be considered to have been of sufficient duration to be "critical," only deviant. State questions more closely reflecting the overall pattern of a period will have high positive or negative loadings, whereas those not conforming to the basic dimension will display weak association. Factor loadings of $+/-.2$ were arbitrarily set as the limits for this pattern.

Although plots for each of the period principal components would reveal an increasing stabilization of electoral response, space constraints prohibit their presentation.[12] However, a quantitative summary of each period is presented in Table 8. The early trends are most characterized by rather rapid surge and decline patterns reflecting instability and confusion inherent in the earliest development of the state. However, by the immediate postwar period the initial principal component was the strongest found in the study, explaining almost half of the total variance (47.8%). None of the state questions considered during these years (1945-1955) assumed a negative factor loading, and no referenda item failed to correlate at the required level with the first principal component. This was a remarkably consistent pattern in an era when 19 of the 27 propositions offered were approved by the Oklahoma electorate. This reflects a stabilizing period following earlier eras characterized by state-building and economic upheaval. The two remaining postwar periods continued this stabilization trend characterized by only four deviating referenda (not loading on the first principal component) in each period when over 50 separate ballot issues were considered.

This form of analysis points to underlying patterns of county referenda voting which have apparently strengthened since statehood. Of the 10 elections considered deviating since 1908, six occurred before 1936 and none occurred between 1946 and 1965. The first 30 years of referenda voting yielded patterns with the most limited explained variance with the first principal component, yet the number of questions was relatively limited. It appears that, once patterns were set, they became quite stable over time. The consistency of this recent period is especially striking; only two deviating elections occurred in 30 years. Of the 138 state questions considered since 1945, only eight (about 6%) did not fit the basic pattern of the period in which they appeared. This stability is even more remarkable given the explosion in the number of state questions considered since 1956 (111). Although, since 1907, 10 elections were found to fit the definition of a deviating election, only two were close to being critical elections (1940 and 1941) within any period. Indeed, the major changes appear to be associated with disturbances reflecting early suffrage extensions, subtle alterations related to the New Deal between 1926 and 1935, and subsequent Depression-related issues appearing in 1940 and 1941.

While the analysis uncovered increasing degrees of stability in county referenda voting patterns within each subsequent 10-year period, we must generalize with great care over the entire 67-year

Table 8. A PRINCIPAL COMPONENTS ANALYSIS OF COUNTY REFERENDA VOTING OVER TIME: 1908-1974

Year	Number of State Questions	Number of Separate Elections	Percent Explained Variance*	Percent of Items Deviating	Deviating Elections	Total Number of Factors (Kaiser's)	Total Percent of Explained Variance (Kaiser's)
1908-1915	33	10	19.1	18.2 (6)	2	9	84.8
1916-1925	26	8	27.6	38.5 (10)	1	6	80.2
1926-1935	34	12	37.1	26.5 (9)	3	6	82.2
1936-1945	30	8	37.2	23.3 (8)	2	5	85.6
1946-1955	27	12	47.8	0.0 (0)	0	5	84.4
1956-1965	52	21	39.0	7.7 (4)	0	10	86.5
1966-1974	59	20	42.6	6.8 (4)	2	10	83.9

*First principal component only.

history. Since it was impossible to factor-analyze the entire era since statehood, it is not possible to dismiss with certitude the likelihood of a larger number of clearly defined deviating elections when the entire era is considered. In order to confirm these findings we calculated successive inter-item correlation coefficients for all state questions considered since 1946 (see Key and Munger, 1959). In effect, these inter-item correlation coefficients decompose more general patterns evident in the preceding factor analyses. The result is a narrowing of extreme coefficients and a tendency for average coefficients to decline over time. While the mean of successive inter-item coefficients for the first period immediately following the war is .63, the two subsequent period means drop to .51 and .55 respectively. The latter two periods are also characterized by a doubling in the number of observations over time. In addition, the standard deviation around mean correlation coefficients is .34 in the first period, rising to a slight peak at .41 between 1956 and 1965, subsequently dropping to a lower standard deviation of .29 in the most recent period. Although the difference in the means is not statistically significant at the .05 level, electoral conflict on state questions tends to occur within narrower boundaries and to be characterized by greater stability in the postwar period.[13]

Table 8 also summarizes the size of the electoral competition space according to number of questions and numbers of separate elections, as well as the amount of variance explained by factor analysis.[14] During the earliest periods (especially the first two) immediately following statehood, the number of state questions and the number of elections in which they occurred was relatively small and, in addition, the amount of explained variance was also slight. In other words, the earliest periods were characterized by greater multidimensionality within a relatively small electoral space. In subsequent periods, however, especially the two most recent periods, there is a stabilization in the amount of explained variance, while the *size* of the electoral space nearly doubles by number of questions and number of separate elections. If we apply the 75% variance criterion to the three most recent periods, as was done in Tables 2, 3, and 4, we see that it takes an additional factor in each postwar period to explain about 75% of the variance, yet the number of observations increases substantially. The *size* of the issue space is greatly increasing, yet its *quantitative complexity* is decreasing; at least it is not increasing relative to size. Over time, political conflict is occurring within a narrower, more consensual range while elites, and to some extent attentive publics, have greatly expanded the policy agenda. At the same time, we have earlier noted that the *qualitative* issue complexity is increasing, particularly in the most recent period; it is less time-bound and more substantively meaningful. In effect, the Oklahoma electorate appears to be reacting more coherently and with greater stability to an increasingly diversified set of issues—an institutionalization of behavior patterns occurring largely in the absence of party system cues.

VI. CONCLUSION

Referenda voting in a state where direct democracy flourishes is indeed a complex political phenomenon. The decline in the use of the initiative petition and the increasing use of legislatively referred measures as a means for placing state questions before the electorate clearly suggests the growing importance of elite agenda-setting. But it would be unwise to ignore the subsequent response by the people. They do, in fact, control the fate of a variety of extremely important policy issues. The foregoing exercise has been an attempt to explore some of the salient features of this aspect of direct democracy in a single state over a period of 30 years. We learned that state question voting is not completely random nor determined solely by patterns of yea-saying or nay-saying, although such did occur to some degree especially in the earlier time period. When related referenda votes were grouped by factor analysis, some relationship emerged between state demographic characteristics and the referenda factors. In most instances, the more urban-industrial counties tended to support referenda measures. The percent of Republican vote for governor was also frequently related to state question voting results, but the impact of this indicator was not altogether consistent. Republican-leaning counties were more inclined than others to vote against revenue-raising measures but were not uniform in their response otherwise.

Another primary focus of the preceding analysis was on developmental processes throughout one state as reflected in the institutionalization of behavior patterns in policy-oriented elections. These patterns share many elements common to general political development studies over time, yet precise analogies must be approached with caution. There is lively debate among comparative politics scholars over the various normative and empirical components of development, and, for the most part, Oklahoma was only momentarily (at statehood) an underdeveloped subculture of a larger developed society. Yet the state progressed through periods of cleavage exhibited by the Oklahoma Territory and the Indian culture, as well as rather enduring regional cleavages over time. Institutional and structural features developed quickly, however. Some early state questions reflected attention to administrative matters and "state-building," later followed by concern for reorganization, change, reform, and moral issues more common to "nation-building."

Although most of the classic prerequisites for political development—administrative and legal appartus, economic development, institutionalization of organizations and procedures, and structural differentiation—were met quite early, changes in other conditions for development are evident in our analysis of state questions. It has been suggested (Packenham, 1970) that a characteristic of development reflects a social system that enables participation and bridges regional, class, and other cleavages—a phenomenon evident in patterns of demographic diffusion in Oklahoma. Agenda-setting elites have also contributed to the "ecology of development" (Riggs, 1967) by providing ranges of choices to enable reshaping the environment. In addition, more explicit value preferences (policy, ideology), which are part of a developing political infrastructure (Ilchman and Uphoff, 1971), have become more apparent. But of all factors most evident, albeit subtle, a form of cultural secularization (Almond and Powell, 1966) has characterized the developmental aspects of referenda voting in Oklahoma. The electorate appears to be increasingly analytical in its political actions, and there is a concomitant movement toward "specificity of orientations" and the development of more specific reactions to policy measures. These overall shifts, from demographic cleavages and alternative electoral moods, to socioeconomic diffusion and policy differentiation, are most characteristic of a developed political culture.

NOTES

1. Much of the research on local referenda voting involves an attempt to resolve two controversies: (1) whether or not issue-specific voting tends to mobilize a portion of the electorate that otherwise may be considered as alienated (Horton and Thompson, 1962; Aberbach, 1969; Shepard, 1975), and (2) whether or not a local political ethos exists that can be characterized as either "public regarding" or "private regarding" (Wilson and Banfield, 1964; Hahn, 1970; Bowman et al., 1972).

2. Survey data best address the attitudinal components of political culture, but they typically exist for only recent periods.

3. The concept of "issue space" refers to the content and organization of individuals' cognitions of issues and their pattern of response to them. Although the concept has previously been reserved for treatment of the underlying dimensions of ideology and "cognitive maps" or spatial organizations of issues based on individual's *attitudes* toward political parties, candidates, and policy, our references are to the total electorate's patterning of response as gleaned from aggregate voting data on referenda items. For spatial attitudinal treatments of issues vis-à-vis partisan political behavior, see Stokes (1963); Kirkpatrick (1970); and Weisberg and Rusk (1970).

4. Using counties as units of analysis slightly overrepresents the rural vote. In Oklahoma, the two largest counties (Oklahoma and Tulsa) account for 36% of the state's population. This fact should be kept in mind in the multivariate analysis to follow.

5. Until 1974 the Oklahoma Constitution required that any constitutional amendment or initiative voted upon in a general election required a majority of *all* votes cast at that election for approval. This resulted in what is called a "silent vote" that could defeat a measure which actually received a majority of "yes" votes on the proposition itself but failed because the percentage "yes" was not over half the vote cast in the general election. In November 1974, the Oklahoma electorate approved two constitutional amendments abolishing the effects of the silent vote.

6. See note 5 for an explanation of the "silent vote" phenomenon.

7. Factor analysis is a statistical technique for reducing a large number of variables to a set of smaller clusters or dimensions containing related variables. Individual variables that have the strongest relationship to a given dimension are said to have the highest "loadings" on that factor. This technique also permits one to derive a factor "score" on each dimension for every case in the analysis (e.g., a score for each county). These factor scores can then be employed as separate variables in subsequent analysis.

In this study we have elected to produce a more limited number of dimensions than would occur following Kaiser's criterion (i.e., selecting only those factors with eigenvalues $\geq$ 1). The standard employed here selects factors which together account for 75% of the total variance in the correlation matrix so long as no subsequent factors explain more than 5% individually (Kirkpatrick, 1974, chap. 4). This results in a manageable set of factors that facilitates interpretation over time.

The factor solutions were also rotated orthogonally using the varimax routine to more clearly isolate independent dimensions. For a more complete discussion of factor analysis see Rummell (1970).

8. For a more complete consideration of the varying roles of political elites, interest groups, and the mass public in agenda setting see Cobb and Elder (1972).

9. Although these two independent variables are themselves closely associated (r = .70), Republicanism is widespread throughout northern rural areas and is not isolated to urban centers. The correlation between Cultural Deprivation and percent Republican for 1950 and 1960 is −.40 and −.56 respectively. In each of the three periods, this was the highest correlation among independent variables.

10. The large number of observations (N = 261) necessitated subsetting the data by period in order to accommodate factor analytic routines. For a discussion of the use of the first principal component, see MacRae and Meldrum (1960) and Baggaley (1959).

11. Our use of the "deviating" label is a more generic reference to empirical deviance from general patterns and should not be confused with the same term often used to classify elections on the basis of partisan loyalties. See Campbell (1966).

12. For detailed plots of the first principal component for each period see Morgan et al. (1975).

13. While this stability is not nearly as uniform nor as marked as trends for inter-item correlation coefficients for presidential, gubernatorial, and senatorial voting during the

postwar era, it is important to note that comparisons between the partisan voting trend lines and the plot for state question voting reveals almost complete independence between the two sets of observations. In other words, state question voting patterns, with the exception of a few unique disturbances, are not reflective of broader partisan electoral trends.

14. When factor solutions by Kaiser's criterion are examined over time (Table 8), the last two periods witness a doubling of variables and a doubling of extracted dimensions, yet the most recent period has an increase of seven observations and a slight loss in total variance. Although the number of extracted factors is high for the last two periods, it does not necessarily suggest greater multidimensionality since Kaiser's criterion permits an unusual amount of empirical "noise" evident in many single-variable factors.

REFERENCES

ABERBACH, J. (1969). "Alienation and political behavior." American Political Science Review, 63(March):86-99.

ALMOND, G.A., and POWELL, G.B., Jr. (1966). Comparative politics: A developmental approach. Boston: Little, Brown.

ALMOND, G.A., and VERBA, S. (1965). The civic culture: Political attitudes and democracy in five nations. Boston: Little, Brown.

BAGGALEY, A.R. (1959). "Patterns of voting change in Wisconsin counties." Western Political Quarterly, 12:141-144.

BLALOCK, H.M., Jr. (1972). Social statistics (2nd ed.). New York: McGraw-Hill.

BONE, H., and BENEDICT, R. (1975). "Perspectives on direct legislation: Washington state's experience 1914-1973." Western Political Quarterly, 28(June):243-262.

BOWMAN, L., IPPOLITO, D.S., and LEVIN, M. (1972). "Self-interest and referendum support: The case of a rapid transit vote in Atlanta." Pp. 119-136 in H. Hahn (ed.), People and politics in urban society. Beverly Hills, Calif.: Sage.

BURNHAM, W.D. (1970). Critical elections and the mainsprings of American democracy. New York: Norton.

CAMPBELL, A. (1966). "A classification of the presidential elections." Pp. 63-77 in A. Campbell, P.E. Converse, W.E. Miller, and D.E. Stokes (eds.), Elections and the political order. New York: John Wiley.

CHAMBERS, W.N. (1967). "Party development and the American mainstream." In W.N. Chambers and W.D. Burnham (eds.), The American party system: Stages of political development. New York: Oxford University Press.

CLUBB, J.M., and TRAUGOTT, M.W. (1972). "National patterns of referenda voting: The 1968 election." Pp. 137-169 in H. Hahn (ed.), People and politics in urban society. Beverly Hills, Calif.: Sage.

COBB, R.W., and ELDER, C.D. (1972). Participation in American politics: The dynamics of agenda-building. Boston: Allyn Bacon.

Council of State Governments (1974). Book of the states. Lexington, Ky.: Author.

DEVINE, D.J. (1972). The political culture of the United States. Boston: Little, Brown.

HAHN, H. (1970). "Ethos and social class: Referenda in Canadian cities." Polity, 2(spring):295-313.

HAMILTON, H.D. (1970). "Direct legislation: Some implications of open housing referenda." American Political Science Review, 64(March):124-137.

HARMAN, H.H. (1967). Modern factor analysis (2nd ed.). Chicago: University of Chicago Press.

HORTON, J.E., and THOMPSON, W.E. (1962). "Powerlessness and political negativism: A study of defeated local referendums." American Journal of Sociology, 67(March): 485-493.

HUNTINGTON, S. (1968). Political order in changing societies. New Haven, Conn.: Yale University Press.

ILCHMAN, W.F., and UPHOFF, N.T. (1971). The political economy of change. Berkeley: University of California Press.

KEY, V.O., Jr. (1955). "A theory of critical elections." Journal of Politics, 17(February): 3-18.

KEY, V.O., Jr., and MUNGER, F. (1959). "Social determinism and electoral decision: The case of Indiana." In E. Burdick and A.J. Brodbeck (eds.), American voting behavior. Glencoe, Ill.: Free Press.

KIRKPATRICK, S.A. (1970). "Political attitudes and behavior: Some consequences of attitudinal ordering." Midwest Journal of Political Science, 14(February):1-24.

––– (1974). Quantitative analysis of political data. Columbus, Ohio: Charles E. Merrill.

KIRKPATRICK, S.A., MORGAN, D.R., and EDWARDS, L. (1970). Oklahoma voting patterns: Presidential, gubernatorial and senatorial elections. Norman: Bureau of Government Research, University of Oklahoma.

MacRAE, D., Jr., and MELDRUM, J.A. (1960). "Critical elections in Illinois: 1888-1958." American Political Science Review, 54(September):669-683.

MORGAN, D.R., KIRKPATRICK, S.A., FITZGERALD, M.R., and LYONS, W. (1975). "Patterns of referenda voting in Oklahoma: A multivariate analysis over time." Paper presented at the annual meeting of the Southwestern Political Science Association, March.

MUELLER, J.E. (1969). "Voting on the propositions: Ballot patterns and historical trends in California." American Political Science Review, 63(December):1197-1212.

PACKENHAM, R.A. (1970). "Political development research." Pp. 169-193 in M. Haas and H.S. Kariel (eds.), Approaches to the study of political science. Scranton, Pa.: Chandler.

PATTERSON, S.C. (1968). "The political cultures of the American states." Journal of Politics, 30(February):197-209.

PRZEWORSKI, A. (1975). "Institutionalization of voting patterns, or is mobilization the source of decay?" American Political Science Review, 69(March):49-67.

RADABAUGH, J.S. (1961). "Tendencies of California direct legislation." Southwestern Social Science Quarterly, 42(June):66-78.

RIGGS, F.W. (1967). "The theory of political development." Pp. 317-349 in J.C. Charlesworth (ed.), Contemporary political analysis. New York: Free Press.

RUMMELL, R.J. (1970). Applied factor analysis. Evanston, Ill.: Northwestern University Press.

SCOTT, S., and NATHAN, H. (1970). "Public referenda: A critical appraisal." Urban Affairs Quarterly, 5(March):313-328.

SHEPARD, W.B. (1975). "Participation in local policy making: The case of referenda." Social Science Quarterly, 56(June):55-70.

State Government News (1974). December.

STOKES, D.E. (1963). "Spatial models of party competition." American Political Science Review, 57(June):368-377.

STURM, A.L. (1970). Thirty years of state constitution-making: 1938-1968. New York: National Municipal League.

SUNDQUIST, J.L. (1973). Dynamics of the party system. Washington, D.C.: Brookings Institution.

WEISBERG, H.F., and RUSK, J.G. (1970). "Dimensions of candidate evaluation." American Political Science Review, 64(December):1167-1185.

WILSON, J.Q., and BANFIELD, E.C. (1964). "Public regardingness as a value premise in voting behavior." American Political Science Review, 58(December):876-887.

WOLFINGER, R., and GREENSTEIN, F. (1968). "The repeal of fair housing in California: An analysis of referendum voting." American Political Science Review, 62(September): 753-769.

Chapter 8

THE POLICY IMPACT OF
ELECTED WOMEN OFFICIALS

SHELAH GILBERT LEADER

I. INTRODUCTION

Politics has long been considered a "manly art," and the absence of women from the political arena has been viewed by many (including some political scientists) as natural and perhaps proper. In response to this situation, feminists have been deliberately seeking a greater voice for women in politics—both within the political parties and as elected or appointed officials. There is, however, some disagreement among feminists about the best way to realize their goals.

Some feminists concentrate on elevating more women to public office in order to achieve numerical equality between men and women in such positions. Others stress the importance of placing in public office women who share the goals of the women's movement for equality and who are committed to using their power to enact policies espoused by feminists.

Those who emphasize the need for equal representation of women in all decision-making bodies do so for both symbolic and instru-

AUTHOR'S NOTE: The views expressed here are those of the author and do not reflect those of the National Commission on the Observance of International Women's Year or any other organization.

mental purposes. As symbols, women politicians illustrate the equal role that women can and should play in the politics of a representative democracy. And, as role models for other women and children, women politicians can encourage the erosion of traditional and rigid sex roles. From this perspective, the actual accomplishments of a woman politician are somewhat less significant than the symbolic impact of her mere presence in an unconventional role. At the same time, these feminists are not merely seeking symbolic change in women's political role. Rather, they assume that, should women control half of the positions of power and influence in America, the policies enacted would be more beneficial to women. The assumption here is that women decision makers are more likely than men to support policies beneficial to women, ceterus paribus.

At its 1972 national convention, the Republican party adopted a rule that is an example of policy changes sought by those who emphasize numerical equality for women. Rule 32(c) requires that "Each State shall endeavor to have equal representation of men and women in its delegation to the Republican National Convention."

A similar effort is taking place within the Democratic party. At the 1976 Democratic National Convention, activists fought for a party commitment to "promote equal division between delegate men and delegate women" and to assist state parties to achieve the goal of equal representation.

The National Commission on the Observance of International Women's Year endorsed the goal of parity for women in the political arena when it adopted, on January 16, 1976, three recommendations of its "Women in Power" committee. The commission recommended that (1) efforts should be made to achieve, by 1985, equal membership of men and women on all state boards and commissions, (2) political parties should seek to insure the equal representation of women in all party activities, and (3) the number of women serving on the judiciary should be increased.

Implicit in the policies just cited are the following assumptions: in a representative democracy, women (who are a majority of the population) should have at least half of the positions of power and influence. And, it is assumed, an increase in the number of women in public office and high party posts is likely to have policy consequences beneficial to women.

Some feminists disagree with this strategy for improving the status and power of American women. They are less concerned with the symbolism of women as politicians than they are with placing particular women with particular policy goals into positions of power. They disagree with the assumption that increasing the number of women in power will necessarily lead to the policy outcomes they seek. In addition, they feel that a woman politician who does not use her position to foster the policy goals of feminism is little more than an "Aunt Jane," i.e., an enemy who is hardly better than a chauvinist man. Whatever symbolic value women politicians might have would be outweighed, in their view, by failure to support particular policies.

Several political organizations have been created by feminists to translate this viewpoint into an explicit strategy. The Women's Campaign Fund was established to help elect "qualified progressive" women to political office through grants of financial aid to selected candidates. The Fund defines "progressive" as "a stand on issues affecting the quality of life and human needs which is substantially more progressive than that of her opponent." The criteria for being considered a progressive are, for example, support for the Equal Rights Amendment (ERA), abortion, and Title IX of the 1972 Education Amendments. Thus, the Fund is less concerned with the number of women elected to office than it is with placing "progressives" in office. Consequently, in the 1974 Maryland Senate election the Fund decided not to use its limited resources to support the candidacy of Barbara Mikulski of Baltimore against Senator Charles Mathias because he had a public record of support for policies endorsed by the Fund.

The National Women's Political Caucus also endorses and assists feminist candidates for political office. The Caucus's standard of evaluation is that the candidate be willing to publicly avow a feminist commitment, be an articulate speaker on behalf of women, and support the ratification of the ERA, abortion, and federally funded child care.

II. METHODOLOGY

We find then that supporters of the women's movement (excluding from consideration here feminists who reject participation in American politics as necessarily co-opting) are committed to two distinct strategies for making the political system more responsive to the needs and interests of women (as defined by feminists). However, the assumptions underlying their strategies have not been tested systematically, and there has been little rigorous effort made to ascertain their effectiveness. This paper represents an initial attempt to test the assumptions upon which feminist strategies have been predicated and to assess the political effectiveness of these two approaches to improving the lot of American women.

We will examine the assumptions underlying the two strategies for achieving the goals of the women's movement by posing the following questions:

(1) Are women legislators more likely than men to support policies espoused by feminists?

(2) Are other factors, such as party or liberalism, better predictors of a legislator's support for policies espoused by feminists than the single factor of sex?

A subsidiary question is whether or not women legislators are more liberal than male legislators.

We can begin to answer these questions by comparing the voting records of male and female state legislators and members of Congress on a number of policy issues of great concern to feminists. If the available evidence indicates that women legislators are, on the whole, stronger supporters than men of policies espoused by feminists, then the strategy of increasing the number and proportion of women in political office would seem to be effective.

On the other hand, if the evidence points to other factors, such as party or liberalism, as stronger predictors of voting behavior in support of feminist policies, then the strategy of selectively supporting the candidacies of women who favor feminist policies makes more sense than simply increasing the number of women in public office.

We will begin to seek answers to these questions by examining the voting records of state legislators on ratification of the Equal Rights Amendment (ERA). This issue is used for several reasons. First, support for the ERA is considered by feminists to be a rock bottom prowoman issue and a benchmark by which legislators can be evaluated. The ERA has attracted the support of the broadest coalition of organizations on any woman's issue and is the "easiest" test of support for the women's movement. Endorsers of the ERA range from the Junior League to the Federation of Women's Clubs and the National Organization for Women. In addition, the ERA provides us with comparable voting data for virtually all 50 state legislatures.

A number of other issues will be used to evaluate the voting behavior of women members of Congress over the past few years. Since many of the policies of the women's movement are identified as "liberal" issues—such as federally funded child care, increased support for welfare, and affirmative action on equal opportunity— the rating system of the Americans for Democratic Action (ADA) will be used to determine if women representatives are, on the whole, more liberal than Congressmen.

In addition, two separate feminist rating systems will be relied upon. One system was compiled by Flora Crater, editor of the feminist newsletter, *The Woman Activist*. She rated members of the 92nd through the 94th Congresses on a number of issues of special concern to feminists.

The Women's Lobby, a registered lobby which seeks support for feminist policies, also began rating members of Congress during the 92nd Congress. Their rating system is used here as well.

Before we move to an examination of the evidence, we must point out an important limitation of the available data. The statistics generated by legislative voting records are somewhat distorted by the gross disparity in the number of male and female legislators. Women comprise only 4% of the members of Congress and less than 10% of the state legislators.

Because the number of women legislators is so small, extreme behavior by one or two women has a disproportionate impact on the average voting score of women. In contrast, extreme voting behavior by male politicians does not skew that group's average score as much because the group is so much larger. In some cases, we are comparing the average voting scores of less than 5 women with more than 100 men. Thus, data describing the extraordinarily small universe of women legislators must be treated with caution.

Keeping this caveat in mind, the assumptions of feminists about the best means to achieve the goals of improving the status and power of women will be examined by a number of measures at both the state and national level of politics. Hopefully, the results of this paper will be of use to women activists and will encourage other scholars to develop better measures of the impact of women on American political life.

III. THE ERA

The proposed Equal Rights Amendment to the Constitution of the United States was first introduced to Congress in 1923 by Alice Paul as a logical follow-up to the acquisition of woman suffrage. Congress refused to pass the ERA until 1972. Congresswoman Martha Griffiths (Democrat, Michigan) was responsible for discharging the ERA from the House Judiciary Committee, where it had languished for 22 years. Thirty-eight states must ratify the ERA before March 22, 1979. By 1973, 30 states had quickly, and without controversy, ratified the ERA. However, an emotional and misleading STOP ERA campaign, mounted by Phyllis Schlafly, slowed the momentum of the ratification movement. As of July 1976, 34 states had ratified. Two states (Nebraska and Tennessee), voted to rescind their ratification; but Congress must decide whether or not it will permit a state to rescind its vote. ERAmerica, an alliance of groups supportive of the ERA is now engaged in an all-out effort to persuade legislators in four of the 16 unratified states to support the ERA.

To begin, we must look at the role of women legislators in the unratified states. Not surprisingly, most of the unratified states are Southern and/or influenced by fundamentalist religious sects (Mormon, Baptist). For example, the Mormon church is openly opposed to the ratification of the ERA. In Utah, most of the state legislators are Mormon bishops and are opposed to the ERA. Thus, in these states, failure to ratify is a deliberate act based on an ideological belief in the inferiority of women. The question for us is whether women legislators in these unratified states transcend dominant regional and religious values to support the ERA.

Unfortunately, legislative voting records in these states are very incomplete. Three states—Virginia, Mississippi, and Louisiana—have never brought the ERA to a floor vote in either house of their state legislatures. While supporters of the ERA have information on the willingness of state legislators to vote for ratification, we will restrict ourselves only to votes cast.

In five unratified states—Alabama, Arkansas, South Carolina, Oklahoma, and Utah—the ERA has been voted on in one house of the legislature. In Alabama, the ERA came up for a vote in the Senate in 1973. Only six of the 35 members (all Democrats, no women) voted for passage. Passage in Alabama is considered unlikely.

The Arkansas Senate also defeated the ERA in 1973. The only

woman member (a Democrat, like all but one of her colleagues) voted against the ERA. The Arkansas House has never voted on the ERA, and the outlook for passage is bleak.

The ERA's fate in South Carolina has been less bleak. In 1972, the Senate (which has no women) passed the ERA on the first two readings, but then recommitted the bill to committee. Since then, there have been three public hearings, but no vote. In 1975, the House voted to table the ERA. Women members of both parties were far more supportive of the ERA than their male colleagues, but Democratic women exceeded Republican women in their support. All three of the Democratic women and one of the three Republican women voted for ratification, while only 35 of the 81 Democratic men (43%) and four of the twelve Republican men (33%) did so.

The state Senates of Oklahoma and Utah have never voted on the ERA. In the lower houses of both states, Democratic women were unanimous in support of the ERA. Only a third of the Republicans (eight men and one woman) in Oklahoma voted for passage, compared with 48% (34) of the Democratic men and both Democratic women. In Utah the two Republican women were half as supportive as the six Democratic women, but far more supportive than men in either party—33% (12) of the Democratic men and 6% (2) of the Republican men. Since religious opposition to the ERA is strong in both states and there are very few women legislators in either state, the fate of the ERA is considered hopeless by state sponsors.

The remaining eight unratified states (Arizona, Florida, Georgia, Illinois, Indiana, Missouri, Nevada, and North Carolina) do have complete voting records on the ERA. The results are shown in Table 1.

What we find in the eight unratified states, for which we have complete votes on the ERA, is that women are demonstrably more supportive of the ERA than men. However, party proves to be a very important factor in influencing voting behavior. While women are far more supportive of the ERA than are the men of their party, Democratic women are much more supportive than Republican women, and there is no appreciable difference between the levels of support of Democratic men and Republican women. This seems to suggest that factors other than sex influence voting behavior.

Is this pattern of support for the ERA also true of the 34 states which have ratified the ERA? Table 2 shows the percentage of male

Table 1. SUPPORT FOR THE EQUAL RIGHTS AMENDMENT IN UNRATIFIED STATES*

| | Democrats | | | | Republicans | | | |
| | Men | | Women | | Men | | Women | |
	%	(N)	%	(N)	%	(N)	%	(N)
Arizona								
Senate	69	(9)	100	(5)	8	(1)		nw
House	60	(17)	71	(5)	11	(3)	0	
Florida								
Senate	59	(16)		nw	8	(1)		nw
House	56	(51)	87	(7)	20	(10)	100	(4)
Georgia								
Senate	39	(20)	100	(1)	40	(2)		nw
House	41	(60)	100	(2)	37	(11)		nw
Illinois								
Senate	61	(21)	100	(2)	24	(6)		nw
House	71	(72)	100	(5)	50	(41)	88	(7)
Indiana								
Senate	82	(19)	100	(1)	8	(2)	0	
House	78	(45)	100	(6)	36	(16)		nw
Missouri								
Senate	55	(12)	0		18	(2)		nw
House	54	(63)	75	(6)	38	(19)	67	(2)
Nevada								
Senate	43	(7)	33	(1)	33	(1)		nw
House	72	(22)	50	(1)	43	(5)	100	(2)
North Carolina								
Senate	54	(19)		nw	29	(4)	0	
House	46	(54)	89	(8)	14	(3)	100	(2)
Total average:	59	(507)	79	(50)	26	(127)	57	(17)

Average total male support = 42%
Average total female support = 68%
Average Democratic support = 69%
Average Republican support = 42%

*Cell entries are percentages of those present and voting in favor of ratification of the ERA. Raw numbers are in parentheses. The notation "nw" means that the legislature contained no women of the party specified.

and female state legislators in each house who were present and voted in favor of ratification.

Again, we find that in the ratified states, women legislators are, on the whole, stronger supporters of the ERA than their male colleagues. Furthermore, this difference persists when we control for party. However, we also find that factors other than sex are important. Democratic men were stronger supporters of the ERA than were Republican women.

Using this national issue, we have data which indicate that women state legislators are more likely than men to support a key feminist

Table 2. SUPPORT FOR THE EQUAL RIGHTS AMENDMENT IN RATIFIED STATES*

	Democrats				Republicans			
	Men		Women		Men		Women	
	%	(N)	%	(N)	%	(N)	%	(N)
Alaska								
Senate	100	(9)	100	(1)	78	(7)		nw
House	100	(27)	100	(2)	71	(5)		nw
California								
Senate	85	(17)		nw	67	(12)		nw
House	89	(33)	100	(3)	60	(18)		nw
Colorado								
Senate	100	(10)		nw	95	(20)	100	(1)
House	100	(25)	100	(1)	100	(36)	100	(4)
Connecticut								
Senate	85	(11)		nw	65	(16)	100	(3)
House	62	(37)	100	(5)	68	(62)	83	(10)
Delaware								
Senate	100	(5)		nw	100	(11)	100	(2)
House	100	(15)	100	(2)	100	(22)	100	(3)
Hawaii								
Senate								
House			voice vote in both houses					
Idaho								
Senate	94	(15)		nw	83	(16)	100	(1)
House	91	(23)	100	(2)	89	(33)	100	(2)
Iowa								
Senate	92	(12)	100	(1)	100	(32)	100	(1)
House	87	(29)	100	(2)	82	(44)	80	(4)
Kansas								
Senate	86	(7)		nw	88	(27)		nw
House	70	(28)	0		70	(58)	0	
Kentucky								
Senate	73	(20)	100	(1)	0			nw
House	69	(45)	67	(2)	47	(9)		nw
Maine								
Senate	80	(8)		nw	52	(12)	100	(1)
House	74	(53)	89	(8)	34	(25)	25	(2)
Maryland								
Senate	100	(26)	100	(3)	100	(8)		nw
House	79	(80)	100	(6)	38	(6)	0	
Massachusetts								
Senate			voice vote					
House	95	(149)	100	(5)	98	(56)	100	(1)
Michigan								
Senate			voice vote					
House	88	(43)	67	(4)	81	(43)		nw
Minnesota								
Senate			nonpartisan election, no women					
House	93	(68)	100	(4)	56	(30)	100	(2)
Montana								
Senate	72	(18)	0		77	(17)	0	
House	87	(47)	100	(6)	60	(26)	100	(1)

Table 2 (continued)

	Democrats				Republicans			
	Men		Women		Men		Women	
	%	(N)	%	(N)	%	(N)	%	(N)
Nebraska								
unicameral,								
nonpartisan body			unanimous					
New Hampshire								
Senate			unanimous					
House			voice vote					
New Jersey								
Senate	100	(13)	100	(1)	100	(21)		nw
House	94	(34)	100	(1)	93	(28)	100	(2)
New Mexico								
Senate	76	(24)	100	(2)	81	(9)		nw
House	70	(35)		nw	45	(9)		nw
New York								
Senate	96	(23)		nw	96	(29)		nw
House	96	(66)		nw	69	(51)	100	(2)
North Dakota								
Senate	81	(14)	100	(1)	39	(14)	33	(1)
House	77	(32)	100	(5)	30	(20)	50	(3)
Ohio								
Senate	87	(14)	100	(1)	36	(6)	50	(1)
House	79	(45)	100	(1)	25	(11)	67	(2)
Oregon								
Senate	87	(15)	100	(2)	67	(8)		nw
House	81	(28)	100	(6)	83	(22)	100	(2)
Pennsylvania								
Senate	88	(23)	100	(1)	83	(20)		nw
House	85	(95)	100	(3)	91	(83)	100	(2)
Rhode Island								
Senate	100	(31)		nw	100	(8)		nw
House	100	(52)		nw	100	(20)	100	(2)
South Dakota								
Senate	88	(16)	100	(1)	35	(6)		nw
House	85	(30)	100	(2)	31	(13)	100	(3)
Tennessee								
Senate	100	(18)		nw	55	(6)		nw
House	100	(41)	100	(2)	100	(31)		nw
Texas								
Senate			voice vote					
House	100	(123)	100	(1)	100	(10)		nw
Vermont								
Senate	83	(6)	100	(1)	68	(13)	50	(1)
House	81	(39)	67	(4)	78	(59)	70	(7)
Washington								
Senate	70	(22)	100	(1)	35	(6)		nw
House	87	(49)	78	(7)	69	(29)	100	(2)
West Virginia								
Senate	100	(22)		nw	100	(8)	100	(1)
House			no roll call					

Table 2 (continued)

	Democrats				Republicans			
	Men		Women		Men		Women	
	%	(N)	%	(N)	%	(N)	%	(N)
Wisconsin								
Senate	92	(12)		nw	85	(17)		nw
House	92	(58)	75	(3)	72	(23)		nw
Wyoming								
Senate	83	(11)	100	(1)	38	(6)		nw
House	93	(15)	100	(2)	55	(25)	100	(2)

Average Democratic female support = 92%
Average Democratic male support = 88%
Average Republican female support = 80%
Average Republican male support = 70%

Average female support = 86%
Average male support = 79%

Average Democratic support = 90%
Average Republican support = 75%

*Cell entries are percentages of those present and voting in favor of ratification of the ERA. Raw numbers are in parentheses. The notation "nw" means that the legislature contained no women of the party specified.

issue. But we also have strong evidence that Democrats are more supportive than Republicans, regardless of sex, at least on this one issue.

Is this also true at the national level, i.e., in the U.S. Congress? To answer this question, we turn next to an examination of the voting record of Congress.

IV. WOMEN IN CONGRESS

LIBERALISM

Are women members of Congress more supportive of liberal legislation than their male colleagues? The liberalism of women legislators is relevant to a study of feminism because the policy priorities of feminists are generally premised on a liberal view of the role of government. For example, feminists desire greater public investment in health and social welfare and would finance it by reducing defense spending. The rationale for these views is that women are disproportionately poor and have a higher incidence of sickness than men (U.S. Bureau of the Census, 1976:7-8, 45-54).

Since women tend to live longer than men, they are more in need of social and medical care and insurance. In addition, as victims of systematic discrimination, women are more supportive of government intervention in the area of civil rights.

Thus, feminism tends to coincide with liberalism: for example, Representative Bella Abzug, a feminist standard bearer in Congress, usually received a 100% rating from the Americans for Democratic Action (ADA). Therefore, we would expect women legislators to be more liberal than men. Evidence for this relationship can be found

Table 3. AMERICANS FOR DEMOCRATIC ACTION'S RATING FOR THE U.S. HOUSE OF REPRESENTATIVES, 94th CONGRESS, 1st SESSION*

	Entire House	*Women*
Average score	49% (434)	72% (18)
Democrats	62% (289)	76% (14)
Republicans	21% (145)	36% (4)
Northern Democrats	78% (313)	75% (15)
Southern Democrats	29% (121)	56% (3)

*Raw numbers are in parentheses. Members of Congress were rated by the ADA on the following issues. Each member is rated on the number of ballots cast in support of the liberal position on a bill. The rating system is then based on the average score of members.

1. Oil depletion: Wilson amendment to the Green amendment to the Tax Reduction Act, February 27, 1975.
2. Social security: O'Neil amendment lifting the cost of living increase limits on the Social Security Act, May 1, 1975.
3. Voting rights: Wiggins amendment applying voting rights act only to the percentage of the population voting, June 3, 1975.
4. Emergency jobs act veto override, June 4, 1975.
5. Override of strip mining bill, June 10, 1975.
6. Flood amendment to concur with Senate deletion of requirement that HEW require schools to integrate all programs by sex, July 18, 1975.
7. Oil price decontrol: veto to disapprove Ford's plan, July 30, 1975.
8. Establishment of a consumer protection agency, November 6, 1975.
9. Findley amendment restricting food stamp eligibility to families below the poverty line, November 13, 1975.
10. Approval of federal loans to New York City, December 2, 1975.
11. Mikva amendment tightening tax loophole on real estate, December 4, 1975.
12. Nuclear disaster insurance, December 8, 1975.
13. B-1 bomber: Aspin amendment deleting authorization for its production, May 19, 1975.
14. Leggett amendment to prohibit testing of MIRV, May 20, 1975.
15. Aspin amendment to reduce authorizations for development of new weapons systems, May 20, 1975.
16. Hicks amendment to end the construction of facilities to produce binary nerve gas, July 28, 1975.
17. Foreign Economic and Assistance bill, fiscal year 1976-1977, September 10, 1975.
18. Boycott of Rhodesian chrome, September 25, 1975.
19. Giaimo amendment requiring disclosure of CIA funds, October 1, 1975.

by examining the ADA rating of Congress and the ratings compiled by the editor of *The Woman Activist.* Since there are no women in the Senate, only the ADA scores for the House of Representatives, 94th Congress, 1st session, are referred to. The votes used by the ADA to score legislators are generally significant issues which generate clear liberal-conservative responses.

According to the ADA rating system, the Congresswomen as a group are more liberal than the House as a whole. But party accounts for a great deal of variation in the voting scores. Democratic women are more liberal than Republican women. And the score of all House Democrats (including that of Southern men) is more liberal than Republican women.

The Woman Activist (March 1976) evaluated the 94th Congress on 20 key issues and found that, as a group, the 19 women members were consistently more liberal than the men.[1] Women voted with the majority on 14 issues and in each case were more supportive of the issue than were the men. The majority of the women bucked the House trend by rejecting the B-1 bomber, suppression of the CIA report, military aid to Chile, and the Casey amendment prohibiting integration of sports by sex. They voted for a trust fund for energy development and lighter trucks on the highways. The Democratic women, on the average, voted liberal 80% of the time, while the majority leader had a 75% liberal score. The Republican women had a 37% liberal score, compared with a score of 10% for the minority leader.

Congresswomen, on the average, tend to be more liberal than their colleagues, more supportive of social welfare legislation, and more opposed to defense spending and an interventionist foreign policy. But party remains an important factor. That is, while Republican women are far more liberal than Republican men, Democrats—except for Southern males—are more liberal than Republican women.

FEMINISM

Is this trend also true of support for feminist policies? Will Congresswomen be more supportive of laws designed to enhance the status of women than their male colleagues? Are Democratic men more supportive of these policies than Republican women? To answer these questions, we will refer to the rating systems devised by *The Woman Activist* and the Women's Lobby.

In 1974, *The Woman Activist* published the first ratings of the 92nd Congress. These ratings were based on several key votes on issues of concern to feminists. The results are shown in Table 4. Based on these ratings, we again find women in Congress, on the whole, to be more supportive of feminist policies than the House as a whole. But party is a key factor. Democratic women are the strongest feminists. While Republican women are far more supportive of feminist issues than their party, the difference between the level of support of Republican and Democratic women is readily apparent.

To confirm this trend, we turn finally to the rating system devised by the Women's Lobby. This rating system is based on examination of five different votes cast on key feminist issues. An absence is counted against the member, and the score represents the percentage of votes cast that were favorable to women. The combined scores are presented in Table 5.

Table 4. *THE WOMAN ACTIVIST* RATING OF THE U.S. HOUSE OF REPRESENTATIVES

	92nd, 1st[a]	93rd, 1st[b]	94th, 1st[c]
Average House score	43%	45%	58%
Average women's score	59	80	77
Average Democratic score	66	51	–
Average Democratic women's score	84	87	88
Average Republican score	23	19	–
Average Republican women's score	58	50	50
Majority (D) leader's score	75	–	100
Minority (R) leader's score	0	–	0

a. The members were rated on four key votes of interest to feminists. Each vote in support of the feminist position was counted as 25%, and an absence was counted as a zero. A perfect record of support for feminist issues was 100% and complete opposition to feminist issues was rated zero. The percentages shown in the chart reflect average House scores. The key votes for the 92nd Congress were (1) the Wiggins amendment to the ERA, (2) the Erlenborn substitute to the Equal Employment Enforcement Act, (3) the Erlenborn Amendment to the Higher Education Act which permitted sex discrimination, and (4) the Brademus Child Development Amendment to the Economic Opportunity Act.

b. The members were rated on the following key issues: (1) rejection of the Erlenborn substitute amendments to the minimum wage bill, (2) override of Nixon's veto of the minimum wage bill, (3) vote for impoundment control to release impounded health and education funds, and (4) rejection of the Hogan Amendment to deny women legal aid for abortion.

c. The members were rated on the following key issues: (1) a House rule change prohibiting discrimination by a member, an officer, or employee on the basis of race, color, sex, or ethnicity, (2) prohibiting HEW from taking action to force schools to integrate physical education classes by sex, and (3) approval of funds authorized by the Women's Conference bill. *The Woman Activist* did not provide the same party analysis of votes as it did for previous sessions of Congress.

Table 5. WOMEN'S LOBBY RATING OF THE U.S. HOUSE OF REPRESENTATIVES

	92nd, 2nd 93rd, 1st[a]	93rd, 2nd[b]	94th, 1st[c]
Average Republican men's score	31%	44%	55%
Average Republican women's score	40	70	80
Average Democratic men's score	61	68	72
Average Democratic women's score	83	78	88

a. These sessions were rated on the following issues: (1) Child Development Amendment to the poverty bill, to establish and expand the comprehensive child development programs and to set up the legislative framework for eventual universally available child development programs (a yes vote is for women; passed September 30, 1971); (2) Wiggins Amendment to the ERA, exempting a person from compulsory military service (a no vote is for women; failed October 21, 1971); (3) Froehlich amendment to Hogan Legal Services Amendment to prohibit Legal Services Corporation lawyers from working to procure a nontherapeutic abortion for a woman or to force a hospital, institution, or doctor to participate in an abortion against their policy or beliefs (a no vote is for women; passed June 21, 1973); (4) HR 4757 to amend the Fair Labor Standards Act to increase the federal minimum wage and to extend coverage to household domestics (a yes vote is for women; passed June 6, 1973); (5) Override of the presidential veto of the minimum wage bill (a yes vote is for women; failed September 19, 1973).

b. This session was rated on the following issues: (1) Erlenborn amendment to the Employee Benefits Security Act to transfer the administration of pension insurance program from the Labor Department to a private government corporation, similar to the FDIC (a no vote is for women; failed); (2) increase in the minimum wage for most nonagricultural workers, extending coverage to 7 million workers, including domestics, not previously covered by the Fair Labor Standards Act (a yes vote is for women; passed); (3) Holt amendment to the supplemental appropriation bill for FY 1975, to prohibit withholding funds from school districts to compel classification or assignment of teachers and students on the basis of race, sex, or ethnicity or keep files on this basis (a no vote is for women; passed); (4) Addabbo amendment to the supplemental appropriations bill to provide $4.5 million for child abuse prevention and treatment programs (a yes vote is for women; passed); (5) Roncallo amendment to the appropriations bill for the Departments of Labor and HEW prohibiting the use of funds for abortion (a no vote is for women; failed).

c. This session was rated on the following issues: (1) Abzug bill calling for state and national women's conferences (a yes vote is for women; passed); (2) reform of the tax law to give tax credit of $400 per year per child for child-care costs (a yes vote is for women; passed); (3) override of the presidential veto of the Kennedy bill giving $2 billion for federal health services, including nurse training and local health services projects (a yes vote is for women; overridden); (4) Stratton amendment to give women equal admissions to military academies (a yes vote is for women; passed); (5) Flood motion to include in the education appropriations prohibition of the use of funds to integrate physical education classes by sex (a no vote is for women; passed).

Once again we find that Democratic women are the strongest feminists and Republican men are the least supportive of feminism. But, while Republican women are far more feminist than their party colleagues, they are less feminist than Democratic women and only slightly more feminist than Democratic men. It is likely that, were

Table 6. COMPARISON OF U.S. CONGRESSWOMEN WITH THEIR
STATE DELEGATIONS*

	93rd	*94th*
California		
entire male delegation	64% (41)	68% (41)
Burke (D)	80 (1)	100 (1)
average D men's score	87 (22)	87 (27)
Pettis (R)	–	60 (1)
average R men's score	–	34 (14)
Colorado		
entire male delegation	40 (5)	50 (4)
Schroeder (D)	100 (1)	80 (1)
average D men's score	60 (1)	90 (2)
Connecticut		
entire male delegation	84 (5)	–
Grasso (D)	80 (1)	–
average D men's score	70 (2)	–
Hawaii		
entire male delegation (one D)	100 (1)	100 (1)
Mink (D)	80 (1)	80 (1)
average D men's score (one D)	100 (1)	100 (1)
Illinois		
entire male delegation	60 (23)	66 (23)
Collins (D)	100 (1)	100 (1)
average D men's score	73 (9)	88 (12)
Kansas		
entire male delegation	–	60 (4)
Keys (only D)	–	100 (1)
Louisiana		
entire male delegation	26 (7)	31 (7)
Boggs (D)	60 (1)	80 (1)
average D men's score	30 (6)	28 (5)
Maryland		
entire male delegation	57 (7)	67 (6)
Holt (R)	40 (1)	40 (1)
average R men's score	33 (3)	50 (2)
Spellman (D)	–	100 (1)
average D men's score	–	75 (4)
Massachusetts		
entire male delegation	84 (11)	95 (11)
Heckler (R)	100 (1)	100 (1)
average R men's score	90 (2)	100 (1)
Michigan		
entire male delegation	60 (18)	–
Griffiths (D)	40 (1)	–
average D men's score	71 (9)	
Missouri		
entire male delegation	64 (9)	62 (9)
Sullivan (D)	40 (1)	60 (1)
average D men's score	70 (8)	68 (8)

Table 6 (continued)

	93rd		94th	
Nebraska				
entire male delegation	–		60%	(2)
Smith (R)	–		60	(1)
average R men's score	–		60	(2)
New Jersey				
entire male delegation	–		86	(13)
Meyner (D)	–		80	(1)
average D men's score	–		85	(11)
Fenwick (R)	–		100	(1)
average R men's score	–		90	(2)
New York				
entire male delegation	61	(36)	78	(36)
Abzug (D)	100	(1)	100	(1)
Chisholm (D)	100	(1)	100	(1)
Holtzman (D)	100	(1)	100	(1)
average D men's score	65	(19)	88	(24)
Oregon				
entire male delegation	53	(3)	–	
Green (D)	40	(1)	–	
average D men's score	80	(1)	–	
Tennessee				
entire male delegation	–		45	(7)
Lloyd (D)	–		60	(1)
average D men's score	–		60	(4)
Texas				
entire male delegation	58	(23)	40	(23)
Jordan (D)	100	(1)	100	(1)
average D men's score	59	(18)	41	(20)
Washington				
entire male delegation	90	(6)	–	
Hansen (D)	60	(1)	–	
average D men's score	88	(5)	–	

*Cell entries are mean scores based on the percentage of votes cast in support of bills selected by the Women's Lobby. Raw numbers are in parentheses.

the votes of Southern Democratic men excluded from the average score of male Democrats, the difference between Democratic men and Republican women would largely disappear.

For a more detailed analysis of the role of party, sex, and region, we turn to a state-by-state examination of the voting behavior of member of the 93rd and 94th Congresses. The scores in Table 6 are based on the Women's Lobby's rating system cited above.

Eight of the 14 Democratic women and one of the two Republican women in the 93rd Congress had more profeminist records than the men from their state. Within state party delegations, eight of the Democratic women and both of the Republican women showed stronger support for feminist policies than male members of their state delegations.

Eleven of the 14 Democratic Congresswomen and two of the five Republican women members were stronger supporters of feminist policies than were the men from their state delegations to the 94th Congress. Eight of the Democratic women and two of the Republican women surpassed the men of their party's state delegations by showing much higher levels of support for feminist policies.

We find that, when we control for region and party, Democratic women continue to show the highest level of support for feminist policies. As examples, Representatives Barbara Jordan (Democrat, Texas) and Lindy Boggs (Democrat, Louisiana) each exceed their state and party delegations in support of feminist policies.

However, Congresswomen as a whole do better than their colleagues in support of feminism. In the 93rd Congress, 63% of the women had better voting records than the men from their state's party delegations, while 53% of the women in Congress were better than their male colleagues from their state parties in levels of support for feminist policies.

V. CONCLUSION

In this paper, we have used six different sets of measures of legislators' support of feminist issues to examine the following questions: Are women legislators more likely than men to support policies espoused by feminists? Or are other factors, such as party or liberalism, better predictors of a legislator's support of policies espoused by feminists than the single factor of sex? The major findings are summarized in Table 7.

Surprisingly, the answer to both of our questions is yes. Women are, on the whole, more supportive of feminist policies than men. But party, rather than sex, is a stronger predictor of voting behavior. Thus, women legislators are stronger feminists than men, but Democrats are more supportive of feminist goals and policies than are Republicans, regardless of sex.

There seems to be a close, but not perfect, fit, between feminism and liberalism. Liberal male politicians, who are usually Democrats, may be more supportive of feminism than conservative women, who are usually Republicans.

Table 7. SUMMARY OF FINDINGS*

Question No. 1: Are women legislators more likely than men to support policies espoused by feminists?

	Women	Men
(1) ERA; % in favor of passage (unratified states)	68% (67)	42% (634)
(2) ERA: % in favor of passage (ratified states)	86 (178)	79 (3129)
(3) Liberalism: ADA rating on selected issues (perfect score 100)	74 (18)	49 (434) (House as a whole)
(4) Liberalism: *Woman Activist* rating on selected issues, general finding	women more liberal	
(5) Feminism: *Woman Activist* rating of 3 Congresses on 4 issues (each worth 25, perfect score 100)	72	49 (House as a whole)
(6) Feminism: Women's Lobby rating of 3 Congresses on 5 issues (each worth 20, perfect score 100)	73	55

Question No. 2: Are other factors, such as party or liberalism, better predictors of a legislator's support of policies espoused by feminists than the single factor of sex?

	Democrats		Republicans	
	Women	Men	Women	Men
(1) ERA: % in favor of passage (unratified states)	79% (50)	59% (507)	57% (17)	26% (127)
(2) ERA: % in favor of passage (ratified states)	92 (105)	88 (1866)	80 (71)	70 (1282)
(3) Liberalism: ADA rating on selected issues (perfect score 100)	77 (14)	62 (276)	46 (4)	21 (140)
(4) Liberalism: *Woman Activist* rating on selected issues (perfect score 100)	80	75 (Maj. leader)	37	10 (Min. leader)
(5) Feminism: *Woman Activist* rating of 3 Congresses on 4 issues (each worth 25, perfect score 100)	86	59	59	21
(6) Feminism: Women's Lobby rating of 3 Congresses on 5 issues (each worth 20, perfect score 100)	83	67	63	43

*Raw numbers of legislators are in parentheses.

We have also found that women politicians in both parties cluster around the liberal wings of their parties. Based on this trend, it is likely that if women were elected to half of the legislative seats in America, the policies subsequently adopted would be more liberal and feminist than they are today.

What conclusions should be drawn from the evidence that we have presented? First, feminists with strong party affiliations should support women candidates within their party. Democratic and Republican women are clearly more feminist than their colleagues. Second, if one is more concerned with policy outputs than with symbolic rewards, it makes more sense to elect a liberal Democratic man than a conservative Republican woman. Finally, we must confront a significant limitation of the available measures. Voting data indicate levels of support for a given issue. Thus, we can safely say that Democratic men constitute a crucial pool of support for feminist policies. But voting is only one kind of political activity and possibly not the most important. It tells us nothing about who initiates the introduction of feminist legislation and who leads the floor fights and mobilizes support. The initiators are invariably women. The essential leadership role played by individual women legislators is not revealed by voting data.

Unfortunately, we cannot here address this important aspect of women's political role in support of feminist policies. Reliable measures of women's leadership role in legislatures must be developed for a fuller understanding of their impact. It is in this role that the impact of women far exceeds that of their sympathetic male colleagues. The few women who have achieved legislative office in the past few years have accomplished far more than their numbers would imply. How much more could they accomplish for women if they occupied half of the seats in American legislatures!

NOTE

1. The 20 votes were for end to discrimination by Congress in employment; closing tax loopholes; adjustment of farm price support; authorization for the B-1 bomber; strip mine act; energy trust fund; emergency housing act; money for community action programs; income tax adjustment; aid to Angola; release of CIA report; deregulation of natural gas prices; public works bill; reduced truck weight on highways; military aid to Chile; ban on use of foreign aid funds for assassination and influencing elections abroad; increase of the debt limit; integration of physical education classes by sex; revision of the Hatch Act; and funding of the National Women's Conference bill.

REFERENCES

U.S. Bureau of the Census (1976). A statistical portrait of the women in the U.S. Washington, D.C.: U.S. Government Printing Office.
Woman Activist (1976). 5(March).

Chapter 9

THE EFFECT OF ELECTIONS
ON DOING THE WORK OF GOVERNMENT

JOHN EHRLICHMAN

THE LONGEST CONTINUOUS MESS HALL LINE IN THE WORLD

When I think about Congressmen, Senators, and Presidents, always necessarily running for reelection, I cannot help but recall the months I spent at the Army Air Corps base at Sioux Falls, South Dakota, during some Great Conflict of the Past. So many men had been sent to that base from Europe for reassignment to the Pacific that the barracks, washhouses, and other facilities were badly overcrowded.

Kitchens and mess lines could not possibly serve the hordes of enlisted men within the 90 minutes they were open at each mealtime. But the military strategists in charge would not deviate from established procedure to alter the standard hours of food service to accommodate the sudden overpopulation on the base. So the survival-wise GI soon learned that if he wished to eat dinner he had better get in the mess hall line 10 minutes after he finished lunch. Thousands of men read, wrote letters, played cards—lived their lives—in the mess hall lines because that was the way the system forced them to act. They adapted.

The freshman Congressman begins to run for reelection 10 minutes after he is elected. Senators usually feel that they can wait until the third or fourth year, since their term is six years and the voters' recollection is at least that short.

In the White House a new President must always have his fourth-year reelection in mind, but his near-run concern focuses on the congressional election in the second year of the President's first term. He must try to improve his congressional support or prevent its erosion in the "off year."

Our federal incumbents are always in the election mess hall line. This chapter will examine how the constantly impending referenda affect the Presidency in one aspect of its operation: the development and execution of domestic policy.

THE WHEAT AND THE TARES

Almost nothing about the President and the Presidency is as stark and simple as journalistic reports make it appear. Reporters deal in the blacks and whites, ups and downs, ins and outs but rarely in the real grays and middles. Decisions which are reported to be "political" in kind or motive are seldom purely political. A notably political President will actually wrestle with the substantive or moral choices, intentionally disregarding the obvious political implications of his decision. But, like the journalists, a chapter of this kind must deal in some unqualified generalities if it is to have any meaning. In an effort to avoid "but on the other hand" disjunctions in every sentence, the actual experience of the Nixon years (1969-1972) comprising the first term will be briefly and selectively examined. Then some generalities will be advanced. The reader will have in mind that some writers assert that the American Presidency is too political because the first term incumbent must face reelection. Some offer a solution in one six-year term. This chapter will also weigh that alternative against the present provision for two successive four-year terms.

THE CONTEXT OF THE 1970-1972 REELECTION CAMPAIGN

Some may argue that President Richard Nixon was running for reelection before 1970. I know that he had decided to seek reelection before the congressional campaign of 1969-1970 was in full swing. But the prospect of a reelection campaign did not overtly intrude on domestic policy work in the White House to a material degree until after the 1970 congressional election.

That election produced a Congress heavily dominated by Democrats. Both Senate and House leaders (Mike Mansfield and Carl Albert) were weak, and the White House had succeeded in moving into the congressional vacuum with countless legislative proposals.

The economy was suffering from an inherited inflation which had direct connection to Lyndon Johnson's guns-*and*-butter economic policy. Unemployment figures were high. The real purchasing power of the dollar was declining. Wages and prices were ratcheting upward.

The Vietnam war, prisoners of war, the Tet offensive, Cambodia, and the Mekong were daily topics. Massive antiwar street demonstrations confronted the administration. Hundreds of bombings took place across the country.

School and housing integration and court-ordered busing divided communities.

President Nixon had narrowly defeated Hubert Humphrey in 1968. The Republican party was statistically outnumbered by both Democrats and Independents in 1970, and Republican candidates experienced significant off-year losses in the 1970 congressional results.

The early polls implied that the central issues in the 1972 election would be the Vietnam War, the economy, crime, busing, abortion, and civil rights. Minor election issues would include veterans' rights, hunger, the environment, health care, and welfare reform, among others.

THE INDEXES AND TRENDS

With regard to the economic issues, as a matter of strategic political decision, President Nixon concluded that *trends* of improvement were more important than the statistical levels themselves. For example, he reasoned that the average voter might more likely vote his fears about unemployment if more and more workers were being laid off at election time. To the contrary, if plants in the voter's region were hiring in November, unemployment would be less a motivating issue. The voter's own personal feeling of insecurity about his job would be assuaged by the favorable trend, even if jobless percentages were in the upper levels. So the strategy would be to ensure that there was hiring in the key states at the critical preelection time. And the White House should make sure that the things done by the departments and agencies and bureaus and offices of the government helped and did not frustrate that objective.

ACTION ON THE ISSUES

In general, it was decided, the administration would respond actively to the other domestic issues which were high on the poll lists.

It was recognized that it is always difficult to know which issues may motivate a voter to support or disfavor an incumbent President. Analysis in 1971 showed that voters weighted the various issues differently, depending on how the pollsters asked their questions. Respondents were invited by pollsters to list issues "of most importance to the nation" and then those "of most importance to you [the voter]"; White House analysis discovered that neighborhood crime, for example, often did not appear high on the national issue list but usually led the list of problems of most importance to the individual responding voter.

So, beginning in 1971, Nixon people began to sift lists of national and local domestic policy questions while, simultaneously, analyzing the geographic and demographic aspects of their findings.

WHERE ARE THE ISSUES?

Demographic aspects of issue analysis are commonplace these days. Political neophytes recognize the demographic alignments in issues like abortion, aid to Israel, and the Rhodesian chromium boycott.

But, as presidential politics has undergone changes, the geographic distribution of those who care passionately about one issue or another has also become important to campaign planners. To the extent that street crime is a motivating issue, obviously it will be less productive to "work" the issue in Red Oak, Iowa, than in Los Angeles, Chicago, or New York.

Unique problems of the aging retired pensioner are highly localized; all but a tiny percentage of these voters are to be found in less than a fifth of the states.

When you plot where the heavy concentration of Roman Catholics (aid to private schools, abortion, morality, conventional values), you find them in about two-fifths of the states.

While some issues are truly national (e.g., foreign affairs and inflation), some which are generally treated by the press as national in scope actually are not. Geographic plotting of where high unemployment exists will show up on the map as pockets; it is an example of a "national" issue which may be successfully identified and attacked by locality.

Electoral College vote proportions require a candidate for national office to analyze which states he can or must try to win to amass the required 270 votes from the electors. In spite of the customary postconvention rhetoric by the nominees, and partly as a result of the disastrous Nixon hyperbole in 1960 ("I shall campaign in all 50 states"), presidential candidates usually will attempt to focus their energy and resources on the 14 or 15 "battleground" states which can elect. Cosmetic campaign appearances in some of the other states will prevent negative reactions but are only made to avoid erosion. No one likes to realize that he is unimportant to the end result or is taken for granted.

The President facing reelection must analyze the key states he needs and must understand the key issues that motivate the voters in those places. When he has gathered that information, as Richard Nixon did in 1971, he is then in a position to act.

SHOTGUN AND RIFLE

It became evident to the Nixon White House that national unemployment trends could be reversed by specific, locally applied efforts in Southern California, western Washington, Dallas-Fort Worth, the Boston suburbs, and one or two other communities where the jobless percentages were very high. Two men were assigned to determine how the federal government could create jobs in those several places. A retired businessman of stature and ability was recruited to serve as full-time liaison between the White House and businessmen in the target communities. Pending government contracts which had bogged down in red tape were quickly signed and funded when local business executives could promise quick hiring. Public works projects received accelerated timetables in the critical localities. Job training, day-care and counseling, data banks to match employers with job seekers, and a focus on unemployment record keeping and statistical methods in the target areas also helped to bring the percentages down. Each of the departments and agencies of the Executive branch were informed of the target areas and enlisted in the effort to create jobs there.

Because the wage-price spiral continued to aggravate the inflation, in spite of "jawboning" and the creation of special watchdog groups like the Construction Council, extraordinary wage-price controls were imposed in the fall of 1971 in an effort to reverse the trend. Whatever one thinks of such an "incomes policy," the problems of Phase II, the Cost of Living Council, and all the aftermath of the New Economic Policy of 1971, students of presidential politics will note that at election time, November 1972, most of the *trends* were right. Prices in the market basket had steadied, the real buying power of the dollar was up, unemployment was heading down, and interest rates were moving down as well. Again, the general direction of movement was more important than the levels of achievement.

While we are looking at trends, it should be noted that in the indicia of foreign affairs favorable directions could also be seen to be the result of similar effort. The draft was down and moving toward extinction. The number of troops abroad and the ratio of defense spending to the budget for domestic problems were also moving in the direction of peace (with honor).

Crime statistics were another matter. In spite of greatly increased budgets, innovative experiments, and morale-building presidential sessions with street cops, the law enforcement hierarchy, narcs, customs people, and rural sheriffs, the incidence, cost, and serious-ness of crime continued to go up in the national statistics. President Nixon and his staff devoted a high percentage of their time to efforts to solve this constellation of problems with only spotty success.

NOT ALL PROBLEM SOLVING IS GOOD POLITICS

When the White House, facing a reelection campaign, creates jobs in battleground states, what should be the political philosophers' judgment about that? Obviously it is good to create jobs, whatever the motive. But for the election, would the jobs have been created? If the answer is "no," then the pending political contest may be said to have had some good effect. If "yes," then is the President to be congratualted on his good motive and perhaps be granted reelection? The fact is that it was usually neither plain "no" nor plain "yes" in the Nixon years; it was usually a mixture, as I suspect it had been with prior Presidents.

Which is not to suggest that *all* acts of presidential omission and commission are mixtures of politics and high-mindedness. Some are pure politics, done to get votes or omitted to avoid antagonism and the loss of votes.

Democratic majorities in Congress are fond of sending Republican Presidents bills to sign or veto which will embarrass him at election time. A President sometimes sends Congress legislative proposals that he hopes Congress will quickly pigeonhole, in order that the President can persuasively campaign against "that do-nothing Congress."

Presidential nominees to high office find it harder and harder to secure senatorial confirmation as an election approaches.

White House decisions on defense base closings are rarely announced in the year before a presidential election. When three or four localities are competing for a new federal installation of some kind, the White House will never gladden one state but antagonize three others by making a preelection selection and announcement, even though a needed program may be stalled for months. Not all problem solving is good politics.

POLICY DETERMINATION IN GENERAL

Every President has had his own unique idea of how domestic policy questions should be framed and moved to him for decision. Some have preferred the departments to handle as many problems as possible, sending the White House only those which the departments decide to send.

Other Presidents, including Nixon, devised machinery within the White House to forecast policy problems and develop orderly procedures for assembling fact, opinion, and alternatives well in advance of the need for a presidential decision.

Some problems are predictable because events force them to the President's attention. For example, the White House knows that the law authorizing Model Cities will expire in 11 months. The Democrats in Congress will surely enact an extension. Should the President sign or veto the extension—or should he now propose an alternative?

Other policy questions are framed by congressional initiative.

The President's annual budget review begins in the early spring and continues until he signs his budget message in December or January. He is called upon to articulate his policy in the choice of alternative recipients of the federal resources.

It may be worth noting an obverse aspect of the problem of determining presidential policy, and that is how one learns and defines the ongoing nonpresidential policy of an office or division of a department which has a life of its own. For example, Presidents may come and go, but, unless a President has occasion to ask for them specifically, the policies of the Anti-Trust Division of the Justice Department will never cross the presidential desk for review. That division will sue, prosecute, approve, and disapprove in specific important cases without ever submitting general questions of policy or philosophy for the President's ratification. Much of the policy of such a division is unwritten, existing only as a part of its functional folklore.

When President Nixon required the Anti-Trust Division to reduce its policy and philosophy to writing for his review, it took months for them to produce it. And they did so with much anguish and objection. The first result was a long, evasive, ambiguous, and remarkably murky statement. In the redrafting process a good many bats were chased out of the cave, at least temporarily. Eventually Nixon was able to read what the division asserted as its policy, and he ordered quite a bit of it changed.

President Nixon created the Domestic Council in order to have a staff to (1) predict policy questions and (2) cause the relevant facts and alternatives to be presented to him in an orderly fashion. The Council staff also had a third and more difficult function, which was greatly aided by the prospect of the reelection campaign of 1972. This was the task of communicating the President's policy decisions to the Executive branch of the government and of securing policy compliance in the caverns and crannies of the bureaucracy.

Dissemination of the President's policy was not nearly as difficult as getting the recipients to listen. We called meetings of the Cabinet and subcabinet to explain the President's decisions. Memoranda were sent. Individual and group luncheons were held to pass the word. Journalists were welcomed in the hope that they would write something where government people might read and learn. And deviations from policy were the subject of quick rebuke. Often the margins of the President's morning news summary were used to note some assistant secretary's West Coast speech advocating something the President had decided to oppose.

POLICY AND THE CAMPAIGN

When the reelection campaign approached, we realized the urgent need for better techniques to insure that everyone speaking on the President's behalf understood his policies and knew something about his performance during the first term. Government people who had been working only on urban problems would be asked questions about agriculture or occupational health and safety or Alaskan native claims. They would be expected to respond accurately because, in the campaign, they spoke for the President, not just their individual agency.

And so the Key Facts sheets (see illustrations) evolved as a campaign tool with much good, if incidental, effect upon government operation. For the first time there was collected, in one package, brief statements of the administration's definition of the nation's domestic issues, its policy and proposals with respect to each of them, and a description of the progress made between 1969 and 1972 in the solution of the stated problems. These summaries and their preparation were also a valuable management device. Meeting the requirement that none exceed two pages was, in itself, a governmental landmark.

A similar value was realized in the preparation of policy briefings for the President. For example, every time he made a political trip to a new locality a separate "trip book" was furnished him describing the local political situation, any recent local polls, the most visible or critical local issues, and the administration "line" or policy with regard to those issues. Occasionally it was the case that there *was* no decided policy on such an issue. Then the Domestic Council staff and the responsible bureaucracy were called upon to amass the necessary information to permit the President to come to grips with it.

This process had been going on more or less constantly in the Nixon staff since the 1968 campaign and after the election. Thick briefing books were prepared for Mr. Nixon in advance of press conferences, predicting likely questions and providing suggested answers. Probable questions dealing with substantive policy issues occasionally required the development of ancillary decision papers when no established policy existed.

Thus the paradox: The political forces at work sometimes dictated that proposed action be enjoined. In other cases political considerations forced sound policy review and decision that otherwise might not have taken place.

KEY FACTS ON EMPLOYMENT

I. The President's economic policies <u>are</u> having the desired impact of reducing unemployment and increasing employment:

    A. The unemployment rate has dropped from 6.1% in August 1971, to 5.5% in September 1972, and is declining.

    B. Jobs are being created at a rate of 2-1/2 million per year. With the effects of defense cutbacks from the wind-down of the war mostly complete, we can expect this job creation rate to sharply cut into unemployment.

    C. Total civilian employment is over 82 million, up from 76 million in 1968.

    D. Job availability has increased sharply from a year ago.

II. Although less than half of those unemployed have actually "lost" jobs, the President has assisted those who have:

    A. extended unemployment compensation benefits (to as much as 52 weeks) for areas of impacted unemployment;
    B. transitional public service employment;
    C. focusing of manpower programs on problem areas;
    D. money to connect engineers and scientists with new jobs;
    E. a national, computerized job bank;
    F. special programs to employ Vietnam-era veterans.

III. The President's expansive economic policies prevented the unemployment rate from rising badly as a result of defense cutbacks and winding down the war.

IV. While the President wants to assure that those who want to work, have work, some points about the <u>raw figure for unemployment</u> should be borne in mind:

    A. 96.7% of heads of households in the labor force have employment;
    B. only 1.3% of the labor force suffers "hardship" unemployment (lasting longer than 15 weeks); and unemployment compensation covers from 26 to a maximum of 52 weeks;
    C. 635,000 left their last job voluntarily to seek new work;
    D. the percentage of heads of households who are unemployed is now substantially lower than the percentage of heads of households who were unemployed 10 years ago when the unemployment rate was at approximately the same 5.5% level.

aj-bc

KEY FACTS ON CENTRAL CITIES

President Nixon is helping America's central cities.

I. The basic problems America's central cities face are:

    A. A severe fiscal crisis; leading to
    B. A decline in the quality of the cities' services;
    C. A need for new housing and waste treatment;
    D. Atrophy of local government; growing Federal power.

II. What President Nixon is doing about these problems:

    A. The President is bolstering the central city fiscal resources:
        1. General Revenue Sharing will pump $8.3 billion of new
           money into states and localities in its first year; and
           more than $3.5 billion per year thereafter.
        2. The President's budget for community development
           and housing has been, on the average, $1 billion a
           year higher than in the previous four years.

    B. The President is helping to improve central city services:
        1. <u>Anti-Crime:</u> The President has helped state and local
           law enforcement officials fight central city crime by
           increasing Federal anti-crime aid by 253% since 1969.
        2. <u>Welfare:</u> The President proposes to replace the present
           system with one that is fair to the taxpayer and to the
           person who must depend on welfare. It is designed to
           reduce abuses in the present system.
        3. <u>Transportation:</u> He secured the passage of a $10 billion
           program to improve urban mass transportation.

    C. The President is meeting central city needs:
        1. <u>Housing:</u> The President has achieved a <u>fourfold</u> increase
           in the production of housing for low and moderate income
           families since 1969. Brought new housing starts to an
           all-time high of over 2 million per year.
        2. <u>Waste Treatment:</u> He has increased the budget authority
           for municipal waste treatment projects from $214 million
           in 1969 to $2 billion in 1973.
        3. <u>Managing</u> their own affairs: His Urban Special Revenue
           Sharing proposal would provide $2.3 billion which urban
           areas can use as they locally decide. No Federal bureau-
           cratic guidelines or matching requirements in this or
           General Revenue Sharing. A historic turnaround.

                                    aj-bc

THE QUALITATIVE QUESTION

When politics or the pendency of a reelection campaign required a policy decision by the President, was it, necessarily, inferior in quality to decisions made in the abstract? Would a lame-duck President make better policy decisions than an incumbent facing a reelection test?

These questions bring us to a question of definition: What is politics? When is a decision political? The dictionary definitions are not conclusive:

> **politics** ... **1 a:** the art or science of government ... **b** ... (2): ... concerned with winning and holding control over a government.... **3:** political actions, practices, or policies.... **4** ... **c:** political activities characterized by artful and often dishonest practices.... **7:** the total complex of interacting and usu. conflicting relations between men living in society. [*Webster's Third New International Dictionary*]

Common usages of journalism add a perjorative quality to the phrase. A political decision is per se less noble than a nonpolitical policy or personnel appointment, according to the television and newspaper reports. But the critical listener or reader will ask himself if such a characterization is necessarily so.

The officeholder who is weighing a decision cocks a wary eye toward his upcoming election. He tries to measure how the voters will react to his forthcoming action. He also attempts to weigh where the merits lie: whose version of the facts is correct? How will each of the competing proposals work? Cost is usually another factor. The officeholder will often feel bound by prior statements or commitments to his constituents ("I will never, never sign a Right to Work bill so long as I am President") which may embody previously recognized political considerations. Rarely will his decision rest entirely upon only one of these factors. Rarely will he disregard all factors except politics. But as an election comes closer and closer the weight any President gives to the voters' probable reaction unquestionably increases. Perhaps that's a law; it should be called Sturdley's Law after Aamon S. Sturdley (1961), the unpublished and recondite political commentator:

> The weight which will be given public opinion in presidential decisions increases in inverse ratio to the number of days remaining before a presidential election. [1]

A ONE-TERM LIMIT?

If an incumbent gets more political as his reelection nears is one term of six years a better alternative? I don't think so.

There is not much historical evidence that bears on the question since our only recent example is President Dwight D. Eisenhower. No one else completed a full second term since Franklin Roosevelt did six Presidents back. And Eisenhower was not a truly political incumbent. But we can reason from some good probabilities.

A lame-duck President would not campaign for himself, of course. But a partisan in that office would probably try to help the successor nominee of his party to a greater extent than Eisenhower did in 1960. And a retiring President would be under great pressure to campaign for the senatorial and congressional candidates of his party as well.

His party's candidates would have a substantial interest in the way a retiring President conducted the office in the waning months of his term. He would be free of the will of the people, but he would surely

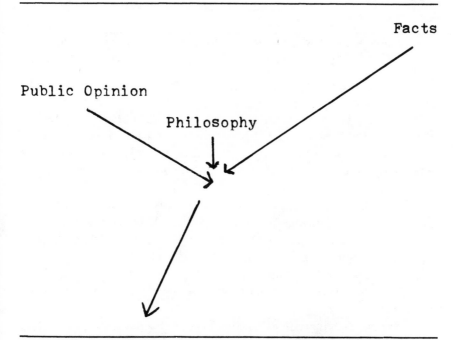

Figure 1: HEAVIER WEIGHT IS GIVEN TO THE FACTS. THE DECISION MAKER
WEIGHS PUBLIC OPINION IN ANTICIPATION OF THE UPCOMING
ELECTION, BUT PUBLIC OPINION IS NOT DECISIVE.

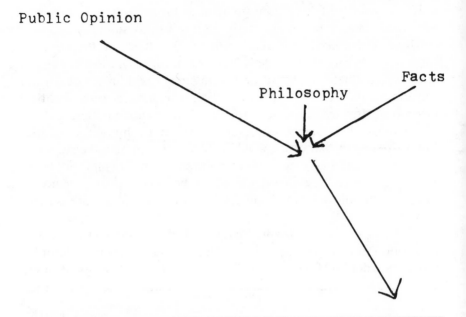

Figure 2: PUBLIC OPINION IS A STRONGER INFLUENCE. STURDLEY'S LAW
IS IN OPERATION.

feel the political will of his fellow politicians who were about to face the electorate.

And what is wrong with requiring an officeholder to go back to the voters halfway through his tenure for a vote of confidence? I believe it can be successfully shown that a "political" President is one who is concerned about how the voters will react to his decisions.

Diagrammatically, an officeholder's actions are almost always the product of a vectoring of considerations. A President weighs the substantive and factual information along with the polls and his best judgment of public opinion. (See Figures 1 and 2.)

Sometimes well-informed public opinion and the facts will coincide, of course, but that relieves the officeholder of the need to resolve the forces.

Add now the ingredient of the President's personal philosophy. Generally it plays a very minor part in the decision process. Political considerations have tended to move all modern Presidents toward the center-left, since that is the locus of voter strength in the United

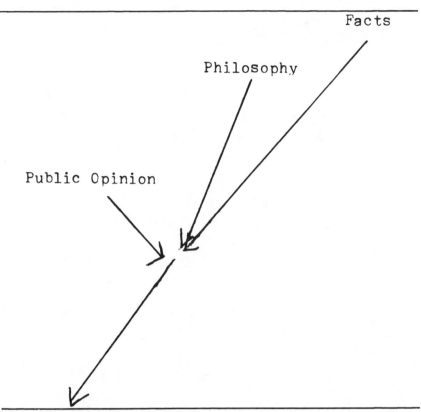

Figure 3: THE DECISION MAKER WILL NOT FACE AN ELECTION. HIS PHILOSOPHY AND THE FACTS ARE COINCIDENT.

States. But if we weaken the political factor by the six-year term innovation, the President may be partly relieved of that restraint, and his personal philosophical convictions will begin to play a much stronger part in the vectoring (Figure 3).

The obvious effect of removing a President from interim account-ability to the electorate would be an increase in the importance of the President's philosophical coloration (Figure 4). Obversely, his independence from the electorate might result in a personal freedom from purely partisan considerations, if the incumbent wished to attempt to forge bipartisan combinations in the Congress and elsewhere (Figure 5).

This combination could produce a very individualistic Presidency but one which would further weaken the political party's role in presidential politics.[2] The six-year term would tend to encourage

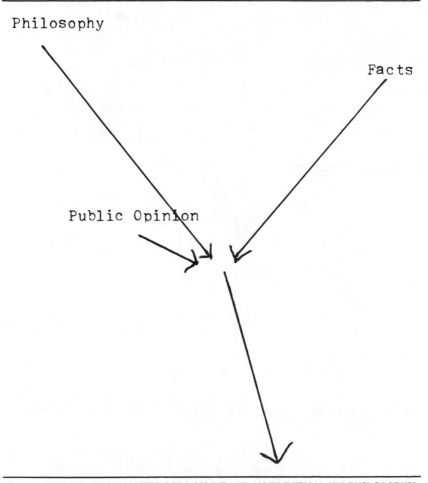

Philosophy

Facts

Public Opinion

Figure 4: **THE DECISION MAKER WILL NOT FACE AN ELECTION. HIS PHILOSOPHY AND THE FACTS ARE OPPOSED.**

the creation of personal political organizations in support of successor presidential candidates, a kind of every-man-for-himself situation, if the incumbent became functionally independent of his party loyalties. President Eisenhower's passive response to his party and its candidate in 1959-1960 offers some evidence of the organizational response that may be expected where the incumbent is an independent lame duck.

In 1960, candidate Richard Nixon constructed a personal campaign organization almost completely detached from the Republican

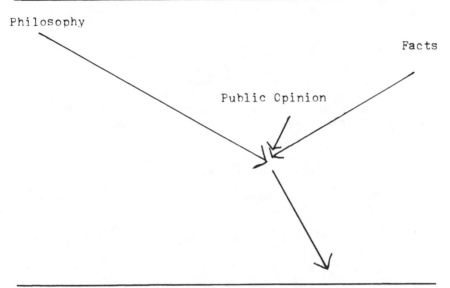

Figure 5: THE STRONGLY FELT PHILOSOPHY OF A SIX-YEAR PRESIDENT WOULD OVERCOME BOTH PUBLIC OPINION AND THE FACTS.

National Committee, which had been seriously weakened by lack of presidential partisanship, indifferent staffing, and the refusal of the Eisenhower White House to aid in its fund-raising efforts.

HOW IT SEEMS

Elections do have an effect on the conduct of the business of government. They tend to cause officeholders to think about public opinion. A constitutional change could bring about more independence from the President's political party and, perhaps, the voters. Such independence might bring with it a greater ideological content in the conduct of the Presidency. So, take your choice, as Terromid Celey said in *The Seed*:

> We seldom gain without
> a loss
> And who is there to
> truly measure?

NOTES

1. This citation is imaginary. However, we felt that we should state at least one political law in this chapter to make it more like the others in this book. And we need a footnote. In the opinion of the author, since Sturdley is also imaginary, it provides a certain symmetry. Almost everything else in this chapter is true.

2. The reader should refer to Sturdley's unpublished article "Why a Presidential Candidate Hates His Political Party."

REFERENCE

STURDLEY, A.S. (1961). "Reflections on the Hoover Presidency." Cundiyo (New Mexico) Chronicle, May.

CONTRIBUTORS

F. CHRISTOPHER ARTERTON is Assistant Professor of Political Science at Yale University. He is coauthor of *Explorations in Convention Decision Making* and has a continuing research interest in political socialization as well as American politics, parties, and campaigning.

HERBERT B. ASHER is Associate Professor of Political Science at The Ohio State University. He is the author of *Presidential Elections and American Politics: Voters, Candidates, and Campaigns Since 1952* and *Causal Modeling* (forthcoming), as well as a number of articles on congressional politics and political methodology.

DAVID WILLIAM BRADY is Professor of Political Science at the University of Houston and Visiting Professor at Rice University. He is author of *Congressional Voting in a Partisan Era* and *Public Policy in America* (forthcoming), as well as of numerous articles that have appeared in leading professional journals.

JOSEPH COOPER is on leave as Professor of Political Science at Rice University while serving as Staff Director of the U.S. House of Representatives Commission on Administrative Review (the Obey Commission). He is author of the monograph *The Origins of the Standing Committees and the Development of the Modern House* as well as of numerous articles on the U.S. Congress.

JOHN EHRLICHMAN was an attorney in Seattle, Washington, before joining the Nixon White House, first as Counsel to the President, then as Assistant to the President for Domestic Affairs and Director of the Domestic Council staff, and finally as Assistant to the President. He is currently appealing his convictions for two Watergate-related offenses.

MICHAEL R. FITZGERALD, Assistant Professor of Political Science at the University of Missouri, Columbia, teaches state and urban politics and has written on the area of electoral behavior. He has a special interest in the politics of school desegregation.

PATRICIA A. HURLEY is Visiting Assistant Professor of Political Science at the University of Houston. Her previous research has been in the areas of electoral behavior and the U.S. Congress.

SAMUEL A. KIRKPATRICK is Professor of Political Science and Director of the Bureau of Government Research, University of Oklahoma. He is author or editor of *Urban Political Analysis, The Social Psychology of Political Life*, and *Quantitative Analysis of Political Data*, as well as of numerous articles.

SHELAH GILBERT LEADER taught political science for several years before joining the Civil Rights Division of the U.S. Department of Justice. Since 1975, she has been a staff associate of the National Commission on the Observance of International Women's Year. Her research interests include the role of women in the People's Republic of China as well as in the United States.

GERALD J. LIEBERMAN is Associate Senior Research Mathematician at the Societal Analysis Division of the General Motors Technical Center in Warren, Michigan. Before joining General Motors, he was Assistant Professor of Mathematics at Colby College. His published research includes a study of apportionment of Maine's school administrative districts.

WILLIAM LYONS, Assistant Professor of Political Science at the University of Tennessee, Knoxville, has written various articles on urban and state politics, electoral behavior, and political methodology. He has special interests in public policy analysis and methodology.

LOUIS MAISEL is Assistant Professor of Government at Colby College. He edited the previous volumes in this series, *The Future of Political Parties* and *Changing Campaign Techniques,* has published a number of articles on parties and the electoral process, and is currently undertaking a comparative study of high-level domestic advising in the United States, Great Britain, and Australia.

DAVID R. MORGAN is Associate Professor of Political Science and Associate Director of the Bureau of Government Research at the University of Oklahoma. He is coeditor of *Urban Political Analysis* and author of several articles on urban and state politics.

ROBERT T. NAKAMURA is Assistant Professor of Government at Dartmouth College. He has worked on the politics of education, coauthoring *The Political Feasibility of School Finance Reform in California,* and has studied the Democratic conventions of 1968, 1974, and 1976 and the Republican convention of 1976.

DAVID H. NEXON is staff Political Scientist and Co-Director of the Program on Civil Liberties and Social Control at the Russell Sage Foundation. Before joining the Russell Sage Foundation, he taught political science at the University of Cincinnati, as a Charles Phelps Taft Post-doctoral Fellow, and at Pitzer College. His previous articles have concerned the behavior of political activists and the legislative impact of realigning elections.

GERALD M. POMPER is Chairman of Political Science at Rutgers-The State University and Professor at Livingston College. His numerous articles on American political parties are well known. Among his books are *Elections in America, Voters' Choice,* and a forthcoming volume on the 1976 election.

JEFFREY L. PRESSMAN is Associate Professor of Political Science at the Massachusetts Institute of Technology. He has specialized in American politics, policy implementation, and presidential nominations. Among his books are *Implementation* (coauthor) and *Federal Program and City Politics.*

DENIS G. SULLIVAN is Professor of Government at Dartmouth College, teaching American politics, political behavior, and the psychological bases of politics. He is senior coauthor of *The Politics of Representation: The Democratic Convention 1972* and *Explorations in Convention Decision Making: The Democratic Party in the 1970s* and has written extensively on simulation and gaming.

MARTHA WAGNER WEINBERG is Assistant Professor of Political Science at the Massachusetts Institute of Technology. Her specialties include American politics, state politics, and executive behavior. Her forthcoming book, *Managing the State,* deals with relationships among governors and bureaucrats.